Development and Regional Cooperation in Central Asia and South Asia

Euro-Asian Perspectives

Development and Regional Cooperation in Central Asia and South Asia

Euro-Asian Perspectives

Editors

Henrik Berglund
Mondira Dutta
Per Hilding

JNU
Jawaharlal Nehru University
New Delhi

Stockholm University
Forum for Asian Studies,
University of Stockholm

PENTAGON PRESS

Development and Regional Cooperation in Central Asia and South Asia: Euro-Asian Perspectives

Henrik Berglund, Mondira Dutta and Per Hilding (Editors)

ISBN 978-81-8274-864-4

First Published in 2016

Published by
PENTAGON PRESS
206, Peacock Lane, Shahpur Jat,
New Delhi-110049
Phones: 011-64706243, 26491568
Telefax: 011-26490600
email: rajan@pentagonpress.in
website: www.pentagonpress.in

Branch
Flat No.213, Athena-2,
Clover Acropolis,
Viman Nagar,
Pune-411014
Email: pentagonpresspune@gmail.com

Printed at Avantika Printers Private Limited.

Contents

Preface

This is an output of a two-day international conference held in Jawaharlal Nehru University, New Delhi from March 13–14, 2014. The conference was organised under the aegis of the Centre for Inner Asian Studies, School of International Studies, Jawaharlal Nehru University in collaboration with Forum for Asian Studies, Stockholm University, Sweden.

Central and South Asia today play at the global centre stage. The troop withdrawal from Afghanistan, the gradual fading of the effectiveness of the sanctions against Iran and a growing insecurity as a result of the increasing violence, crime, conflict and terrorism is disturbing to the region as a whole. Amidst the emerging connectivity and transport corridors, Central Asia is struggling and is in the process of transformation through a chain of regional cooperation and institution building. The newly independent states have turned out to be the focus of superpowers due to their rich natural resources and are confronted with various threats besides the struggle for domination. Security concerns faced by the region include a combination of social disorders, crime, illegal drug trafficking, extremism, terrorism, ethnic and civil conflicts, border tensions, water and transport disputes, illegal narcotic movements and so on. These conditions have had a disastrous impact not only on the region but also on the neighbouring region and on India in particular.

Considering the relatively limited level of regional economic integration achieved in the region, the book attempts to focus on some of the major challenges as envisaged by the other regional cooperations, particularly through the experiences of the EU. The book envisages to explore a deeper and wider understanding of the region of Central and South Asia within the given background. Such an approach will facilitate a critical and constructive discourse for identifying some of the obstacles and challenges for marching ahead towards a closer political, economic and legal cooperation in the region.

The book draws attention to the potential benefits of closer cooperation between Central Asia and South Asia concerning energy, trade transports, security and cultural ties. The close relationships— historically, politically and culturally—could weld the Central Asian countries and India and lessen the threats from mighty neighbours such as China and Russia. Also, the need of combating trafficking and violence against women, which are obstacles to social and economic progress, are discussed in the volume. The book is an humble attempt in flagging off important issues in the areas of concern from different perspectives. It is hoped that it will contribute to the hitherto slender collection on the various challenges from a wider perspective of Central Asia, South Asia and the European Union.

Henrik Berglund
Mondira Dutta
Per Hilding

List of Contributors

1 **Anuradha Banerjee,** Ph.D, Professor, Centre for the Study of Regional Development, School of Social Sciences, and Jawaharlal Nehru University, New Delhi & President, Indian National Cartographic Association. Her research interests include Population & Settlements, Urbanization, Women and Child Development, HIV/AIDS, Remote Sensing & GIS. She has published two books, 29 articles, chapters in books and various projects.

2 **Anwesha Ghosh,** Doctoral Researcher at Willy Brandt School of Public Policy, University of Erfurt (Germany) under the DAAD International Conflict Management Programme. Her field of research includes issues related to South and Central Asian region particularly on Afghanistan. Her latest book is '*A Leap Forward: Capacity Building, Education and India-Afghanistan Cooperation*, 2014.

3 **B.C. Upreti,** Ph.D, Currently Senior Fellow, ICSSR, Jaipur, Rajasthan. Professor & Former Director, South Asia Studies Centre, University of Rajasthan, Jaipur. His research interests are South Asian Affairs.

4 **Haseena Hashia,** Ph.D, Professor, Department of Geography, Jamia Millia Islamia, New Delhi. Her research interests include Gender Geography, Disaster Management, Environmental Management, with a special focus on Issues of Indian women particularly within the Muslim community.

5 **Henrik Berglund,** Ph.D, Associate Professor, Department of Political Science, Stockholm University, Sweden. His research areas include globalization, democratization, development, civil society, religion and nationalism. He has been teaching at Stockholm University since 1993, mainly within the field of global development and politics. He

is currently the co-ordinator of the Forum for Asian Studies, Stockholm University.

6 **Koyel Sarkar,** Doctoral Researcher, Centre for the Study of Regional Development, Jawaharlal Nehru University , New Delhi. Her research interests include Women's Family Transformations particularly Marriage, Domestic Violence, Fertility Behaviour and Reproductive Health.

7 **Mahesh Ranjan Debata,** Ph.D, Assistant Professor, Centre for Inner Asian Studies, School of International Studies, Jawaharlal Nehru University, New Delhi. His research interests include studies on China's Xinjiang region, Silk Road and Central Asia.

8 **Malini Prava Sethi,** Doctoral Researcher, Centre for Inner Asian Studies, School of International Studies, Jawaharlal Nehru University, New Delhi, Research interests include Tourism and Development in Central Asia. She has recently published an article in the "I-START Entrepreneurship Energy of Youth", Almaty Management University, Kazakhstan, April 2015.

9 **Mondira Dutta,** Ph.D, Professor & Former Chairperson, Centre for Inner Asian Studies, School of International Studies, Jawaharlal Nehru University, New Delhi, Areas of interest include, Gender Studies (Violence against Women), Trafficking, Human Security and Human Development in Central Asia, South Asia and Afghanistan.

10 **Mukesh Mishra,** Ph.D, Research Associate, UGC Area Studies Programme, Centre for Inner Asian Studies, School of International Studies, Jawaharlal Nehru University, New Delhi. His area of interest include Central Asia. His most recent book is entitled 'Democratisation and Constitutional Reforms in Kazakhstan'.

11 **Netajee Abhinandan,** Ph.D, Assistant Professor, Dept of Political Science, Ravenshaw University, Cuttack, Odisha. Author of innumerable articles published in journals on Asian Affairs and India's foreign Policy in addition to two books. He was nominated by the US Department of State under International Visitor Leadership Programme (IVLP) in 2013.

12 **Per Hilding,** Ph.D, Senior Lecturer, Section for International Relations, Department of Economic History, Stockholm University. His research interests include development theory, family and household economy, trade and regional development.

13 **Sharad K Soni,** Ph.D, Professor & Director, Area Studies Programme, Centre for Inner Asian Studies, School of International Studies, Jawaharlal Nehru University, New Delhi. He specializes in Inner Asian Studies with a focus on Mongolia and Inner Mongolia Autonomous Region of China.

14 **Sideek Mohamed Seyad,** Ph.D, Former Crown Counsel from Sri Lanka. Currently Associate Professor in EU Financial Law, attached to Stockholm University. He teaches EU Law in Sweden, China and Russia and is the author of four text books and have published numerous articles in international law journals.

15 **Sudhir Singh,** Ph.D, Asst Professor, Department of Political Science, Dayal Singh College, University of Delhi, India. His research interests relate to Pakistan and Afghanistan for the last two decades.

16 **Thomas Jonter,** Ph.D, Professor of International Relations, Department of Economic History & Director Graduate School of International Studies, Stockholm University. His research focuses on Nuclear Non-proliferation and Energy Security.

17 **Umarov Khojamahmad,** Ph.D, Professor, Tajik National University, Dushanbe, Tajikistan. With more than 520 publication in the field of theories of economic and agrarian reforms, macroeconomic analysis, international trade and economic relationship, regional integration of Central Asian economies. He is a member of the editorial boards of several magazines, journals and a number of international research Organizations.

PART I

Power Dynamics in Asia: Relevance for India

1

Sino-Indian Collaboration in Post-2014 Afghanistan

Anwesha Ghosh

ABSTRACT

With America's declaration of its longest war coming to "a responsible end" in Afghanistan, one of the most pressing concerns that have emerged happens to be about the potential role the regional countries can play in ensuring stability. China and India are amongst the two most significant players in Afghanistan's neighborhood and post-2014 Afghanistan offers both challenges as well as compelling opportunities for strategic cooperation between the two countries. Although bilateral relations between the two remain troubled by territorial disputes and imbalanced trade, yet both countries' interests appear to overlap in Afghanistan. Over the past decade, both the countries have been involved in Afghanistan and have contributed in its developmental process. They do acknowledge that a stronger and more coordinated regional cooperation is crucial for addressing the challenges faced by Afghanistan and the region at large. Accordingly, several efforts have been undertaken from different quarters; however, it is believed that the key to regional cooperation in securing Afghanistan's future lies in the interactions of Asia's two giants. This paper will begin by highlighting China and India's involvement in Afghanistan over the past decade. It would then attempt to identify the factors that have propelled them to continue their involvement and trace the major areas where their interests converge. It further aspires to locate certain areas wherein the two can cooperate and finally puts forward certain recommendations that can optimise the India–China cooperation in Afghanistan.

Keywords: Afghanistan, India, China, interest, collaboration.

As NATO and Western powers begin to withdraw from Afghanistan, one of the most pressing questions that has emerged pertains to the potential role the regional countries can play in helping the country to become a stable one. China and India are amongst the two most significant players in Afghanistan's neighbourhood. The current situation in Afghanistan presents challenges as wella as compelling opportunities for strategic cooperation between Asia's two giants. Although bilateral relations between the two remain troubled by territorial disputes and imbalanced trade, both countries' interests appear to overlap in Afghanistan. The most obvious areas of concern for both India and China are: First, security outcomes in Afghanistan, which have a direct bearing on the larger regional security framework. Second, maintaining the sovereignty and integrity of Afghanistan by strengthening its institutions, both civilian and military, and by facilitating a smoother political transition. Third, protecting their respective commercial interests and investments. Finally, the economic integration of Afghanistan at the regional level.

Over the past decade, both the countries have been involved in Afghanistan and have contributed in its developmental process. As part of their efforts to contribute towards stabilisation there, both countries have undertaken several programmes individually. They do recognise that a stronger and more coordinated regional cooperation is crucial for addressing the challenges faced by Afghanistan and the region at large. Several efforts are already underway through several platforms, yet the key to regional cooperation in securing Afghanistan's future is believed to lie in the interactions between these two countries. The aim of this paper would be to briefly highlight China and India's involvement in Afghanistan over the past decade and identify the four major areas of converging interests that propel them to continue their involvement. It also attempts to locate rooms for cooperation and puts forward certain recommendations to optimise the India-China cooperation in Afghanistan.

China and India in Afghanistan

There is a perceptible convergence of India and China in Afghanistan where both have been involved and have provided financial assistance and have invested a great deal and are increasingly looking for avenues of cooperation. However, considering China's current politico-economic stature and its geographical proximity, its involvement in Afghanistan has lacked both depth and scale. Between 2002 and 2011, Beijing pledged approximately \$230 million[1] to Afghanistan's reconstruction process while

India's assistance programme touched $ 2 billion,[2] making it the most extensive Indian foreign aid programme till date. However, in the recent past, Beijing has upgraded bilateral cooperation with Afghanistan and with that, enhanced its diplomatic profile. For the first time in nearly fifty years, Zhou Yongkang, a senior Chinese official visited Afghanistan and signed a series of agreements in 2012.[3] Further, the Chinese Foreign Ministry spokesman Hong Lei's statement, "As a close neighbor of Afghanistan, China is ready to work with countries in the region and the international community to support the peaceful reconstruction and reconciliation process in Afghanistan and jointly maintain peace, stability and development of Afghanistan and the whole region"[4] and the Kabul visit of the Chinese Foreign Minister Wang Yi himself in February 2014, reiterated the Chinese interest to play an active role in Afghanistan beyond 2014.[5]

China's Afghan policy has been influenced in recent years by the security imperative of protecting its border regions, particularly the Xinjiang province, and to contain the separatist activities of the East Turkestan Islamic Movement, which has links with militant groups fighting in Afghanistan.[6] Wang Yi, addressing a press conference in Kabul, stated: "Afghanistan has special and important influence. The peace and stability of this country has an impact on the security of Western China and more importantly it affects tranquility and development of the entire region," and that "China will play a constructive role" to achieve that beyond 2014.[7] On the other hand, India's approach to the reconstruction efforts has been to focus on the underlying structural problems and has thus carved out an effective role in the political, security, economic and institutional rebuilding process.[8] The development assistance that India provides to Afghanistan increasingly has an underlying goal of facilitating India's access to the natural resources within Afghanistan and through Afghanistan in Central Asia. Indian investors have shown great interest in the emerging opportunities in mining, hydrocarbons, infrastructure development and other sectors of Afghanistan. But more than India's formidable commercial interest, it is the security angle that has propelled India to adopt a proactive Afghanistan policy. It cannot afford a situation where the country succumbs to domestic instability and the Afghan territory gets used for attacks against India.

The sources of threats for India and China are not the same. The major cause for the Chinese concern is the Al Qaeda-linked East Turkistan Islamic Movement (ETIM) which China alleges is fighting for the independence of Xinjiang.[9] Groups known for targeting Indian interests include the

Pakistan-backed Lashkar-e-Taiba, which was blamed for the 26/11 attack on the Indian city of Mumbai, and the Haqqani network, which is known to be "a veritable arm of Pakistan's Inter-Services Intelligence Agency"[10] and has been held responsible for attacks on the Indian Embassy and Consulate in Afghanistan. Therefore, although both China and India have convergent interests in seeking an outcome that ensures that the Afghan territory is not used to destabilise another country, yet their areas of concerns are divergent. The alleged involvement of China's close ally Pakistan as a destabilising factor makes the equation even more complex. Nonetheless, both India and China would look forward to a stable Afghanistan and to achieve that goal both acknowledge the importance of a sustained international support for Afghanistan beyond 2014. Both countries concur that the rehabilitation of Afghanistan should be 'Afghan-owned and Afghan led'[11] and they significantly agree on the importance of investment and economic development of the country. Though they foster differing attitudes towards Pakistan and its militant proxies, still they manage to see eye-to-eye on a number of fundamental issues about the security situation in Afghanistan. Even though both experience a similar domestic threat from extremism and terrorism and are worried about the its spillover effect, yet neither sees the answer to this crisis in sending troops to the country. As part of their efforts to contribute towards the stabilisation of Afghanistan, both countries have undertaken several programmes individually. They also recognise that stronger and more coordinated regional cooperation is crucial to addressing the challenges of more effective development in Afghanistan.

Indian and Chinese Aid Programmes in Afghanistan: A Brief Glance

The governments of Afghanistan and India have capitalised on their mutual trust, based on centuries of common history and civilisation. Importance of the role played by India in Afghanistan's reconstruction and rehabilitation in the past decade has been widely acknowledged. India's Afghanistan policy is based on the understanding that democracy and development are the key instruments in ensuring that Afghanistan becomes a source of regional stability and does not slide back to extremism. For a non-traditional donor, India's contribution to Afghanistan is rather significant. The cumulative level of Indian assistance amounts to US$ 2 billion, out of which a total of US$ 1,229,793,372 has been allotted to various developmental projects.[12] The focal point of India's approach has been people-to-people contact in order touch the lives of common Afghans. New Delhi has maintained that its assistance programme has been designed as per Afghan requirements and is not based on what India thinks is right for Afghanistan.

A major portion of the Indian assistance to Afghanistan has come in the form of aid, particularly in infrastructure. Several big construction projects have been undertaken by India like the strategic Zaranj–Delaram highway which connects Afghanistan with the Iranian port of Chabahar. India has also constructed a 200 km long transmission line from Pul-e-Khumri to Kabul and a substation at Chitmala. India is constructing the Salma Dam in the Herat Province and a new Parliament building, among other things.[13] The former Indian Prime Minister, Dr Manmohan Singh, during his 2011 visit committed US $ 500 million in aid for developing infrastructure.[14] Figure 1 (Ministry of External Affairs, Government of India, 2013) provides a sectoral breakdown of India's development cooperation with Afghanistan. The former Indian Ambassador to Afghanistan, Mr Jayant Prasad expressed that "Over 90 percent of Afghan either approve or strongly approve of India's presence in Afghanistan because they believe India is making contribution towards their development."[15]

In the period 2002–2013, China's aid commitment to budget the Afghan reconstruction has been quite weak at around US $ 252 million.[16]

> Chinese undertook (or will have undertaken) 7 complete plant projects (including the Jamhuriat Hospital and Parwan Irrigation Project); 15 batches of materials and equipment, 4 bunches of emergency humanitarian donations, trained over 600 Afghan officials and professionals; wrote off the debt of 9.6 million Pounds (Ministry of Finance, Islamic Republic of Afghanistan 2010).

The scale of China's foreign assistance kept expanding from 2010 to 2012. Besides complete projects, goods and materials, which were the main forms of China's foreign assistance, technical cooperation and human resource development cooperation also saw a remarkable increase.[17] The Chinese framework for engagement with Afghanistan has four dimensions: promoting peace and security; assisting in economic development; supporting "political reconciliation" and strengthening international cooperation. Although Beijing's aid to Afghanistan is significantly less than its assistance to the other developing countries, its contributions in various areas has been encouraged and welcomed by Kabul. Various sources provide differing estimates of the Chinese aid to Afghanistan over the course of the past decade. The Afghan Ministry of Finance (MoF)'s Donor Assistance Database offers the figure of US$ 146 million.[18] The Carnegie

Endowment's Report of 2010 gave the figure of US$ 200[19] million and this figure of Chinese aid has been commonly cited in the most available literature on the subject. Chinese President Hu Jintao announced a further "selfless" amount of US$ 23 million in 2012 making the total contribution to amount to US$ 253 million.[20]

Figure 1

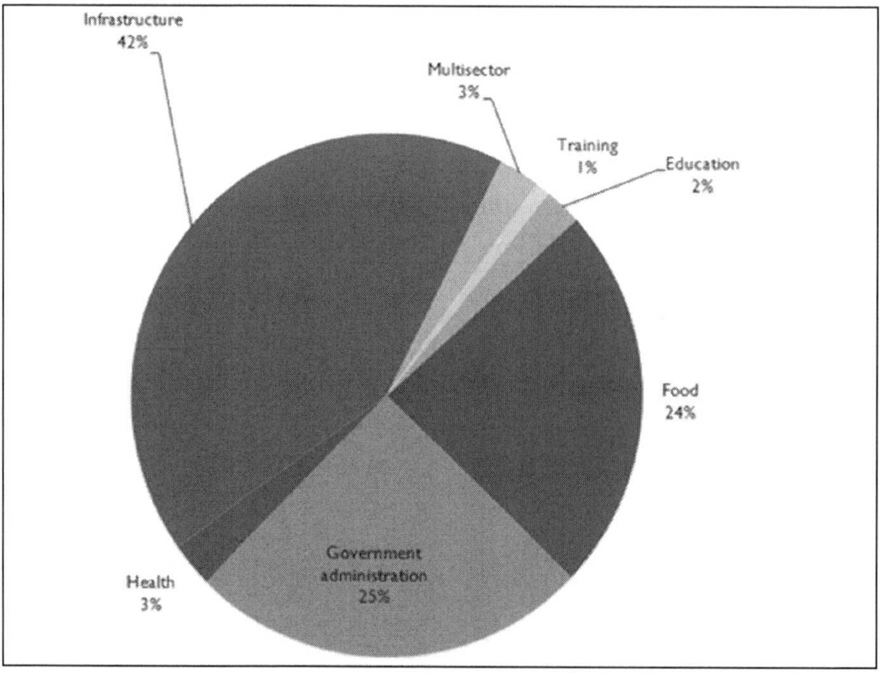

Source: Mullen 2013.

In 2011, China pledged a further US$ 75 million for Afghanistan over a five-year timeline according to the *Foreign Policy* magazine.[21] The Chinese administration under President Xi Jinping, which came in power in 2013, has placed a particular premium on its border relationships and there has been a clear signal in the past few years that China is increasingly focused on what Wang Jisi, the Dean of the School of International Studies at Peking University, has termed 'Marching Westward'.[21]

Pillars of Sino-Indian Cooperation in Afghanistan

There are areas of converging interests of the two counties in Afghanistan, which has led them to undertake the above-mentioned projects there. The cooperation between Beijing and New Delhi regarding Afghanistan thus can broadly be structured under four pillars: security, economics, politics and regional cooperation.

Security

The security situation in Afghanistan holds the key to its future. This is the basic requirement for achieving political and economic stability and without it Afghanistan can never be attractive to external investors. The security situation within Afghanistan and the region at large does not look too optimistic. According to Zhang Xinfeng, the Director of the SCO's Regional Anti-Terror Structure or RATS, "SCO members are facing complicated threats from the south of Afghanistan" and the NATO withdrawal "leaves behind uncertainty in the security situation of the country."[22] During and post the Presidential elections last year, there has been a serious surge in Taliban attacks on civilian and military targets. This has led to President Ghani's government being criticised for serious security failures. Additionally, the problems of insurgency and warlordism are in part fed by an underdeveloped economy that weakens the influence and capacity of the central state. The solutions to these problems is not immediately apparent, but Afghanistan's long-term stability is ultimately contingent on the as-yet distant goal of a strong economy—something that will, in turn, be dependent to some degree on the cessation of, or reduction of violence.[23] Both India and China provide some support to both the military and the police in the form of equipment.[24] Furthermore, they play a role in the capacity building and training of the ANSF. Since 2012, China has agreed to train some 30 members of the Afghan National Police over the next four years.[25] India on the other hand has provided training to at least 650 Afghan Special Forces and officers.[26]

Here, it is important to make a distinction between the Indian military presence in and military aid to Afghanistan. There have been several discussions at different levels about India's presence and the majority thinks it would be counterproductive. Kabul wants to augment its counter-insurgency capacity and hence requires related equipment—from helicopters to communication tools and India has promised to help.[27] As of 2013, there were a total of 334,852.[28] Afghanistan National Security Force (ANSF) personnel and will probably shrink to 228,500 (in line with the declarations made at the NATO Chicago Summit 2012).[29] Even if the ANSF could operate without a significant US or NATO troop presence, which is far from clear, it will remain dependent on international financial and training assistance for some time to come. In 2012, the ANSF budget was US$4.1 billion; US$3.6 billion of which was provided by international donors.[30] NATO estimates that sustaining the ANSF could cost as much as US$5 billion annually. Considering that the Afghan government's entire budget is only US$7.4 billion,[31] it is apparent that Afghanistan will remain unable to maintain it on its own. So far, China and India's contributions in the arena of security have been minimal. So while their physical proximity means that China and India are the countries that are most likely to feel the immediate impact of growing instability in Afghanistan, their contributions do not reflect this fact. Having watched the NATO and Western struggle of the past decade, it is unlikely that the two would be willing to get too closely involved in the difficult quandary of Afghan security.

Economics

In the summer of 2010, the US and Afghan officials trumpeted survey findings which they claimed showed that the nation was sitting on a US$1 trillion of untapped copper, iron and lithium deposits.[32] For a nation whose 97 per cent of the GDP, excluding opium production, is dependent on foreign aid, the development of the mineral industry—whatever its actual worth—is vital to the state's survival. To access these deposits, the Afghans are heavily dependent on foreign countries such as India and China for their technical and industrial expertise. This is one area where the interest of the two powers overlaps. For example, according to one report, China's push for a Turkmenistan-Afghanistan-China gas pipeline (almost at the cost of the long-planned TAPI pipeline) has raised concerns in Delhi, as did the success of a Chinese consortium in securing the rights to a copper mine in Aynak. Although, these concerns have reduced somewhat following the successful Indian bid for rights to the Hajigak mines.[33] The China National Petroleum Cooperation (CNPC) along with the Watan Group (an Afghan Exploration company) has secured the rights to three oil blocks in the province of Sar-i Pul and Faryab in north-western Afghanistan; for its development, the CNPC expects to invest $ 400 million.[34] India has ventured more gingerly into Afghanistan's mining sector, with SAIL AFISCO (the seven-company Afghan Iron and Steel Consortium, led by the Steel Authority of India) holding back on committing to the contract it had won to exploit the Hajigak Iran ore mines while it waits for Afghanistan's mining legislation to be passed.[35]

The trend of the mining sector is likely to accelerate as the Chinese administration develops its 'Silk Road Economic Belt', which will comprise a vast network of transport arteries and trade routes between China's Xinjiang, Central and South Asia and ultimately Europe. Figure 2 depicts

China's vision of the Silk Road Economic Belt as well as the Maritime Silk Road as published by China's state owned *Xinhua* News Agency.[36] India, meanwhile, launched its own 'Connect Central Asia Policy' in 2012 that envisions Afghanistan as a regional trade hub, crossed by energy pipelines and air, rail and road links which it is hoped will one day link up with the subcontinent. In other words, both India and China have a vision for Afghanistan and its neighbourhood as a thoroughfare for regional trade and prosperity.

It is in this context that the BRICS bank could open up possibility for new and virtuous cycles of trade and financial flows among the emerging economies. The announcement of the BRICS (Brazil, Russia, India, China, South Africa)-led development back, to be headquartered in Shanghai, China, is a promising step in the India–China relations. The newly elected Modi Government is strategically positioning itself to play an important role in the Bank's success by attempting to transform India into a manufacturing powerhouse.[37]

Politics

Afghanistan completed its first, however imperfect, transfer of power through ballot with the swearing in of Dr Ashraf Ghani Ahmadzai as the new President in 2014. One of his first acts as the President was to sign a decree appointing his principal opponent Dr Abdullah Abdullah as the Chief Executive Officer (CEO) of a Government of National Unity (GNU) agreed upon to prevent the country from plunging into an abyss. This latest attempt at a GNU has met with mixed reactions; while some have applauded the move, the others being more circumspect, have raised questions over the longevity of what they see as a 'fragile arrangement'. Thus, the outcome of the elections has re-opened the long simmering debate not only on who is to rule but also on how such rule is to be exercised. The GNU is still in its nascent stage and its eventual success or failure will depend upon several variables.

The real test for the GNU begins as it gets down to the business of governance and the excruciating task of executing the long overdue political and administrative reforms and in steering a faltering economy. How the GNU addresses these challenges will be seminal in the realisation of "stability" which Ghani in his inaugural address underlined as "the fundamental goal of our national unity government."[38] Notably, President Ghani linked stability to good governance which he asserted was the key to ensuring economic development, which in turn would foster stability and security. At this juncture, it is important to note that some of the

Figure 2

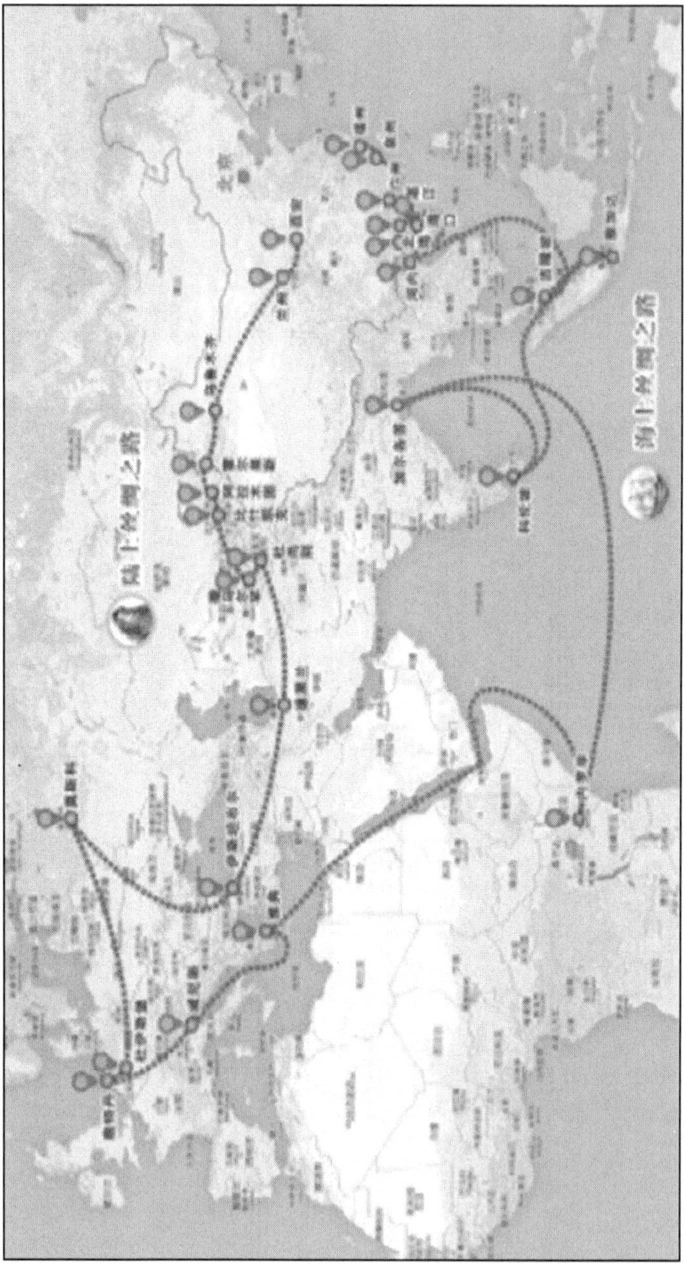

Source: Xinhua News Agency.

realities are not unlikely to change. In particular, Pakistan's fraught relationship with Afghanistan will continue to play a significant role in the country's future and its political process. China might have some role in addressing that. It can continue to use its close relationship with Pakistan as a way of ensuring that Pakistani concerns and interests in Afghanistan are maintained, while the new government in India could reiterate that its relationship with Afghanistan is not being shaped in any way which can be directed against Pakistan. Both China and India are convinced that any reconciliation process has to be Afghan led. While powers such as Pakistan undoubtedly have a role to play, however, their maintaining a veto over the process will not be acceptable. Calling on their regional big-power status, China and India can use their accumulative influence to bring Afghanistan's other border partners, such as Iran and Turkmenistan, into any political process.[39]

Regional Cooperation

Afghanistan has a series of particularities that deeply connect its fate to Central and South Asia such that its internal crisis has a spillover effect on the entire region. In this sense, a regional approach seems to be the most appropriate way to deal with the issues of post-2014 Afghanistan. The SCO member states have recognised the need of a regional framework to deal with the situation there. The fear of an unstable Afghanistan was behind the creation of the SCO itself; as Vorobiev puts it, "One should not forget that the SCO emerged as a response to immediate threats of terrorism and drug trafficking, which came from Afghanistan in 1990s. The SCO idea was born from the collective demand for a regional coalition to combat that."[40] Afghanistan's situation gives SCO the opportunity of moving to the next level and putting the Afghan issue within its scope area. However, despite the many demonstrated and tangible achievements, the organisation has historically remained relatively ineffective. Its decisions on economic cooperation and anti-terrorist efforts, and the situation in Afghanistan have remained on paper.[41] These shortcomings are highlighted when one notes that the SCO does not have a standing military force. According to the Russian envoy to the SCO, Kirill Barsky, "The SCO is not prepared to assume the responsibility of ensuring security in Afghanistan itself."[42]

Although India is still only an observer in the organisation, Indian diplomats have never hesitated to highlight the potential benefit of SCO's involvement in Afghanistan. In a speech given by former Indian Foreign Secretary Sujatha Singh at Tashkent, she called for the SCO to have 'a greater role' in 'rebuilding Afghanistan'.[43] Chinese President Xi even assured the former Afghan President Karzai that "China is also ready to push the Shanghai Cooperation Organization to play a bigger role on the Afghan issues".[44] India sponsored Afghanistan's membership in the South Asian Association for Regional Cooperation (SAARC) in 2006 and was the first country to sign a strategic partnership with Afghanistan in 2011 and has generally enjoyed a cordial relation with Kabul except for the period when the Taliban was in power. Now, India wants to showcase that its inputs to Afghanistan's security and economic welfare especially in the context of the US/NATO withdrawal would be crucial. India at this juncture has to convince China that its participation will add value to the possible cooperative framework and identify resources that it can bring to bear. India has to impress upon China that its membership in the SCO will be beneficial for the entire region and also help to ease the traditional India–China suspicions. Given the political leadership role that China has in the SCO, it would be in India's best interest to avoid the competition for energy.

A Possibility for Cooperation?

At a multinational level, China and India are already engaging in the many initiatives in the region driven by the World Bank and Asian Development Bank (ADB). The Central Asia Regional Economic Cooperation (CAREC) partnership, CASA 1000 (an electricity and trade project for South and Central Asia), the ADB led Turkmenistan-Afghanistan-Pakistan-India project and the Heart of Asia process initiated in 2011 in Istanbul to bring Afghanistan's regional neighbours to take on a greater role in its future development are among the important initiatives taken for reconnecting the region with Afghanistan. China and India have been working along with each other in such projects; however, a greater coordination of the two countries' position within these organisations would ensure more effectiveness in the process of implementation.

Following the electoral victory of Narendra Modi in India, China attempted an early foreign policy reset. The Chinese Foreign Minister Wang Yi—in his capacity as President Xi Jinping's Special Envoy to India—referred to Modi as an 'old friend' of China, and stated that his election injected a 'new vitality into an ancient civilization'. Corroborating Wang's comments, another Chinese Foreign Ministry spokesperson commented that the visit signified a new and positive age in Sino-India relations.[45] Heralding 2014 as the 'Year of China–India Friendly Exchanges', the Chinese State Councilor Yang Jiechi declared that "since the beginning of the 21st century, China and India have both embarked on a modernization drive and became world's most dynamic emerging markets".[46] These gestures however do not underplay the issues of long-standing tensions over disputed borders or for that matter the two countries' differing relationship with Pakistan. They very much continue to be irritants to the bilateral relationship; nonetheless, it is important to acknowledge that over the past year, some notable diplomatic successes have taken place and now both sides would be eager to sustain the momentum.

It would not be realistic to talk about Afghanistan's security situation without taking Pakistan into consideration. The Indian government has to tread carefully. If India adopts an approach on the lines of counter-terrorism with Afghanistan, indicating the role played by Pakistan, it is likely to jeopardise both the prospects of trilateral cooperation and the progress with China. At the same time, if India does not appropriately highlight Pakistan's role in the worsening of the security situation within Afghanistan and the region at large, it may undermine India's position in the eyes of the Afghan policymakers. So considering China's soft stance on Pakistan, this paper suggests the following approaches:

Firstly, India and Afghanistan can attempt to engage a dialogue with China with the evidence of the threats coming from Pakistan. This would provide a counter-narrative to the explanations and arguments forwarded by Pakistan.

Secondly, even though the SCO has provided a great framework for cooperative actions between New Delhi and Beijing in Afghanistan, it would be better to keep the other options open. For example, China has an observer status at SAARC while India and Afghanistan are members of that multilateral organisation. This platform can be utilided to advance regional causes in a way that complements the initiatives taken at SCO.

Thirdly, to set the ball rolling, if they have to identify an area where the two powers can work jointly in Afghanistan, this paper recommends it to be the sphere of human resource development. Over the years, both the countries have undertaken capacity building projects in Afghanistan separately. In future, they can undertake joint ventures in that sphere. Since the costs involved in such projects are lesser, these can be undertaken as pilot projects to test the working compatibly of the two powers. Such small steps might not lead to an overnight change in Afghanistan but these may contribute towards building the foundation for a long-term improvement in the quality of life in Afghanistan. If some of the joint ventures are successful in Afghanistan, the model could be replicated in Central Asia.

Finally, the Indian establishment should bear in mind that it does not rub the sensitivities of its Pakistani counterpart in a wrong way. These capacity building initiatives for the common people of Afghanistan in partnership with its ally, ideally should not generate much suspicion in Islamabad.

Conclusion

Most analysts now believe that the Asian continent is going to become the new centre of gravity in global politics.[47] In the evolving economic and security architecture, most Asian countries would be looking towards China or India for future economic and security alignments; more so in relation to post-2014 Afghanistan where their interests merge to a large extent. This could be partly because they are viewed as the only regional actors with the capacity to take effective action or perhaps because they have the most to lose should the situation falter further. Afghanistan, so far, has been viewed as a part of the larger security matrix of the Central Asian region. It is true that the two countries do not have the same presence in Central Asia. India is expected to play there the role of a balancer in the backdrop of increasing Chinese dominance and declining Russian presence; however, its interests and stakes in Afghanistan and the region at large have forced New Delhi to recast its attention on the region. The proposition of linking the Central and South Asian regions through various networks can only be feasible in a situation when Afghanistan is stable. The groundwork for cooperation between India and China should be worked out both at bilateral and multilateral levels. Though there are uncertainties pertaining to the exact approach that they need to undertake to address the situation in Afghanistan, it remains certain that Afghanistan will continue to be the epicentre of geopolitical interest for the region.

NOTES AND REFERENCES

1. Hornung, Jeffrey W. (2012), "Why China Should Do More in Afghanistan", *The Diplomat*, 1 August. http://thediplomat.com/2012/08/why-china-should-do-more-in-afghanistan/(accessed on 17.1.2015)
2. Mullen, Rani D. (2013), "India-Afghanistan Partnership", Indian Development Cooperation Research, May 16. http://idcr.cprindia.org/blog/india-afghanistan-partnership (accessed on 17.1.2015)
3. *Aljazeera* (2012), "China and Afghanistan Sign Landmark Deals", September 23. http://www.aljazeera.com/news/africa/2012/09/2012923522833684.html (accessed on 17.1.2015)
4. Panda, Ankit (2014), "Is Trilateral China-India-Russia Cooperation Possible in Afghanistan", *The Diplomat*, January 16. http://thediplomat.com/2014/01/is-

trilateral-china-india-russia-cooperation-in-afghanistan-possible/(accessed on 8.1.2015)

5. Harooni, Mirwais (2014), "Top Official says Chinese Security Depends on Afghan Stability", *Reuters*, February 22. http://www.reuters.com/article/2014/02/22/us-afghanistan-china-idUSBREA1L0D720140222 (accessed on 18.1.2015)
6. Lodhi, Maleeha (2013), "China's Afghanistan Policy", *The International News*, December 24. http://www.thenews.com.pk/Todays-News-9-222149-Chinas-Afghan-policy (accessed on 18.1.2015)
7. Gul, Ayaz (2014), "China Increases Focus on Afghanistan", *Voice of America*, February 22. http://www.voanews.com/content/china-increases-focus-on-afghanistan/1857937.html(accessed on 18.1.2015)
8. D'Souza, Shanthie Mariet (2007), "India's Aid to Afghanistan: Challenges and Prospects", *Strategic Analysis*, Vol. 31, No. 5, pp 833-851.
9. *DNA India* (2014),"China wants Afghan Crackdown on Xinjiang Militants", February 23. http://www.dnaindia.com/world/report-china-wants-afghan-crackdown-on-xinjiang-militants-1964479 (accessed on 18.1.2015)
10. *BBC News* (2011), "Pakistan 'Backed Haqqani Attack on Kabul": Mike Mullen", September 22. http://www.bbc.com/news/world-us-canada-15024344 (accessed on 18.1.2015)
11. *Times of India* (2010), "Peace Process Should be Afghan Led, Afghan-Owned", July 21.
12. Royal United Services Institute for Defence and Security Studies and Vivekananda International Foundation (2012), "Towards a Stable Afghanistan: The Way Forward", Occasional Paper, January. https://www.rusi.org/downloads/assets/Towards_a_Stable_Afghanistan.pdf(accessed on 18.1.2015).
13. Embassy of India, Kabul, Afghanistan, (2015), "Indo-Afghanistan Relations: A Development Partnership", January 28, http://eoi.gov.in/kabul/?0707?000 (accessed on 28.1.2015)
14. Mitra, Devirupa (2011), "India Pledges $ 500 Million to Afghanistan", *The Indian Express*, May 11.
15. Ghosh, Anwesha (2014), *A Leap Forward: Capacity Building, Education and India-Afghanistan Cooperation*, New Delhi, KW Publishers, p. 28.
16. Ministry of Finance, Islamic Republic of Afghanistan (2010), "Development Cooperation Report, 2010". Between 2002 and 2011, China committed US$ 139 million of which only US$ 58 million was disbursed. http://mof.gov.af/Content/files/Development%20Cooperation%20Report%202010.pdf) (accessed on 18.1.2015).
17. *Xinhua.net* (2014), "China's Foreign Aid 2014", Report by Information Office of the State Council, The People's Republic of China, Beijing, July http://news.xinhuanet.com/english/china/2014-07/10/c_133474011.htm (accessed on 24.1.2015)
18. Zyck, Steven A. (2012), "The Role of China in Afghanistan's Economic Development and Reconstruction", Civil-Military Fusion Centre (CFC) Report, pp 1-8, March.
19. Ibid.
20. Hornung, Jeffrey W. (2012), "Why China Should Do More in Afghanistan", *The*

Diplomat, August 1. http://thediplomat.com/2012/08/why-china-should-do-more-in-afghanistan/(accessed on 18.1.2015).

21. Pantucci, Raffaello (2010), "In Afghanistan its only Chinese Take Out", *Foreign Policy*, November 29. http://www.foreignpolicy.com/articles/2010/11/29/in_afghanistan_its_only_chinese_takeout?page=full (accessed on 18.1.2015).
22. Peng, Han (2014), "SCO Anti-Terror Chiefs Meet Press", CCTV.com, 15 June. http://english.cntv.cn/2014/06/15/VIDE1402812120558890.shtml (accessed on 24.1.2015)
23. Shisheng Hu, Pantucci, R. and Sawhney, Ravi (2014), "A Roadmap For Sino-Indian Cooperation In Afghanistan", *Royal United Services Institute*, Occasional Paper, July.
24. Weitz, Richard (2014), "Beijing Braces for Afghanistan 2014", *China-US Focus.com*, 18 January.
25. *BBC News* (2012), "China and Afghanistan Sign Economic and Security Deals", September 23.
26. Houreld, Katherine and Mirwais Harooni, (2014), "India and Pakistan Ramp up Aid as They Jostle for Influence in Kabul", *Reuters*, 4 March.
27. Roy, Shubhojit (2013), "India to Give Three Helicopters to Afghanistan Next Year", *The Indian Express*, December 15. http://archive.indianexpress.com/news/india-to-give-3-helicopters-to-afghanistan-next-year/1207793/ (accessed on 14.1.2015).
28. Centre for Security Governance (CFSG) (2014),'The Afghan National Security Force beyond 2014: Will They be Ready?" e-Seminar Series, No. 2, Feb.
29. NATO (2012), Chicago Summit Declaration, 20 May. http://www.nato.int/cps/en/natolive/official_texts_87593.htm?mode=pressrelease (accessed on 24.1.2015)
30. *The Economist* (2012), "All Change: Afghanistan's Hard Road to 2014", October 27; *Transparency International* (2013), "Country Profile – Afghanistan", www.transparency.org/country#AFG (accessed on 24.1.2015).
31. Ministry of Finance (2014), "1393 National Budget Approved by WJ", Kabul: Ministry of Finance: http://mof.gov.af/en/news/1393-national-budget-approved-by-wj (accessed on 24.1.2015)
32. Risen, James (2010), "U.S. Identifies Vast Mineral Riches in Afghanistan", *New York Times*, 13 June, http://www.nytimes.com/2010/06/14/world/asia/14minerals.html?_r=0
33. Bose, Srinjoy (2014), "India and China: An Agenda for Cooperation on Afghanistan", *Institute of Chinese Studies*, Occasional Paper No.19.
34. Downs, Erica (2012), "China Buys into Afghanistan", *SAIS Review*, Vol XXXII, No.2, Summer-Fall.
35. *Economic Times* (2014), "SAIL-Led Firms Await Afghan Law to Negotiate Investment Plan", March 14.
36. *Xinhua* News Agency website http://www.xinhuanet.com/world/newsilkway/index.htm (accessed on 24.1.2015).
37. Modi, Narendra (2014), 'My Government Will Focus on Manufacturing, Infrastructure: Narendra Modi", e-mail interview with IANS, 4 May, http://

www.narendramodi.in/our-government-will-be-a-truly- representativetrans parent-and-sensitive-government-narendra-modi/(accessed on 26.1. 2015)

38. Sharma, Raghav (2014), "Afghanistan After the Elections", *Khaama Press*, October 30.
39. Shisheng Hu, Pantucci et al (2014), op.cit.
40. Vorobiev, Vitaly (2012), "SCO as the Rising Master of the Heartland: How to Elevate the Most Promising Organization in Eurasia to a Next Level", *Russia in Global Affairs*, March 25.
41. Malashenko, Alexey (2013), "So Much Hot Air Expected in Bishkek", Carnegie Moscow Centre, September 12.
42. *RIA Novosti* (2014), "SCO wont Take over From NATO in Afghanistan: Envoy", January 15. http://en.ria.ru/world/20140115/186554000/SCO-Wont-Take-Over-From-NATO-in-Afghanistan—Envoy.html(
43. *The Hindu* (2013), "India Feels SCO Can Play a Bigger Role in Afghanistan", December 1.
44. Shisheng Hu, Pantucci et al, 2014, Op.cit.
45. Panda, Ankit (2014), "China: Foreign Minister's India Trip Has 'Great Significance'", *The Diplomat*, 11 June, http://thediplomat.com/2014/06/china-foreign-ministers-india-trip-has-great-significance/ (accessed on 27.1.2015).
46. Shisheng Hu, Pantucci et al, 2014, Op.cit, p.1.
47. Tellis, Ashley J. (2005), "Military Modernization in Asia" in Ashley J. Tellis and Michael Wills (eds.), *Strategic Asia 2005–06: Military Modernization in an Era of Uncertainty*, Washington: The National Bureau of Asian Research.

2

The Uyghur Factor in India's Relations with China

Mahesh Ranjan Debata

ABSTRACT

The Uyghurs, who are a Sunni Muslim minority group living in China's northwest region of Xinjiang, have never been so important in India's relations with the People's Republic of China, in the way that they have been a factor in the Sino-Turkish, Sino-Central Asian and Sino-Russian relations. However, both the Chinese and the Uyghurs feel that India could play the Uyghur card in the near future. Against this backdrop, this paper discusses the relationship between India and the people of Xinjiang, which has been a major link between China and India since ancient times till the independence of China in 1949. While rejecting the proverbial Uyghur factor in the Sino-Indian relations, the paper argues that the Xinjiang region—and not the Uyghurs—is important for India as it could serve as a land bridge to Central Asia, and is thus poised to be a significant factor in India's relations with China. This paper constitutes of two parts: the first part describes vividly the historical–cultural linkage between India and Xinjiang since the early times till 1949 and the second part delineates the developments in the last two decades, particularly since 2004 till date, that have prompted the two neighbours to come closer on three important areas of cooperation: economic partnership, energy needs and counter-terrorism efforts.

Keywords: Uyghur, Xinjiang, India, historical-cultural linkage, energy, Central Asia

Introduction

The Uyghurs, a Sunni Muslim minority group in China's northwest region of Xinjiang,[1] have never been so important in India's relations with the People's Republic of China, in the way they have been a factor in the Sino-Turkish, Sino-Central Asian and Sino-Russian relations. However, both the Chinese and the Uyghurs feel that India could play the Uyghur card in the near future. There were two important issues that led the Chinese leadership to suspect, particularly in the year 1950 and onwards, that India could play a Uyghur card against its mighty neighbour. Firstly, following the Communist takeover of China in 1949, China eyed India with suspicion after the two top Uyghur leaders, Mohammad Amin Bughra and Isa Yusuf Alptekin, left Xinjiang for the Indian state of Kashmir, along with over 100 Uyghur families. Since both Bughra and Alptekin were spearheading the Uyghur movement in Xinjiang in the 1930s and 40s, China suspected an Indian patronage of these two Uyghur leaders keeping in view India's strong historical and cultural bonds with the people of Xinjiang. Secondly, India's favourable tilt towards Russia (the then USSR), a country which was not only an important actor in Xinjiang from 1920 to 1949 wielding considerable influence in the political circles and having a major say in the economic sector, but also, as per Chinese belief, had helped the Uyghurs establish a Turkic Islamic Republic of East Turkistan in the 1940s. The Chinese feared Russia might persuade or use India to play its part in its troubled northwest. However, both the above Chinese notions were proved wrong when both Bughra and Alptekin left for Turkey in 1950 without getting any patronage or help from Indian leadership. Further, Russia has never brought the issue of Uyghurs before Indian leadership to tinker with the situation in Xinjiang.

It is imperative to cite here another important angle to the whole issue of India, China and Xinjiang that is a staunch belief among the Uyghurs that in due course of time, *Hindistan* (as they address India) will support the Uyghur movement; even help them establish an independent East Turkestan republic.[2] A couple of reasons they ascribe to justify this argument are: i) historically, there were cultural and economic linkages between Uyghurs and the people of India; ii) use of the Uyghur card by India. The disagreements between India and China are many; both are involved in competition and even confrontation, and most importantly, India is worried—even concerned—about the Chinese encirclement[3] following a conspicuous Chinese presence in India's neighbourhood, which will force India to use the 'Uyghur card' against China, once it outmanoeuvres China as an important economic and military power in the coming 30/40 years. However, no one in India buys or will buy this argument, at least as far as the present surge in India's relationship with China is concerned.

Even today, the Uyghurs do not curry India's favour or sympathy for their cause—a separate Islamic republic exclusively for the Uyghurs. India, having its own problems of separatism and terrorism in the State of Jammu and Kashmir, deplores any kind of separatist and terrorist violence not only in Kashmir or Xinjiang, but also anywhere across the globe. What is worth noting in this context is the vehement condemnation of a violent attack in Urumqi on May 22, 2014 by the spokesperson of India's Ministry of External Affairs (MEA), who stated: "We strongly condemn the terrorist attack which took place earlier today at Urumqi, China. India opposes terrorism in all its forms and manifestations. We extend condolences to the families of the victims."[4]

Following are some of the reasons why India may not sacrifice its relationship with China for the sake of the Uyghurs:

1. India does not want to add one more irritant (in the form of the Uyghur issue) to its relationship with China, as major irritants like the boundary issue, Tibet, Arunachal Pradesh, Aksai Chin, etc. still persist.
2. Business interests and energy needs are the other issues which have prompted India to think wisely and cautiously. When trade between India and China is about to reach 100 billion US dollars and India's desire to a get a sub-pipeline from the Central Asian (Kazakh and Turkmen) energy from Xinjiang to India gets stronger after the disappointment over the Iran-Pakistan-India (IPI) and Turkmenistan-Afghanistan-Pakistan-India (TAPI) pipelines, supporting the Uyghur cause could prove to be a blunder.
3. Many in India argue that India's sympathy or support for the establishment of a separate Uyghur nation, will prompt China to raise the Kashmir issue on which it has been maintaining a stand (though not an out-and-out pro-India one) that will not go in the favour of India. Even during the Kargil war between India and Pakistan in 1999, China maintained a neutral position and desired the issue to be solved bilaterally.[5]
4. Most importantly, India and China have one common stand on the issue of three evil forces—separatism, extremism and terrorism.[6] There have been exchanges of experience and intelligence information between India and China in tackling the common

> menace of terrorism. Xinjiang and the Indian state of Jammu and Kashmir, which share a 350-km long border, have been victims of violent terrorist activities. Since links between some Uyghur cadres and the Al Qaeda, Taliban and jihadi groups in Pakistan are being ascertained, India will not support at all any anti-Chinese activity by the Uyghurs which may have a deleterious effect on its relationship with China.

Against this background, this paper discusses the relationship between India and the people of Xinjiang, which has been a major link between China and India since the ancient times till the independence of China in 1949. While rejecting the proverbial Uyghur factor in the Sino-Indian relations, the paper argues that the Xinjiang region—andnot the Uyghurs—is important for India as it could serve as a land bridge to Central Asia, and is thus poised to be a significant factor in India's relations with China. This paper constitutes of two parts: the first part describes vividly the historical–cultural linkage between India and Xinjiang since early times till 1949 and the second part delineates the developments in the last two decades, particularly since 2004 till date, that have prompted the two neighbours to come closer on three important areas of cooperation: economic partnership, energy needs and counter-terrorism efforts.

At the first instance, it is imperative to discuss here the importance of Xinjiang both for China and India. Xinjiang is China's largest province covering an area of 1.6 million sq km in the north-western part of the country, where 10-million strong Uyghurs have been demanding a separate homeland. The region is strategically located, having borders with three nuclear powers—Russia, India and Pakistan; three Central Asian Republics (CARs)—Kazakhstan, Kyrgyzstan and Tajikistan as well as Mongolia and Afghanistan. A sizeable Muslim population in almost all the countries bordering this region, a complex geography, history, ethno-cultural and religious diversity as well as abundant natural resources like oil, natural gas and other minerals have catapulted the region into one of the most important and strategic regions of China. For India, the importance of Xinjiang stems from a number of factors—historical, cultural, economic and trade exchanges. The biggest gain of this relationship will be the opening of the old Ladakh–Xinjiang route, which will pave the Indian access to Central Asia and its resources[7] that India has been constantly trying for the last two decades or so.

Civilisational Links

India's 2500-years-old relationship with Xinjiang is based on historical contacts, exchange in trade and business and cultural linkages. The Silk Route, being witness to the integration of the rich cultural heritage of India and Xinjiang, promoted exchanges of ideas and intellect, and most importantly, trade and commerce. The civilisational linkage between the two regions was spruced up with the introduction, spread and prevalence of Buddhism, one of the foremost precursors of Indian culture, that spread from India to Tibet, Xinjiang, Central Asia and then to Mongolia. Till the advent of Islam in the region, Buddhism remained as the most important religious faith among the people of Xinjiang. Even the Uyghurs followed Buddhism before being converted to Islam. India's rich cultural heritage and spiritual thought and gospels of Buddhism percolated into the hearts and minds of the people of the entire region further leading to a cultural efflorescence of Xinjiang. A well-known Indian scholar, who contributed to the spread of Buddhism in Xinjiang, was

Kumarajiva (344 AD–413 AD), one of the greatest sutra translators in China.[8] Also known as the "Light of Kuqa", Kumarajiva's bronze statue in Kuqa bears testimony to his popularity as a well-known Buddhist scholar and also as the chief protagonist of the India–Xinjiang cultural exchanges. By the seventh century AD, all the kingdoms in Xinjiang's Tarim Basin region had embraced Buddhism.[9] Sanskrit became the main religious lingua franca. The Kumtura Thousand-Buddha Caves lying 30 km to the southwest of the Kuqa Prefecture not only symbolise Buddhism but also glorify its noble principles. The Buddhist texts were translated from Sanskrit into local dialects such as Tocharian.[10] By 658 AD, Kuqa became the main hub of Hinayana Buddhism. Teh famous Chinese travellers, Fahien and Hiuen Tsang, who visited India and tread along the Silk Route, confirmed that most of the small and big kingdoms in Kashgar, Kizil, Karashahr and Kuqa followed the Hinayana form of Buddhism, whereas the Mahayana form of Buddhism flourished in cities like Khotan and Yarkand. The discovery of Buddhist images, murals, frescoes, some symbols of lotus, mandala, swastika, etc. and inscriptions in Sanskrit, Brahmi and Kharoshthi scripts and artefacts depicting Indian traditions in Kuqa, Kizilgaha, Kumtura, Khotan, Kashgar, Dunhuang, Yotkan, Dandan Uiliq, Niya, Loulan and Turfan bear testimony to the Indian cultural influence in the entire landmass.[11] An ivory plaque collected by the Swedish explorer, Sven Hedin from the Khotan region of Xinjiang, now preserved in the Ethnographic Museum, Stockholm (Sweden), is believed to be more than a thousand years old. It presents a very intricate composition in the form of a *Yantra* or *Mandala*. According to it, Tantric Buddhism, which originated in India, was popular in the Khotan region in the ninth–tenth century AD. Other sources confirm that the Khotan region was an important centre of Tantric Buddhism during the early medieval period.[12]

India and Xinjiang in Modern Times

In the modern and contemporary period, Xinjiang became important due to the British interests there. The British authorities in India paid great attention to Xinjiang, especially for political reasons, and remained active in the region from 1891 to 1947.[13] They wanted to gain a foothold in Xinjiang so that any move by the Tsarist Russian ruler to expand beyond his empire could be staved off. At that point in time, Russia had taken control of the khanates in Central Asia (Kokand, Khiva, Fergana, Samarkand and Bukhara). The British Indian authorities apprehended a further expansion of the Tsarist empire towards India either through Afghanistan or through Xinjiang. As a precautionary measure, the British rulers in India first tried to get a foothold in Afghanistan, but failed miserably after being vanquished in the Anglo-Afghan wars. Then to establish their presence in Xinjiang, the British authorities found a favourable ally in Yakub Beg, who established an Islamic Emirate in Kashgar from 1867 to 1877.[14] Yaqub's dislike for the Qing rulers prompted him to build harmonious relations with the British Indian authorities, which augured well for the overall relationship between the two regions, especially trade. In 1874, the British authorities signed an agreement with Yakub in order to obtain the freedom to trade with low duties in the region. However, the ouster of Yakub Beg in 1877 and the consolidation of the Qing rule in Xinjiang seriously affected the British interests in the region. The British loss in the region was Russia's gain. Russia remained a dominant force in Xinjiang during the last leg of the Qing rule and throughout the republican rule in the region from 1911 to 1949.

When the Tsarist government first set up a consulate in 1881 in Kashgar, British India too set up a consulate there to contend and collude with Tsarist Russia. From 1890 onwards, the Government of India appointed an official resident to be stationed at Kashgar. Colonel Francis Younghusband was the first British official resident in Kashgar, and was replaced by George Macartney in 1891 who stayed there until his retirement at the end of World War II. The Jammu and Kashmir is the northernmost state of India. It is situated mostly in the Himalayan mountains. Jammu and Kashmir shares a border with the states of

Himachal Pradesh and Punjab to the south and internationally with the People's Republic of China to the north and east and the Pakistani...

British consulate in Kashgar was the only British diplomatic organisation in Xinjiang in the early twentieth century. It handled business activities and other diplomatic activities in the Tianshan region on behalf of the British Empire and its colonies such as India.[15]

However, its activities in China were a short-term gain for the British empire, but a long-term loss for India. By annexing Kashmir through the Treaty of Amritsar in 1846, the British bequeathed independent India with a boundary problem with China that exists till date; almost six decades after the establishment of diplomatic relations between the two neighbours. The India–China border, which is 4,000 km long and being divided into the western, middle and eastern sectors, stretching from the trijunction of India, China and Afghanistan in the west to the trijunction of the borders of India, China and Myanmar in the east,[16] has become a border of contention. What adds insult to injury is the thorny issue of Aksai Chin, which continues to haunt the relationship between the regions even today. Aksai Chin was ceded to British India by Tibet through a treaty in the early 1900s. But since China does not recognise Tibet's independence from China at that point of time, it does not recognise that treaty as well. The Aksai Chin region, which had been controlled by Pakistan illegally since 1947, was gifted to China on March 3, 1963, immediately after the Sino-Indian war (October 1962), and now it forms part of the Khotan County of Xinjiang.[17]

Trade Exchanges

The relationship between the two regions began with regular contacts between the traders/merchants from India's Ladakh and Kashmir regions and the southern and south-eastern regions of Xinjiang through the Silk Route. Traders travelled between India and Xinjiang on the Himalayan caravan routes over the Karakoram Pass between Kashgar in Xinjiang and the Gilgit and Hunza valleys (presently in Pakistan). During Han rule, links with India got a major boost, particularly when the Han General Zhang Qian sent his assistant to India to find ways and means for the promotion of bilateral trade between the two regions.[18] The main items exported from India to Xinjiang were opium, cotton, piece-goods, spices, Indian tea, sugar and indigo and the imports from Xinjiang included gold and silver, *charas*, shawl wool, carpets and felts, tea, Chinese teacups, leather-ware, coarse cotton cloths, raw silk, precious stones, ponies, horses and mules. The bulk of the Indian trade with the oasis towns of Yarkand, Kashgar and Khotan was carried through Kashmir and Ladakh. Under a barter system, the traders from Yarkand used to bring these goods to Ladakh where they used to exchange the same with their Indian counterparts. They even moved further to Kashmir, Punjab and Himachal Pradesh to expand their flourishing trade. Similarly, the Indian traders went beyond Ladakh towards Yarkand to purchase goods at relatively low prices. Ladakh was connected with the Silk Route at Yarkand by a caravan route running across the Karakoram Pass.[19]

In eighteenth century, King Gulab Singh (1792–1857), the Dogra ruler of Jammu, and his military commander General Zorawar Singh looked beyond the frontiers of Ladakh and took measures to safeguard the trade routes from marauders, raiders and plunderers, besides ensuring the steady flow of trade from Xinjiang into Ladakh and Kashmir, particularly the lucrative shawl-wool trade. Gulab Singh's son Ranbir Singh (1830–1857) went one step ahead. He abolished all the transit duties on the merchandise passing to and from Xinjiang through Kashmir and Ladakh so that the existing trade would get a major boost. The Srinagar-Leh-Yarkand route became the most important thoroughfare between India and Xinjiang during the Dogra rule in Kashmir. The Karakash Valley served as an important caravan route for the north–south trade between Yarkand (China) and Leh over the Karakoram Pass in the Leh district of Jammu and Kashmir.[20]

The British rulers in India encouraged trade exchanges between the two regions. In 1874, the British authorities had signed an agreement with Yakub in order to obtain the freedom to trade with low duties in the region. However, the ouster of Yakub Beg by the Qing rulers had affected India's trade with Xinjiang. In 1885, a mission headed by Ney Elias, an official of the Foreign Department of the Government of India, arrived in Kashgar to negotiate a trade agreement. The Jammu and Kashmir is the northernmost state of India. It is situated mostly in the Himalayan mountains. Jammu and Kashmir shares a border with the states of Himachal Pradesh and Punjab to the south and internationally with the People's Republic of China to the north and east and the Pakistani...

British consulate in Kashgar handled business activities too on behalf of the British empire.[21] Further, the period from 1890 to 1908 saw an increase in the export of coral ornaments to Xinjiang from India. During the rule by the Chinese warlords in Xinjiang in the republican era, India's trade with Xinjiang continued unabated. In the period from 1917 to 1931, India exported goods worth 30 million rupees that constituted cotton goods and silks, dyed skins, indigo, spices and tea to Xinjiang through Kashmir and Ladakh. A merchandise worth 33 million rupees was imported from Xinjiang into Ladakh and Kashmir of which *charas*, Russian gold and paper currencies, gold dust, raw silk, carpets and felts were the main import items. The India–Xinjiang bilateral trade through Kashmir and Ladakh was worth seven million rupees during the years 1920–21.[22] From the late 1930s onwards, the internal disorders in Xinjiang that had arisen out of the creation of the East Turkestan Republic (1933–34) and the subsequent opening of the Russian overland trade with Xinjiang dealt a fatal blow to the Indo-Xinjiang trade. Later in 1949, the century-old relationship between both the regions ceased to exist after China came under communist rule.

The end of the Cold War in the early 1990s following the disintegration of the former Soviet Union heralded the dawn of a new era. With the emergence of five independent republics of Central Asia, the importance of the strategically located Xinjiang region has increased further. It has brought new hopes for India since both the Central Asian and Xinjiang regions have been historically and culturally important for it. There is also hope for the revival of trade between the regions, which was a continuous affair since ancient times, with a five-decade interregnum from 1949 to 2004. The year 2004, which has been a watermark as far as the issues related to India and Xinjiang are concerned, witnessed a serious Chinese endeavour to develop Kashgar—one of the most underdeveloped regions of Xinjiang. And in this regard, a process of economic integration of Kashgar started, which will be discussed later in greater detail. The Xinjiang provincial governors were sent to India as special emissaries of the Chinese Central Government to revive the old cultural linkage between the two regions.

Political Initiatives

A six-member delegation led by the then Governor of Xinjiang, Ismail Tiliwaldi, visited India in October 2004 in order to revive the old ties and promote a bilateral interaction with India. Both the sides made proposals for the India–Xinjiang land link, air route (Delhi–Kashgar via Urumqi), laying a natural gas pipeline from Xinjiang to India through Ladakh and bilateral cooperation in four fields—agriculture and food processing, traditional medicine and herbs, energy and oil production and tourism. Both sides believe that the road link could transform the two economies. With a reliable land link through Pakistan to Central Asia still being a distant dream, linking Ladakh, which is in eastern Jammu and Kashmir and borders Tibet, to Xinjiang and then reaching out to Central Asia, will not only tap the resources of the region but also result in a greater cooperation in diverse fields. For India, the pipeline proposal with Xinjiang will open a new connectivity between India and Central Asia. Since the much-talked about Turkmenistan-Afghanistan-Pakistan-India (TAPI) and Iran-Afghanistan-India (IPI) pipelines to bring the energy resources from Central Asia and Iran respectively have become "pipedreams"[23] now due to the turbulent situations in Afghanistan and Pakistan, a pipeline bringing energy resources from Xinjiang could be a feasible proposition.

Further, in November 2011, the present Governor of Xinjiang Nur Bekri visited India under the India–China Distinguished Visitors' Programme, which assumed considerable importance as this was the second time that the Governor of Xinjiang had visited India in the past eleven years. Nur Bekri, leading an official delegation of 19 officials and prominent businesspeople from Xinjiang, held official talks with the then Minister for Commerce and Industry of India, Anand Sharma, high-profile officials of the Ministry of External Affairs, business leaders, academia and media. While addressing a Business Session organised by the Confederation of Indian Industry (CII) in New Delhi on November 2, 2011, Nur Bekri called for the building of a trade and investment relationship between India and Xinjiang. Bekri said that with the extensive economic reforms of the last three decades, Xinjiang has developed greatly and now offers huge business and investment opportunities in the sectors like oil and natural gas, mining, agriculture, tourism, Information and Technology, pharmaceuticals and biotechnology. Besides, Bekri emphasised the strengthening of cultural exchanges between India and Xinjiang to revive the people-to-people contact both the regions had had earlier.[24] Further, officials from Xinjiang's Political and Legal Committee who had accompanied Nur Bekri expressed their readiness to work with India on the important issue of counter-terrorism. Earlier, the Xinjiang government's Development and Reform Committee (DRC) had extended its support for increasing frontier trade with India. The DRC welcomed the Indian companies to invest in Kashgar, spoke in favour of the opening of international flights from Kashgar to India, and even encouraged the foreign airlines to open direct flights between the two regions.[25] Shi Dagang, Vice Chairman of Xinjiang's provincial government, expressed his government's desire to boost the land trade with India. Speaking ahead of the start of the Shanghai Cooperation Organisation (SCO) Summit meeting in Beijing on May 30, 2012, Shi stated, "we have no land port with India, so our trade with India has to be routed through Pakistan, through places like Rawalpindi. It only takes 50 minutes by air from New Delhi to Kashgar, while the land distance is only 1,200 km. I believe that with our relationship deepening, this trade link will be utilised further."[26] The above-mentioned facts are found to be interesting and give a positive signal for both India and Xinjiang and there is a renewed hope that Xinjiang is going to be an important factor in India's relationship with China in the near future.

One unusual thing on part of the Chinese leadership is its view about Pakistan and its position on the issue of Uyghurs, which is important for India too. Though, Pakistan has been China's all-weather friend, China accuses Pakistan of harbouring the Uyghur separatists and imparting training them to launch jihad in Xinjiang. The Chinese officials have been making claims time and again that the Uyghur separatist movement in Xinjiang has received religious and ideological materials and literature from several Muslim countries via Pakistan. Beijing believes that the Karakoram Highway that links Xinjiang with Pakistan has been facilitating the spread of Islamic ideology into Xinjiang and the movement of the radical Uyghur militants.[27] China has pointed an accusing finger at Pakistan after an attack in the Yecheng city of Xinjiang on February 28, 2012. The Chairman of the Xinjiang Regional Government remarked a week after on March 7, 2012 that the attackers had "one thousand and one links" to Pakistan. China further implicated Pakistan, when profiles of six Uyghurs from China, who allegedly operate in "South Asia" as members of the ETIM, were published on the website of China's Ministry of Public Security on April 6, 2012.[28] The Chinese stand on Pakistan's involvement in the terrorist activities in Xinjiang is an indication for India to bolster up its cooperation with China on the issue of combating the evil forces. In this context, the view of the Development and Reform Committee (DRC) of the Xinjiang government sounds good for India. The DRC acknowledged India's claims to Pakistan-occupied Kashmir (PoK) by describing the Kashgar region as bordering India, and not Pakistan.[29] These developments clearly show that though Xinjiang remained a non-descript factor between the two neighbours for a period of five decades from 1949 to 2004, it is becoming a vital cog in the common relationship between the two global powers.

Economic Initiatives

The economic boom in Xinjiang[30] and the proximity of Xinjiang to the resource-rich Central Asia have prompted India to think about the renewal of links with Xinjiang and for acting immediately. With Xinjiang prospering by leaps and bounds under the Chinese Central Government's Great Western Development Programme,[31] a new and dynamic region in their neighbourhood would be available to the Indian entrepreneurs for their trade and business activities. Now, Xinjiang has an effective border trade with three Central Asian republics of Kazakhstan, Tajikistan and Kyrgyzstan, besides Mongolia and even Pakistan. Even the trade between India and Xinjiang has reached US$ 47 million by 2011,[32] and is supposed to reach the US$ 100 million mark. In order to strengthen the business relations with India, four trade delegations from Kashgar hve arrived in India in the recent years and have been welcomed by India's business community. Another important issue is energy. There has been a tremendous increase in India's energy consumption after it experienced a rapid and robust economic growth. Since China has been able to bring the oil and natural gas pipelines from Kazakhstan and Turkmenistan, India's purpose to get energy from Central Asia could be solved once the Central Asian energy is diverted from Xinjiang to India. In this context, this section will discuss three important issues: (i) Economic integration of Kashgar; (ii) China–Eurasia Expo and (iii) The Silk Road Economic Belt and the Maritime Silk Road.

Economic Integration of Kashgar

Since June 2004, the authorities in Xinjiang have been promoting a nationwide campaign to achieve the economic integration of Kashgar,[33] a town known for its historic role in the matters of China's trade through the ancient Silk Route with eight countries in Central and South Asia including India. The main thrust of Kashgar's economic integration with Central and South Asia is to ensure the security, stability and prosperity of the volatile region of Xinjiang. The Chinese endeavour to integrate Kashgar with the outside world, at least in economic terms, primarily aims at improving the security situation in Kashgar, which has been a theatre of violent activities since the Communist takeover of China in 1949; the recent being the incident in the Sache County of Kashgar in December 2013. The Chinese government feels that by integrating Kashgar with South and Central Asia, it can kill two birds with one stone: the first is to ensure the security and stability of Kashgar and the second is the tapping of the resources of the region. In 2009, Kashgar was made a Special Economic Zone (SEZ) on the model of Shenzen and Guangdong. Shenzhen and Hong Kong signed an agreement to invest US$ 3.7 billion in Kashgar in 2011 and offered US$ 15 million to help the local enterprises to expand and to provide employment to 30,000 people. The Chinese Central Government has decided to provide financial subsidies to the Kashgar SEZ from 2011 to 2015, to exempt qualified enterprises from business income tax, to subsidise fixed-asset investment and offer government loans to qualified companies at discounted rates. The government also intends to give discounts to qualified farm product-processing enterprises and other labour-intensive companies by reducing their power consumption and transportation fees. Investments in the major infrastructure facilities' construction projects in the two zones, including the construction of the China-Kyrgyzstan-Uzbekistan railway and the China-Pakistan railway, have increased.[34] For India, the proposal for Kashgar's economic integration with the outside world assumes greater significance on two counts. Firstly, India has strong historical–cultural affinity with Kashgar, which is also known as Kashi. In India, Kashi is one of the holiest places of the country. Secondly, India has an emotional relation with Kashgar, where an Indian Consulate existed from 1890 to 1947. But most importantly, the opening of Kashgar will provide India an opportunity to have access to the resources in Xinjiang and Central Asia, as it used to have earlier on the Silk Route.[35] India and China now consider the opening of the trade route from Kashmir to Xinjiang on the lines of the Nathu La border point in Sikkim which was opened in July 2006. The border trade with Ladakh and Kashmir will not only revive the ancient cross-border trade between the two regions but will also help in renewing the people-to-people contact as part of the historical and cultural relationship both the regions had nourished earlier.

China–Eurasia Expo

Since 2011, the China–Eurasia Expo has been a continuous business fair attracting world attention. Further, during the third Expo in 2013, some $121 billion worth of domestic deals were announced. The German–Chinese joint venture company VW-SAIC is opening a car factory outside Urumqi; a Sino-Turkish investment park is being opened in Urumqi, while companies from across China are being actively encouraged to invest in the region.[36] India too participated in this Expo in October 2011 and India's Ambassador to China, S. Jaishankar visited Urumqi, where he met officials from the energy companies TBEA and Goldwind.[37] This author, during his visit to the TBEA Headquarters in Changji (Urumqi) on June 25, 2014, interacted with the Deputy Secretary of Party Committee and the Deputy General Manager of TBEA CO Ltd, Ms Wu Wei. Ms Wei gave information about a US$ 200 million investment by the TBEA in establishing the Green Energy Park at Karjan, Vadodara (Gujarat). Ms Wei also informed this author about the training of some 200 Indian personnel at the TBEA Headquarters in Changji, who will be part of the Green Energy Park at

Karjan. And finally on June 28, 2014, the Energy Park in Karjan saw the light of the day, when the Gujarat Chief Minister inaugurated it along with high-profile Chinese officials.

The Silk Road Economic Belt and the Maritime Silk Road

The Silk Road Economic Belt and the Maritime Silk Road are two ambitious initiatives launched by the Chinese Central Government to revive the old route of trade, commerce and people-to-people contacts. The Silk Road Economic Belt, which covers 18 Asian and European countries with a total area of 50 million square km and a population of 3 billion people, is a reservoir of energy, mining, tourism, cultural and agricultural resources[38] and can serve as a driver for growth, bringing access to the global value chain to all countries and people along the Belt.[39] Since energy cooperation is the warp and weft of the region's development, the Belt will ensure regional energy security and support sustainable economic growth.[40] The Belt would link the different regions in Eurasia, enable the convergence of their different interests for complementary advantages and enable the sharing of development opportunities to achieve common development.[41] And at large, it will help in achieving peace, progress and prosperity of the entire region.

The Belt begins in Xi'an in central China before stretching west through Lanzhou (Gansu), Urumqi (Xinjiang) and Khorgas (Xinjiang), which is near the China–Kazakhstan border. Then it runs south-west from Central Asia to northern Iran before swinging west through Iraq, Syria, and Turkey. From Istanbul, the Belt crosses the Bosporus Strait and heads northwest through Europe, including Bulgaria, Romania, the Czech Republic and Germany. Reaching Duisburg in Germany, it swings north to Rotterdam in the Netherlands. From Rotterdam, the path runs south to Venice (Italy) where it meets up with the Maritime Silk Road. The Maritime Silk Road will begin in Quanzhou in Fujian province and also hit Guangzhou (Guangdong), Beihai (Guangxi) and Haikou (Hainan) before heading south to the Malacca Strait. From Kuala Lumpur, the Maritime Silk Road heads to Kolkata, India, then crosses the rest of the Indian Ocean to Nairobi, Kenya. From Nairobi, the Maritime Silk Road goes north around the Horn of Africa and moves through the Red Sea into the Mediterranean, with a stop in Athens before meeting the Silk Road Economic Belt in Venice.[42]

One scholar sums up the features of this initiative as the following:

> (i) This initiative will bring about unity among nations and a commitment to cooperation, by means of a greater connectivity and complementarity among East Asia, Central Asia, South Asia,

> Southeast Asia and West Asia, thus bringing the pan-Asian and Eurasian regional cooperation to a new level; (ii) the initiative will boost infrastructure development and structural innovation in order to improve the business environment of the region, besides facilitating an orderly and unimpeded flow of production factors and their efficient distribution, accelerating the development of landlocked countries and remote and inaccessible pockets, lowering costs and barriers of trade and investment and driving greater reform and an opening up by the regional countries and (iii), this will strengthen the people-to-people contact, irrespective of nationhood, regions, classes and religions, further consolidating the foundation of friendship among the people and contributing positively to peace and development in Asia.[43]

For India, these two plans seem to be interesting and can bring about new opportunities. Some of the existing projects of India's cooperation with China, like the Bangladesh-China-India-Myanmar Economic Corridor and the Chinese industrial parks in India, can be part of this cooperation. India's Look East policy as well as the BIMSTEC Cooperation can also be integrated with the above two initiatives.[44] To popularise these two economic initiatives, the Chinese government has been organising conferences and discussions collecting views, information and stands by the foreign countries on these issues. In one such international conference on the theme, *Silk Road Economic Belt: An Opportunity to Work, Share, Prosper and Succeed Together*, from June 26–27, 2014, organised by the State Council Information Office of China at Urumqi, Xinjiang, this author spoke on what India is going to gain from this ambitious initiative.[45] Almost 80 delegates from 23 countries from Asia and Europe participated in the Seminar. The biggest gain for India wiould be energy. Over the last one decade, China has been able to pipe 60 million tonnes of crude oil and 81 billion cubic metres of natural gas from Central Asia to its territory. Further, the building of a US$ 30 billion oil pipeline from Russia to Xinjiang as part of the US$ 400 billion worth of the Sino-Russian energy cooperation agreement for 30 years provides a glimmer of hope. Now, India is making efforts to persuade Russia for the extension of this pipeline to India while perceiving Xinjiang as the connecting bridge in this process.

Conclusion

Now, the onus is on the leadership of both the countries on how to reap the benefits from these golden opportunities. It is crystal clear that whatever differences India and China may have had in the last six decades, both the regions share at least two similar views now: i) trade and economic partnership and ii) the fight against separatism, religious extremism and terrorism. In this era of globalisation, when economic development has become the main buzzword, India and China have emerged as two important global actors and responsible world powers with economic prowess and military might. Xinjiang is important for both these two mighty neighbours. While on the one hand, it is China's gateway to the resource-rich Central Asia region, on the other, it could be India's land bridge to Central Asia. The development in Xinjiang, whether positive or negative, will have impact on both India and China. Since India and China have been moving in the right direction in the recent period, with bilateral trade projected to touch 100 billion US dollars in the coming couple of years and a meaningful engagement at the political and diplomatic levels, there is a glimmer of hope for a relationship based on mutual trust and understanding. The last few initiatives such as the economic integration of Kashgar, the visit by two of Xinjiang's provincial governors to India in 2004 and 2011 and the Silk Road Economic cooperation have been interesting and positive signs for both India and Xinjiang. The visits by the Xinjiang Governors clearly show that the Chinese leadership is keen to revive the age-old India–Xinjiang linkage. Even the Indian Embassy in China has been participating regularly in the China–Eurasia Expo in Urumqi for the last few years. In the recent times, the leadership of both the countries has shown a desire to strengthen their cooperation. The new Indian government under the leadership of Narendra Modi that came to power in May 2014 has expressed its desire to extend the hand of friendship to China in order to resolve all the outstanding issues between the two neighbours. As a corresponding gesture, the Chinese Foreign Minister visited India from June 7–9, 2014 as the Special Emissary of Chinese President to facilitate the new vistas of cooperation among the two neighbours. India's Vice President Hamid Ansari visited China from June 28–30, 2014 and participated at the commemoration of the 60th Anniversary of the Five Principles of Peaceful Coexistence (Panchsheel) in Beijing on June 28, 2014. The Indian Minister of Commerce and Industry had accompanied the Vice President. The Indian side signed two MoUs and one document with its Chinese counterparts. During the Chinese President Xi Jinping's visit to India from September 17–19, 2014, as many as sixteen agreements were signed between the two countries. From the Indian side, the Minister for External Affairs has reciprocated through a visit to China. The Indian Prime Minister Modi's visit to China this year could also be a beacon of hope towards the establishment of more meaningful relations. Out of these goodwill gestures, a simple conclusion can be deduced that perhaps the 'good days are ahead' for both the regions.

NOTES AND REFERENCES

1. As per the Chinese Census 2010, the Uyghur population in Xinjiang is 12 million out of the total population of 22 million. Uyghurs, who are the majority nationality in Xinjiang, are one of the 47 minority groups and one of the 13 Muslim minorities living in Xinjiang, and have been demanding a separate "East Turkestan" republic out of China.
2. Many Uyghurs, including academics, scholars and leaders of various organisations, living in the USA, Turkey and Europe, whom this author interviewed during the period 2005 to 2013, have expressed their feelings that India should play an important role in the Uyghur movement for a separate state of East Turkestan.
3. Some Indian analysts and policymakers fear a possible Chinese encirclement of India, which they call China's "string of pearls strategy", considering the Chinese presence in India's neighbourbood (Pakistan, Bangladesh, Sri Lanka, Nepal, Bhutan, Myanmar, etc.). For details see, Maloy Krishna Dhar, "Chinese String of Pearl around India", 14 August 2011, http://maloykrishnadhar.com/chinese-string-of-pearl-around-india; Also see, Deepak Kapoor, "India's China Concern", *Strategic Analysis*, vol. 36, no. 4, July 2012, pp. 663-679.
4. *"Official Spokesperson's Response to a Media Query on the Terrorist Attack at Urumqi, China", 22 May 2014, http://www.mea.gov.in/media-briefings.htm?dtl/23345/Official+Spokespersons+response+to+a+media+query+on+the+terrorist+attack+at+Urumqi+China*
5. Srikant Kondapalli, "China's Response to the Kargil Incident", ***Strategic Analysis,*** vol. 23, no. 6, September 1999, pp.1039-1044; Also see Swaran Singh, "Kargil Conflict: Why and How of China's Neutrality", *Strategic Analysis,* vol. 23, no. 7, October 1999, pp. 1083-1094.
6. For a detailed analysis of the three evil forces, see Mahesh Ranjan Debata, "Discourse on 'Three Evil Forces' within the Ambit of SCO" in Rashpal Malhotra et al (eds.) *Central Asia and its Neighbours: Prospects of India's Cooperation,* Chandigarh: Centre for Research in Rural and Industrial Development (CRRID), 2014, pp. 39-56.
7. At present, India does not have any direct border with the resource-rich Central Asian Republics. India has been trying to gain access to Central Asia through Iran and Afghanistan at the cost of billions of dollars. But unfortunately, due to political and security issues, India's efforts have ended in a fiasco. Even India's bid to get the hydrocarbon resources from Central Asia through the Turkmenistan-Afghanistan-Pakistan-India (TAPI) pipeline has not materialised so far.
8. Kumarajiva's father, Kumarayana, who was from a noble family in the Indian state of Kashmir, went to Kuqa and married the king's sister, Princess Jiva. Jiva renounced family life and travelled to India along with her son, Kumarajiva, and studied under renowned Buddhist masters. By the tender age of seven, Kumarajiva had memorised many sutras and texts, and his name, fame and glory spread across the entire region. He translated 74 texts in 384 fascicles from

Sanskrit into Chinese, which not only spoke volumes about his wisdom, but also greatly contributed to the propagation of the Dharma in China. For more details, see the conference proceedings of the International Seminar and Exhibition on "Kumarajiva: Philosopher and Seer", Indira Gandhi National Centre for the Arts, New Delhi, 3–5 February 2011; Also see Sunita Dwivedi, *In Quest of the Buddha: A Journey on the Silk Road*, New Delhi: Rupa, 2009.

9. Kashgar, Yarkand and Khotan in the western part of Xinjiang; Tumsuk, Aksu, Kumtura and Kizil in the north; Loulan, Karasahr and Dunhuang in the east and Miran and Cherchen in the south became important learning centres of Buddhist philosophy and thought at that point of time.
10. *Tocharian* was an independent member of the group of languages that includes the modern European languages such as German and French, the modern Asian languages including Persian, Hindi and Urdu branches of the northern Indian language. See Michael Dillon (2004), *Xinjiang:China's Muslim Far Northwest*, London and New York: Routledge Curzon, p. 8
11. "Buddhism and its Spread along the Silk Road", Silk Road Foundation, http://www.silk-road.com/artl/buddhism.shtml
12. For more details, see Mahesh Ranjan Debata, "India and Xinjiang", *World Focus*, vol. xxxi, no. 11-12, Annual Number, November–December 2010, pp. 528-531.
13. James Onley, "The Raj Reconsidered: British India's Informal Empire and Spheres of Influence in Asia and Africa", *Asian Affairs*, vol. 40, no.1, 2009, p. 58.
14. For details, see Kim Ho-Dong, *China's Holy War: The Muslim Rebellion and State in Chinese Central Asia, 1864-1877*. Stanford: Stanford University Press, 2004.
15. "British Consulate", http://www.kashi.gov.cn/english/Context/History40.htm
16. Mohan Guruswamy and Zorawar Daulet Singh, *India-China Relations: The Border Issue and Beyond*, New Delhi: Viva Books, 2009, p. 3; Also see A.G. Noorani, *India-China Boundary Problem, 1846-1947: History and Diplomacy*, New Delhi: Oxford University Press, 2011.
17. Under China's "east–west swap" proposal, China would abandon its claim on the Indian State of Arunachal Pradesh, recognising Indian sovereignty over that area, in exchange for India giving up its claim on Aksai Chin, recognising Chinese sovereignty over that area. The East–West swap was first proposed unofficially by Zhou Enlai in 1960 when he talked of a 'reciprocal acceptance of present realities in both sectors.' In 1980, the proposal was revived in an interview to an Indian defence journal by Deng Xiaoping. He suggested the package deal of China accepting the McMohan Line in the east in return for India recognising the status quo in the west. For details, see Bharat Bhushan, "Sino-Indian Relationship beyond Tibet", *The Daily Times*, 5 July 2003.
18. P. Stobdan, "China's Xinjiang Problem", *IDSA Comments*, 9 July 2009, http://www.idsa.in/strategiccomments/ChinasXinjiangProblem_PStobdan_090709
19. K. Warikoo, "India's Gateway to Central Asia: Trans-Himalayan Trade and Cultural Movements through Kashmir and Ladakh, 1846-1947" in K. Warikoo (ed.) *Himalayan Frontiers of India: Historical, Geopolitical and Strategic Perspectives*, London & New York: Routledge, 2009, pp. 1-13.
20. Ibid.
21. "British Consulate", http://www.kashi.gov.cn/english/Context/History40.htm

22. K. Warikoo, "India's Gateway to Central Asia: Trans-Himalayan Trade and cultural Movements through Kashmir and Ladakh, 1846-1947" in K. Warikoo (ed.) *Himalayan Frontiers of India: Historical, Geopolitical and Strategic Perspectives*, London & New York: Routledge, 2009, pp. 1-13; Also see Madhavi Thampi, "Indian Traders in Xinjiang in Nineteenth and Twentieth Centuries", *China Report*, vol. 46, no. 4, pp. 373-375.
23. For more details, see Mahesh Ranjan Debata, "Turkmenistan-Afghanistan-Pakistan-India (TAPI): Pipeline or Pipedream" in K. Warikoo (ed.) *Central Asia and South Asia: Energy Cooperation and Transport Linkages*, New Delhi: Pentagon, 2011, pp. 178-192.
24. "Build Economic Relationship: Xinjiang Governor", 4 November 2011, http://indiacurrentaffairs.org/build-economic-relationship-xinjiang-governor/
25. Ananth Krishnan, "Xinjiang Keen on Reviving Historic Trade Ties with India", *The Hindu*, 2 November 2011.
26. Ananth Krishnan, "Xinjiang Eyes Direct Land Trade with India, Afghanistan", *The Hindu*, 5 June 2012.
27. Ziad Haider (July–August 2005), "Sino-Pakistan Relations and Xinjiang's Uyghurs: Politics, Trade, and Islam along the Karakoram Highway, *Asian Survey*, vol. 45, no. 4, p. 523.
28. Jacob Zenn, "Insurgency in Xinjiang Complicates Chinese-Pakistani Relations", *Terrorism Monitor*, vol. 10, Issue: 8, 20 April 2012.
29. See Note 25.
30. Economic development in Xinjiang includes an elaborate communication network (roads, railways, telecom), besides development in industries and oil refineries. For details, see K. Warikoo, "China's Policy in Xinjiang and India's Experience in Kashmir", *Himalayan and Central Asian Studies*, vol. 14, no. 4, October-December 2010, pp. 5-19.
31. The Great Western Development Programme focuses on the development of the entire western part of the country of which the north-western region of Xinjiang forms an important part. The programme lays stress on the all-out development of the region for which trade and economic cooperation with the neighbouring regions/countries is very much essential.
32. See Note 26.
33. D.S. Rajan, "Making Kashgar a Centre for Central and South Asia Economic Grouping", Paper No. 1190, 15 December 2004, http://www.southasiaanalysis.org/papers12/paper1190.html
34. For details, see Bhavna Singh, "China's Modernization Rush: Kashgar at Crossroads", No. 3556, 16 January 2012, http://www.ipcs.org/article/China/Chinas-modernization-rush-kashgar-at-crossroads-3556.html
35. For details, see Mahesh Ranjan Debata, "Kashgar's Economic Integration with Central and South Asia: Opportunities for India" at the National Seminar on *Rising India, China, South Africa & Brazil: Challenges & Strategic Options*, on 27–28 January 2014, organized by Centre for South African and Brazilian Studies, Aligarh Muslim University, Aligarh.
36. For details, see Raffaello Pantucci and Alexandros Petersen, "Tightening the Silk

Road Belt", 18 September 2013, http://thediplomat.com/2013/09/tightening-the-silk-road-belt/

37. "India-China Bilateral Relations", http://meaindia.nic.in/mystart.php?id=50042452
38. "Xinjiang to Promote Silk Road Economic Belt", 16 January 2014, http://www.china-embassy.org/eng/zt/Xinjiang/t1119718.htm
39. He Na and Xue Chaohua, "Revival of Ancient Silk Road, Essential for Asian Nations", *China Daily*, 29 May 2014, p. 7.
40. "Energy Cooperation to Lead Silk Road Economic Belt", 25 May 2014 http://www.china.org.cn/business/2014-05/25/content_32484567.htm
41. Chen Yurong and Tang Zhongchao, "Summary of the International Symposium on the Silk Road Economic Belt in the Context of Economic Globalization", organised by the China Institute of International Studies (CIIS) in Beijing on 11 December 2013, China International Studies, January/February 2014, pp. 159-170.
42. Shannon Tiezzi, "China's 'New Silk Road' Vision Revealed", 9 May 2014, http://thediplomat.com/2014/05/chinas-new-silk-road-vision-revealed/
43. Wei Wei, "Silk Route: The Way to Prosperity for India, China and the Entire Asia", 14 April 2014, http://economictimes.indiatimes.com/opinion/comments-analysis/silk-route-the-way-to-prosperity-for-india-China-and-the-entire-asia/articleshow/33712755.cms
44. Ibid.
45. For details, see Mahesh Ranjan Debata, "Silk Road Economic Belt and India: Challenges and Opportunities", *World Focus*, Annual Issue, Series 2, Vol. 35, No. 12, December 2014, pp. 121-126.

3

Changing Dynamics of Power in Asia and the Asian Century: Challenges and Opportunities for India and ASEAN

Netajee Abhinandan

ABSTRACT

The dream of the 'Asian Century' still remains unfulfilled. The concept that germinated during the famous meeting between Deng Xiaoping and Rajiv Gandhi in 1988 has not moved beyond the level of an 'idea'. Though counties like China, India and Japan have risen dramatically in recent times in terms of their economic and political prowess acquiring global power status, they have not been able to provide collective leadership to other countries of Asia in bringing them together to a common platform for advancing the interests of the region as a whole countering the dominance of Europe and America in world politics. In fact, Asia, of late, has become a hotbed of conflicts, controversies and contradictory claims and counterclaims among the various countries, as evident during the South China dispute. The differences have only intensified further following the dispute resulting in an atmosphere of deep mutual distrust and rivalry. While China wants to position itself as the 'sole' leader representing the interests of the Asian countries in global regimes and multilateral institutions, India, Japan and other South-East Asian countries are determined to counter the growing power and influence of China in the region. The lack of rules of engagement and confidence-building measures, unresolved disputes, competition for scarce resources and status considerations and the jostling for greater power among the countries have the potential to seriously threaten peace and stability in Asia in the long term.

Asia has certainly lagged behind, in comparison to North America and West Europe, in achieving regional integration. Despite the economic imperatives and interests in the current phase of globalisation pushing for a strong and formal institutional arrangement among the countries for a better and smoother facilitation of trade and commerce along the lines of the European Union (EU), the Asian countries have not been able to pursue a cohesive and common agenda of growth and development for the region. The regional organisations like the South Asian Association for Regional Cooperation (SAARC) and the Shanghai Cooperation Organization (SCO) have failed to achieve their proclaimed goals and objectives. The Association of South East Asian Nations (ASEAN), on the other hand, has proved to be relatively more successful in bringing the countries together for negotiation and agreement on important economic issues and problems. Still, it has not been to resolve the long-standing political and security-related issues among the member countries and to make them agree to collective self-regulation and common rules of political engagement, thus affecting its functioning.

In this context, it is imperative to explore whether the ASEAN would be able to get its act together and move towards establishing the Asian Economic Community in 2015 and also arrive at solutions to the substantial issues of governance. Moreover, India's role assumes crucial significance in this regard as it tries to leverage its strategic partnership with the ASEAN to attain greater power for itself vis-à-vis China in the South and South East Asian region. The paper would endeavour to analyse the dynamics of engagement between India and ASEAN on the one hand and India and China on the other in effecting a greater Asian solidarity. Also, it would try to examine whether the ASEAN would be able to go the EU way towards realising the dream of the 'Asian Century'.

Keywords: Asian Century, India, China, ASEAN, regional cooperation, integration, economic challenges.

In the twenty-first century, Asia can no more be ignored as a continent of poverty and underdevelopment as countries like Japan, China, South Korea, India along with other East Asian economies account for more than 40 per cent of the global output. It is believed that if Asia continues to grow at the current speed, it could, by 2050, account for more than half of the global Gross Domestic Product (GDP), trade and investment and enjoy a greater prosperity and affluence. Its per capita income could rise six-fold to reach the global average and match the European levels of today. If Asia succeeds in achieving this feat, it could very well control more than half of the total global financial assets and occupy the most dominant position in the global economic structure. The remarkable economic transformation of Asia along with a relative decline in the American power and the inability of the European countries to manage the global crises have made the analysts believe that the current century would indeed be an 'Asian Century' ushering in the resurgence and dominance of Asia in the coming years.

During Prime Minister Rajiv Gandhi's path-breaking visit to China in 1988, Deng Xiaoping hoped that the impending century would be an 'Asian Century', if China and India would choose to join hands and forge a strategic partnership setting aside their outstanding differences. Subsequently, this term has been used on several occasions by the Asian leaders, theoreticians and political analysts to signal the emergence of Asian countries like China, Japan and India as new 'centres' of power and as important stakeholders of the global system. As the twentieth century was characterised as the American Century and the nineteenth century as the British, it was hoped that the twenty-first century would belong to the Asian countries leading the world based on their strong economic performances and technological achievements. The hope was not far-fetched or unrealistic as Asia accounted for nearly 60% of world population and around 25% of the global economic output. The ushering of a 'free market economy' in the Asian economies along with the end of the Cold War in the early 1990s unleashed a great potential for the economic development for these countries and also opportunities for the Western countries seeking markets for their businesses. The strong economic performances of the Asian countries in the last three decades along with the intensification of the globalidation processes provided excellent opportunities for the realisation of the dream of the 'Asian Century'. Kishore Mahbubani presents seven pillars that would enable the Asian countries to excel and make them 'equal' with the Western counterparts. The seven pillars include: free-market economics, science and technology, meritocracy, pragmatism, culture of peace, rule of law and education.[1] Mahbubani argues that the time has come for the West to recognise the importance of Asia and include it in the global decision-making processes. The control over the key global forums and institutions such as the UN Security Council (UNSC), the WTO, the International Monetary Fund (IMF), the World Bank the G-8, etc. must shift to the Asian countries corresponding to their rising power and influence. The changing dynamics of power in favour of Asia was quite evident in the way India and China led the other Asian and African countries during tough negotiations in the WTO and Earth Summits demanding a greater accommodation of their interests. In fact, they were largely successful in preventing the imposition of a 'Western' agenda over the global trade and environmental policies. Moreover, as there has been a perceptible decline in the American power and dominance on the world scene, either any European country individually or the European Union (EU) as a whole has not been able to assert its authority and assume leadership.

The Asian Century: A Dream or a Reality?

Many analysts believe that despite the adversities and political differences, the Asian economies would surely play a vital role in the global economic order, eventually paving the way for a greater political assertion by them. In the twenty-first century, Asia can no more be ignored as a continent of poverty and underdevelopment as countries like Japan, China, South Korea, India along with other East Asian economies account for more than 40 per cent of the global output. It is believed that if Asia continues to grow at the current speed, it could, by 2050, account for more than half of the global Gross Domestic Product (GDP), trade and investment and enjoy a greater prosperity and affluence. Its per capita income could rise sixfold to reach the global average and match the European levels of today. If Asia succeeds in achieving this feat, it could very much control more than half of the total global financial assets and occupy the most dominant position in the global economic structure. The report of the Asian Development Bank (ADB), published in 2011, outlines Asia's economic future:

> Asia's rise will be led by PRC, India, Indonesia, Japan, Republic of Korea, Malaysia, and Thailand. In 2010 these seven economies had a combined total population of 3.1 billion (78 percent of Asia) and a GDP of $14.2 trillion (87 percent of Asia). By 2050 their share in population is expected to fall to 73 percent of Asia, while the share of GDP rises to 90 percent. These seven economies alone will account for 45 percent of global GDP. Their average per capita income of $45,800 (PPP) would be 25 percent higher than the global average of $36,600.[2]

Also, Asia presents a huge market having millions of middle-class consumers, which the European countries and the US could hardly afford to ignore. It is estimated, rather conservatively, that the middle class will grow to 3.2 billion by 2030 and would remain under a billion in Europe and North America. Moreover, the humongous human resources in the Asian countries, which earlier were seen rather as a liability, are currently being considered as the most essential drivers of economic growth and development. The increasing economic prowess of the Asian countries has led to their growing political influence in world politics. Particularly, the rise of China and India challenges the role of the established industrial powers of Europe and North America in many ways and also forces them to come to the negotiating table on contentious trade issues. Especially, after the global financial crisis of 2008, the Western world looked towards Asia to sort out the trade imbalances and help it in warding off the economic disaster. The emerging powers of Asia were incorporated into the global economic governance and were made members of G-20. It signalled a marked shift in the centre of power towards Asia underlining its importance as one of the most integral stakeholder in the global governance structure. The remarkable economic transformation of Asia along with a relative decline in the American power and the inability of the European countries to manage the global crises have made the analysts believe that the current century would indeed be an 'Asian Century' ushering in the resurgence and dominance of Asia in the coming years.

However, to fulfil the dream of an 'Asian Century', some long-term problems and issues have to be addressed and future agendas have to be clearly defined. The biggest challenge would be the eradication of poverty and an equitable distribution of resources among the people so that inequalities and polarisation within the countries do not happen. Some countries require a greater capital investment and technological innovations so that they can gradually move into the 'high-income' groups. While countries like China and Japan face the problem of ageing populations, populous countries like India stand to reap demographic dividends only if they could create sufficient jobs for their bourgeoning labour force. As Asia's urban population will likely double up to 300 billion by 2050, it has to grapple with the stress and constraints that rapid urbanisation creates. Moreover, the Asian countries while surging ahead towards a greater economic growth and development must ensure that environmental concerns and issues are duly considered and taken care of. Apart from the domestic policy adjustments, the Asian countries need to shoulder new challenges, responsibilities and obligations at the global level. The ADB Report of 2011 delineates the future road map for Asia, if it has to play a proactive role in global affairs proportionate to its growing economic and political clout:

> The region will need to take greater ownership of the global commons, including an open trading system, stable financial system, climate change, and peace and security. It will need to gradually transform from a passive onlooker in the debate on global rule-making and a reticent follower of the rules, to an active participant in the debate and a constructive formulator of the rules. While formulating its domestic or regional policy agenda, the region as a whole, but also the larger economies—PRC, India, Indonesia, Japan

and Republic of Korea—will need to take into account the regional and global implications. The region will need to delicately "manage" its rapidly rising role as a major player in global governance in a non-assertive and constructive way. As an emerging global leader, Asia should act as—and be seen as—a responsible global citizen.[3]

The Jostle for 'Power' in Asia: Can Integration Really Happen?

Regional integration, cooperation and collaboration among the major powers of Asia are critical for achieving the goals of development. Unless the countries come together on issue areas such as energy security, poverty alleviation, sustainable use of natural resources, technological development, disaster preparedness, etc. setting aside their differences, the dream of an 'Asian Century' can never be realised. However, the Asian countries have failed to get their acts together. Despite the economic imperatives pushing for a grand alliance among the Asian countries along the lines of the European Union, any such formation has not been possible even after more than a decade into the twenty-first century. In fact, Asia, of late, has become a hotbed of conflicts, controversies and contradictory claims and counterclaims among the various countries. The increasing tensions over territorial disputes, rising military budgets and dawdling economic growth threaten to "impede trade, tourism and investment especially if incidents occur between rival air or naval forces operating in close proximity over or around disputed waters and territories. Cyberspace is another domain in which competition could get out of hand."[4] As Asia is passing through a phase of transition—from poverty and political irrelevance to prosperity and political dominance—it has to contend with power imbalances and growing security challenges. The resurfacing of the Cold War-era territorial and maritime disputes has led to the formation of alliances and counter-alliances and reconfiguration of power equations in the region. The intensification of the geopolitical competition among the major Asian countries has thwarted any attempt towards political integration that would have resulted from a greater economic interdependence.

The dispute over the South China Sea best exemplifies the crisis in Asia. While on the one side is China asserting its sovereignty over this entire area claiming it as part of its territory, on the other side the ASEAN countries like Malaysia, the Philippines and Vietnam are vehement in opposing the Chinese claims as they seek equal rights to explore the natural resources from it. The tensions arising out of these claims and counterclaims in the recent times have posed a serious challenge to regional security raising grave concerns in the international community.[5] The differences have only intensified further following the dispute resulting in an atmosphere of deep mutual distrust and rivalry. While China wants to position itself as the 'sole' leader representing the interests of the Asian countries in global regimes and multilateral institutions, India, Japan and other South-East Asian countries are determined to counter the growing power and influence of China in the region. In this context, Richard N. Haas asks, "Will twenty-first-century Asia resemble Europe – the dominant region of much of modern history—during the first half of the twentieth century, when it experienced two wars of unprecedented cost and destruction, or the second half, when tensions with the Soviet Union were effectively managed and Western Europe experienced unprecedented peace and prosperity?"[6] The Western analysts see contemporary Asia as a conundrum—alternately swinging between extreme situations—as integration eludes it despite the opportunities and as dissensions take the centre stage. The question arises whether Asia would be able to overcome the long-standing differences among the countries and move towards greater unity and integration.

Most of the outstanding disputes among the Asian countries date back to the times of the World Wars or even before. Korea and China still nurture anti-Japanese sentiments. Both Russia and Japan claim the Kuril Islands as part of their respective territory. The long-standing border dispute between China and India (that triggered the war in 1962) remains unresolved despite several rounds of negotiations. The continuing conflict between the two Koreas, the threat posed by a nuclear-armed North Korea, China's assertions over the East and South China seas and instability in South Asian countries like Pakistan, Afghanistan, Bangladesh and Nepal present serious difficulties for any attempt towards an Asian integration. Moreover, the rapidly growing economic, political and military power of China has made many countries anxious, prompting them to invite other major external powers to engage in the region. Many believe that their political and strategic interests would be adversely affected with the rise of powerful China and its assertions over the maritime resources in the region. These concerns have led to the promotion of the concepts of 'Asia-Pacific' and 'Indo-Pacific', which is evident with the US pivot to Asia and the direct mention and discussion in Australia's Defence White Paper (2013).[7] Incidentally, the former Indian Prime Minister Manmohan Singh too referred to this terminology in December 2012, when he moved to enhance India's relations with the ASEAN.

Asia has certainly lagged behind, in comparison to North America and

West Europe, in achieving regional integration. The lack of the rules of engagement and confidence-building measures, unresolved disputes, competition for scarce resources, status considerations and the jostling for greater power among the countries have the potential to seriously threaten peace and stability in Asia in the long term. Though counties like China, India and Japan have risen dramatically in recent times in terms of their economic and political prowess acquiring global power status, they have not been able to provide collective leadership to other countries of Asia in bringing them together to a common platform for advancing the interests of the region as a whole, countering the dominance of Europe and US in world politics. Moreover, there have not been meaningful regional agreements or institutions in the political and security spheres to enhance the level of understanding and for creating a more amiable atmosphere for cooperation. Thus, despite the economic imperatives and interests in the current phase of globalisation, pushing for a strong and formal institutional arrangement among the countries for a better and smoother facilitation of trade and commerce along the lines of the European Union (EU), the Asian countries have not been able to pursue a cohesive and common agenda of growth and development for the region. The regional organisations like the South Asian Association for Regional Cooperation (SAARC) and the Shanghai Cooperation Organization (SCO) have failed to achieve their proclaimed goals and objectives. In this context, it is imperative to explore whether the ASEAN would be able to get its act together and move towards establishing the Asian Economic Community in 2015 and also arrive at solutions to the substantial issues of governance.

India in the Asian Century: Can It Play a Pivotal Role?

India, economically growing at a rapid pace, still remains a middle-income country, lagging behind its BRICS counterparts. India has the largest concentration of poor people: in 2010, more than 840 million Indians lived on less than $2 a day, and 400 million on less than $1.25 a day.[8] By the time India becomes the most-populated country in the world, it would face serious problems in making adequate provisions for food, drinking water, shelter, health facilities, infrastructure and jobs for its people. In this context, many questions do arise with regard to India's possible role in the Asian Century. Can India contribute to the Asian Century? What opportunities will Asia's rise offer India? Can India forge partnerships with its South Asian neighbours and other countries in the South East Asian region and emerge as one of the leaders? Can India counter the Chinese influence and dominance in Asia and help in establishing an accommodative and collaborative framework for regional cooperation?

India has to address these challenges if it were to realise its full potential and join the league of high-income countries like China and Japan. It has to devise and most importantly effectively implement the suitable policy mechanisms to achieve the goal of 'faster, sustainable, more inclusive growth' that the government's 12th Five Year Plan (2012–17) has set for itself. Analysts believe that there were mainly seven factors that have helped the industrialising countries of Asia in rapidly transforming their economies: policies that have supported free markets, science and technology, meritocracy, pragmatism, a culture of peace, rule of law and education.[9] India has to factor in these aspects while pursuing its growth agenda. Also, it has to curb corruption at all levels of public life, make governance transparent, responsive, efficient and people-centric and ensure that the benefits of development reach all sections of the society.

On the external front, India needs to intensify its trade relations not only with the Asian countries, but with North American, European and African countries also. Apart from economic initiatives, it has to have a greater interaction with all the major powers of Asia and try to leverage its strategic importance vis-à-vis its biggest competitor China. India has clearly outlined its foreign policy framework on how to grapple with the changing dynamics of power in Asia over the years. The former National Security Advisor Shiv Shankar Menon sketched out the following fundamental principles of India's policy for the emerging Asian Century:

- The new order must be inclusive, comprising all powers—regional and extra-regional—relevant to the practice of Asia's security.
- India's geographic outreach must be extensive, extending from the Suez to the Pacific, seamlessly enfolding the maritime periphery with the rising continental core.
- Its security structure must be plural and open ended, having learnt its lesson from the past collective security failures.
- Finally, its institutional mechanisms must be consultative and non-prescriptive, respectful of the region's preference for consensus-based approaches to problem-solving, and centred in that cross-roads of the Asian inter-civilisational interaction—Southeast Asia.[10]

These principles prescribed by Menon have provided a sense of the probable path that India would like to embark on in the coming years to maximise the opportunities that a rising Asia would offer. However, the actualisation of these principles would require India to project its power in such a way that it could win the trust and support of not only its South Asian neighbours but also the other major actors of the South East Asian region, without antagonising any of them. Moreover, it has to play a proactive role in the deliberations and negotiations on various issues at the different regional forums such as SAARC and ASEAN.

ASEAN: Challenges and Opportunities

The Association of South East Asian Nations (ASEAN) has been the most significant multilateral group in Asia for almost the last half-decade. Since its inception in 1967, ASEAN has largely achieved its initial purpose of preventing Southeast Asia from further outbreaks of war following the India–China War, and has also succeeded in bringing the countries together for negotiation and agreement on important issues and problems in the economic and non-proliferation realms. The main objective of ASEAN—managing Southeast Asia's diversity for peace rather than conflict—has been fulfilled. There has been no major and sustained conflict between the member states in recent years, despite persistent bilateral tensions over historical territorial claims, ethnic or separatist insurgencies and controversies over natural resource management. ASEAN serves as the core of other important regional organisations such as ASEAN+3 (including China, Japan and South Korea) and ASEAN+6 (with India, Australia and New Zealand), the Asian Regional Forum and the East Asian Summit among others. In the absence of any other credible regional forums, ASEAN has been at the forefront in devising the commonly acceptable norms and practices for the various issue areas. It is, nowadays, being popularly referred to as the 'ASEAN Way'. Its two main principles are decision-making by consensus and non-interference in the internal affairs of member countries. These principles have been infused into other regional organisations such as the ASEAN Regional Forum (ARF) and the East Asian Summit.[11]

ASEAN has been able to build strong economic networks among the member countries as well as all its partners and associated members creating opportunities for a faster growth and development of the whole region. Economic growth, coupled with the normalisation of political relations among the former Cold War adversaries, has encouraged new trade routes and infrastructure development at the subregional level. Apart from the economic issues, it has made efforts to arrive at a common agreement on other issues of vital importance such as climate change, energy and food security, counter-terrorism, non-proliferation, cyber safety, human trafficking, gender equality, etc. It aims to establish an Asian Economic Community along with a Political Security and Socio-Cultural Community by 2015 that would ensure a free flow of goods, services, investment, skilled labour and capital among the member countries. It would help in setting up of a highly competitive single market promoting an equitable economic development for the member states, as well as facilitating their integration with the global community.

However, despite many success stories, the ASEAN has not been to resolve the long-standing political and security-related issues among the member countries and to make them agree to collective self-regulation and common rules of political engagement, thus affecting its functioning. In July 2012, the ASEAN Ministers Meeting in Phnom Penh, for the first time in its 45-year history, failed to issue the traditional joint communiqué due to differences over the South China Sea territorial disputes. It is clear that even after decades of bonhomie and institutional togetherness, the ASEAN countries have not been able to mutually work out the threat perceptions, defence policies and military doctrines. As the efficacy of the ASEAN has been challenged in the recent years following a number of unfortunate bilateral disputes among the member countries, questions are being raised regarding the future of regional cooperation in South East Asia in particular and in Asia in general. As the ASEAN attempts to reinvent itself as an economic union and to present a common front in the international community, it is often undermined by its diversity. As the member countries greatly differ in terms of their political ideologies, convictions, priorities and stages of development, guided by their respective national interests, they very often choose not to rally behind the ASEAN, unless there are significant political and economic benefits. As ASEAN was preparing to face the challenges of the post-globalised world order by launching ambitious initiatives on all major fronts, the debilitating effects of an economic crisis, growing differences on political issues and a very slow progress on regional security have led most analysts to raise doubts about the future of this regional organisation and its ability to enforce a commonly acceptable framework for the member countries to deliberate upon all issues pertaining to security, political engagement and economic development.[12]

The ASEAN members have failed to evolve a broad common understanding over the questions of the role of major powers, the regional balance of power, bilateral security arrangements, etc. as many ASEAN countries still repose a greater faith in bilateralism than multilateralism. The US has tried to undermine the influence of ASEAN by strengthening its alliance partnerships with countries like Japan, Australia, South Korea and Taiwan and thereby gaining greater leverage in the East Asian and South East Asian regions. The dispute between China and Vietnam, Philippines, Japan and other countries over the control over the South

China Sea has not only reflected the limitations of the conflict-resolution capabilities of the ASEAN but also underlined the deep fissures and trust deficit existing within the organisation. What the ASEAN lacks is an institutional mechanism to deal with the various contentious issues. The Secretariat of ASEAN, based in Jakarta, has played a rather limited role and it does not offer any policy directions to the member states. Unless the ASEAN addresses these issues, its effectiveness as a united front against any external attempt at destabilisation of the region can never be realised. This is a major challenge that the ASEAN will have to address sooner than later in view of the developments in the South China Sea. Any failure on the part of the ASEAN, which has assumed and played a central role in regional security, has far-reaching implications not just for South-East Asia, but for the larger Pacific Asian region too.

India and ASEAN in the Asian Century: The Road Ahead

In the post-Cold War period, India made a significant leap towards greater engagement with the countries of the East and South-East Asia by announcing a "Look East policy" that redefined its foreign policy goals and aspirations. It was a well-calculated strategic initiative by India to counter the growing influence of China in the region and to project itself as a natural partner for rapid economic growth and development. This policy that was adopted during the Narasimha Rao regime in 1991 was earnestly pursued by the successive governments under Atal Bihari Vajpayee and Manmohan Singh. India established strong commercial, cultural and military ties with countries like the Philippines, Singapore, Vietnam and Cambodia and signed numerous free trade agreements with the ASEAN member states.

India's relations with ASEAN have improved rapidly and dramatically in the recent years. Since becoming a full-dialogue partner in December 1995, India has intensified its engagement with ASEAN by holding annual Summit Meetings, signing important agreements and actively participating in its deliberations. India participates in a series of consultative meetings with ASEAN under the ASEAN–India Dialogue Relations, which includes summit, ministerial meetings, senior officials meetings and meetings at an expert level as well as through dialogue and cooperation frameworks initiated by the ASEAN, such as the ASEAN Regional Forum (ARF), the Post Ministerial Conference (PMC) 10+1, the East Asia Summit (EAS), Mekong–Ganga Cooperation and Bengal Initiative for Multisectoral Technical and Economic Cooperation (BIMSTEC), which help in contributing to the enhancement of regional dialogue and in accelerating regional integration. India has undertaken some bilateral and multilateral projects for boosting connectivity between the North-East and South-East Asia. The important ongoing and potential infrastructure projects in this regard are the Moreh-Tamu-Kalewa Road, India-Myanmar-Thailand Trilateral Highway, Trans-Asian Highway, India-Myanmar rail linkages, Kaladan Multimodal project, the Stilwell road, Myanmar-India-Bangladesh gas or oil pipeline, Tamanthi Hydroelectricity project and the optical fibre network between North-East India and South-East Asia.[13] The collaboration between India and ASEAN has transcended the realm of functional cooperation to cover the political and security dimensions. Apart from the economic sphere, India and ASEAN share similar concerns in the field of terrorism, piracy, drug trafficking, sea-lane protection, climate change, natural disaster management and most notably, the rise of China.

More than two decades after the initiation of the "Look East policy", India has established itself as a key player in the South-East Asian region by galvanising its relations with all the major countries and in finding common ground on various issues such as terrorism, human rights, environmental sustainability, drug trafficking and trade facilitation. It now looks forward to enter a new phase of strategic engagement in the region and expand its influence further by deepening ties with the ASEAN. At the ASEAN–India Commemorative Summit held on December 20, 2012 in New Delhi, the ASEAN–India Vision Statement was adopted which declared the elevation of the ASEAN–India relations to the level of Strategic Partnership. India is keen to leverage its strategic partnership with the ASEAN to attain a greater power for itself vis-à-vis China in the South and South-East Asian regions. India's then External Affairs Minister Salman Khurshid outlined the vision for future relations during his inaugural address at the recent India–ASEAN Delhi Dialogue VI named 'Realizing the ASEAN–India Vision for Partnership and Prosperity',

> A very important dimension to the ASEAN India strategic partnership is its increasing relevance to the political-security space in East Asia. With power equations being re-drawn, the ASEAN India relationship provides an egalitarian balance for the maintenance of peace and stability. An inclusive, open architecture is our common objective. It is pertinent now more than ever to reinforce existing international law on maritime security. India's naval footprint is essentially that of a net security provider even as it is set to expand. There is also potential for greater engagement between ASEAN and India in the ARF, ADMM+ and ASEAN Maritime Forum.[14]

Shri Narendra Modi, after taking over as the Prime Minister, underscored the importance of India's relations with the East Asian countries as he upgraded the "Look East policy" into "Act East policy" at the 12th ASEAN Summit at Myanmar in November last year. During the first few months of his regime, Modi and Foreign Minister Sushma Swaraj have visited countries like Bhutan, Nepal, Bangladesh, Japan, South Korea, Myanmar, Maldives, Mauritius, Singapore, Fiji and Vietnam signaling a more proactive and action-oriented policy towards East and South-East Asia. As China positions itself as the most dominant power in Asia, as evident during the South China dispute, India is keen to leverage its strategic partnership with the ASEAN countries to attain a greater power for itself vis-à-vis China in the South and South-East Asian region.

On the other hand, ASEAN also realises that India has a much greater role to play in South-East Asia in the second decade of the twenty-first century. India's role is becoming critical in shaping the regional strategic discourse that has been drifting towards uncertainty, mutual suspicion and deep distrust for each other with the fight for control over natural resources also increasing. While both Manila and Hanoi called for New Delhi's active participation in the regional security discourses, such as the resolution of the South China Sea issue, Phnom Penh requested India for a financial assistance of US$ 57 million. This trend gained ground during the proceedings of the Delhi Dialogue III at the track-II level in March 2011 when demands for India's active role in the region were sought by experts and leaders in the backdrop of China's growing assertion in the South China Sea since May 2010.[15] Thus, there is mutual recognition on the part of both India and ASEAN that their close partnership in the Asian Century would certainly help in establishing peace and stability in Asia and give a definite and positive direction to the process of development in the continent.

The South-East Asian nations look towards India to play a kind of 'balancing role' vis-à-vis China in the region. They prefer to jointly manoeuvre against the Chinese strategy rather than individually engaging with China in any conflict. China's growing economic and strategic power and influence in the region, makes it imperative for South-East Asia to intensify ties with India. However, while countries like Japan, Vietnam, Singapore and Malaysia would be proactive in seeking formal arrangements with India to counter China with the backing of the US, India would prefer to be cautious, avoiding any direct alliance with countries. It would rather be ambivalent and equivocal, maintaining flexibility and the freedom of action that India associates with its non-alignment policy.

The strategic analyst Brahma Chellany summarises India's position, "Its hesitancy notwithstanding, India may invariably find itself a part of this collective security framework, within which it will need to work with countries such as the US, Japan and Australia. Notably, the US pivot to Asia entails a strategic realignment that would accord an important role to India and the Asia-Pacific in the near future. But undoubtedly India is an important stakeholder in the Asia-Pacific region and as a responsible actor, it will have to employ some astute diplomacy by demonstrating that it can work equally well with China given the latter's respect for Indian concerns."[16]

With the decline in the US power and its engagement with the region, many believe that India will provide an added stability and security to the region. In the immediate future, India and the ASEAN countries must intensify their cooperation both at the bilateral and regional levels to fight the common threats to the security and stability of Asia. Since India's north-eastern region is being recognised as the 'corridor to South-East Asia', integration with the traditional neighbouring regions like Myanmar, Bangladesh and Thailand should be facilitated through transportation networks which would contribute to a sustained peace and development. As India deepens its ties and employs pragmatic diplomacy to increase its influence in South-East Asia, the repercussions in the India–China relations are inevitable. However, if India manages to maintain its relations with both China and the ASEAN countries on parallel tracks without any friction between the two and make all the stakeholders agree to a common agenda of peace and development, the 'Asian Century' would reach its zenith.

NOTES AND REFERENCES

1. Mahbubani, Kishore (2008), "The New Asian Hemisphere: The Irresistible Shift of Global Power to the East", *Public Affairs*, pp. 51–99.
2. Asian Development Bank (2011), *Asia 2050: Realizing the Asian Century*, ADB: Singapore, pp.15-28.
3. Ibid, pp.7-8.
4. Richard N.Haas, "Which Asian Century?" available at *http://www.project-syndicate.org/commentary/richard-n—haass-on-asia-s-need-for-reconciliation-and-integration*
5. For some plausible interpretations of the Chinese assertions, see Carlyle A. Thayer, "Recent Developments in the South China Sea: Grounds for Cautious Optimism?"RSIS Working Paper, no. 220 (December 14, 2010), pp. 2-6, available at http://www.rsis.edu.sg/publications/WorkingPapers/WP220.pdf; Michael D. Swaine, "China's Assertive Behavior, Part One: On 'Core Interests'", *China Leadership Monitor* no. 34 (Fall 2010), pp. 8-11, available at http://carnegieendowment.org/files/Swaine_CLM_34_1114101.pdf.

6. Richard N. Haas, op.cit.
7. Government of Australia (2013), *Defence White Paper*, available at http://www.defence.gov.au/whitepaper2013/docs/WP_2013_web.pdf
8. Shekhar Shah (2013), " How will India be Part of Asia Century?" available at http://www.eastasiaforum.org/2013/06/26/how-will-india-be-a-part-of-the-asian-century/
9. Ibid.
10. Shiv Sankar Menon (2013), Closing Remarks at the 13th Asian Security Conference, available at http://idsa.in/keyspeeches/AmbShivshankarMenon_13ASC
11. For a detailed analysis of ASEAN's role and functioning see, Amitabh Acharya (2009), *Constructing a Security Community in Southeast Asia: ASEAN and the Problem of Regional Order*, New York: Routledge.
12. Ibid.
13. Kripa Sridharan (2005), "The ASEAN Region in India's 'Look East' Policy" in K. Raja Reddy (ed.) *India and ASEAN: Foreign Policy Dimensions For the 21st Century*, New Delhi: New Centuries Publications, p.130.
14. Keynote Address at the Inaugural Session of Delhi Dialogue VI 'Realizing the ASEAN-India Vision for Partnership and Prosperity' by Salman Khurshid, Minister of External Affairs on March 6, 2014, available at http://www.mea.gov.in/Speeches-Statements.htm?dtl/23040/Inaugural+Address+ by+External+Affairs+Minister+at+Delhi+Dialogue+VI
15. Vibhanshu Shekhar(2013), "India-ASEAN Relations Enter a New Discourse" available at http://www.icwa.in/pdfs/VPIndiaasean.pdf
16. Brahma Chellany (2014), " Asia's Changing Power Dynamics", Project Syndicate Paper available athttp://www.project-syndicate.org/commentary/asia-s-changing-power-dynamics#dRph1ViOYDGlvTet.99

4

Security Dimension of Mongolia's Foreign Policy: Relevance for India

Sharad K. Soni

ABSTRACT

Mongolia's foreign policy in the recent past has witnessed a marked shift in terms of priorities from what it used to be during the two decades after the Soviet collapse. This policy shift gave way to the emergence of new dimensions in the existing "multi-pillared" foreign policy that came into force in 1994. Since then, Mongolia has been maintaining friendly and balanced relations with the direct geographical neighbours—Russia and China—while at the same time fostering its ties with the "third neighbours" on the basis of mutually beneficial cooperation. However, in February 2011, the Mongolian Parliament passed a revised Foreign Policy Concept which redefined Mongolia's main foreign policy strategy as ensuring security, be it strategic or economic. In that sense, China has become more central in the foreign policy outlines as it is not only territorial security but also the economic security concerns in the minds of the Mongolians. No wonder then, as to why the 2011 Foreign Policy Concept has focussed more on adding a "balance of influence" element to its already existing strategy of diversification of dependence. This balance of influence behaviour in Mongolia's foreign policy strategy suggests that the need to manage its relations with China has become crucial to the Mongolian strategic thinking, and hence the balance of influence approach by wooing the "third neigbours" will provide the bulwark to ensure the country's overall security. This new security dimension of Mongolia's foreign policy is also relevant for India as New Delhi occupies a prominent place among Mongolia's "third neighbours". The relationship between the two sides has now changed from bilateral relations to a comprehensive partnership, and is moving ahead towards a strategic partnership. The paper, therefore, argues that the latest push to boost Mongolia's relations with India is obligated to Ulaanbaatar's "third neighbour" policy and is driven by strategic concerns. India, on its part, has been patiently expanding its defence and security links with Mongolia as part of an effort to build strategic ties with China's neighbours in line with New Delhi's more action-oriented "Act East" policy; the hitherto "Look East" policy. Hence, as a third neighbour, India may well fit into the balance of influence approach of Mongolia's foreign policy.

Keywords: multi-pillared foreign policy, "third neighbours", balance of influence, realpolitik, nomadic elephant, Khaan Quest, Act-East Policy.

Introduction

Occupying an important strategic position at the heart of Inner Asia, Mongolia is a landlocked country sandwiched between two great powers—Russia and China. In recent years, its foreign policy has witnessed a marked shift in terms of priorities from what it used to be during the two decades after the Soviet collapse. This policy shift gave way to the emergence of new dimensions in the existing "multi-pillared" foreign policy that was adopted in 1994. For over two decades now, the basis of the Mongolian foreign policy has been to balance relations with its direct geographical neighbours—Russia and China—in economic, military and political domains while at the same time nurture close ties with the "third neighbours" which are powerful but distant countries. This basis of Mongolian foreign policy, since its inception, has been well maintained largely due to the absence of alternative safeguards for Mongolia's security. However, in February 2011, the Mongolian Parliament passed a revised Foreign Policy Concept which redefined the country's principal foreign policy strategy by putting more emphasis on safeguarding security, be it strategic or economic. China, therefore, has become more central in the foreign policy outlines, particularly within the security dimension fold, as Beijing remains at the centre of not only the territorial security but also of the economic security concerns in the minds of the Mongolian policymakers. Conceivably, economic security concerns have led to the adding of the economic component to the revised foreign policy focussing further on collaborating with "third neighbours" to achieve the country's economic security. The official acknowledgement of a "third neighbour" policy in the 2011 revised Foreign Policy Concept is an indicative of the fact that Mongolia has now stressed on adding a complex "balance of influence" component to its prevailing strategy of "omni-enmeshment", a term coined by Evelyn Goh (2005) in the context of Southeast Asia's diversification of dependence.[1] Later, in her another work, Goh clarified that omni-enmeshment does not intend to concentrate on any single state because the followers of omni-enmeshment prefer "neither to pick sides nor to exclude certain great powers, but rather to try to include all the various major powers in the region's strategic affairs".[2] Such a foreign policy perspective has been contextualised in this paper which not only examines the security dimension of Mongolia's foreign policy but also its relevance for India so far as bilateral security ties are concerned. The paper argues that Mongolia factors importantly into India's "Eurasia policy" as well as the "Look East Policy", recently rechristened as the "Act East Policy", while India remains an important country for Mongolia both in regional and international contexts, and that as a third neighbour it could well be fitted into balance of influence approach of Mongolia's foreign policy.[3]

Evolution of Mongolia's Foreign Policy

The collapse of the erstwhile Soviet Union in 1991 provided Mongolia a rare opportunity in its history to become part of the new international order. Without wasting time, Mongolia went ahead in search for a new national identity and recast its ties with the external world on a new basis. Democratic reforms paved the way for framing the governmental policies in such a manner that it could benefit Mongolia both internally and externally, particularly on security issues at a time when it was no longer under a protective shield of the former Soviet Union. The key policy issues revolved around Mongolia included "national interest in the first place, depending upon how constructively the policy and strategy can achieve the defined goals".[4] Thus, the issue of national security was given prime importance while defining the goals of Mongolia's foreign relations.

No wonder then that the national security of Mongolia was figured out in the global, regional and subregional contexts and the Mongolian foreign policy was outlined accordingly. But what was the key reason for adopting quite a fresh post-Soviet foreign policy? It was essentially to discard "reliance on just one state and one ideology in favour of embracing a multi-pillared foreign policy."[5] The intention was quite clear, i.e., to have a balanced, though not necessarily equidistant, relationship with Mongolia's two geographical neighbours—Russia and China—besides the aim to integrate itself into the Asia-Pacific region by declaring the Mongolian civilisation and national identity as unquestionably Northeast Asian.[6] Lastly, Mongolia came up with its "Multi-Pillared" foreign policy, also described as "Multi-Dimensional" or "Omni-Directional" foreign policy, the basic tenets of which were spelled out in the three interrelated documents, i.e., Concept of National Security, Concept of Foreign Policy and the Military Doctrine which were adopted by the State Great *Khural* (Mongolian Parliament) in July 1994.[7]

Indeed, this "Multi-Pillared" foreign policy from the initial stage took an inclusive account of traditional and non-traditional aspects of national security which helped reshape Mongolia's external relations fairly on a new base. The core principle was that it will not adopt the line of either Russia or China but will maintain a balanced relationship with both of them and will promote an all-round neighbourly cooperation. This aim of balancing the two neighbours articulated the "third neighbour" policy.[8] As such, Mongolia's foreign policy activity focused on developing friendly relations with the highly developed countries of the West and East and creating and bringing to an appropriate level their economic and other interests in Mongolia. Taking such concerns into consideration, one of the general provisions of the 1994 Concept of Mongolia's Foreign Policy clearly remarked that "in formulating Mongolia's foreign policy and determining its priority directions and objectives, flexible approach shall be applied, paying close attention to the development of international relations and to the regional and world political situations."[9] In order to pursue its objectives the whole policy has been guided by the following directions:[10]

1. To maintain friendly relations with both the Russian Federation as well as the People's Republic of China. Mongolia shall not adopt the line of either country but shall maintain in principle a balanced relationship with both of them and shall promote an all-round neighbourly cooperation. In doing so, the traditional relations as well as the specific nature of Mongolia's economic cooperation with these two countries will be taken into account.
2. To develop friendly relations with the highly developed countries of the West and East such as the United States of America, Japan and the Federal Republic of Germany. At the same time Mongolia will also pursue a policy aimed at promoting friendly relations with such countries as India, the Republic of Korea, Thailand, Singapore, Turkey, Denmark, the Netherlands, Finland, Austria, Sweden, Switzerland and at creating and bringing to an appropriate level their economic and other interests in Mongolia.
3. To strengthen Mongolia's position in Asia and securing a constructive participation in the political and economic integration process in the region. Within the framework of this objective, greater

attention shall be given to Asia and the Pacific region, in particular to North-East and Central Asia. Mongolia shall take an active part in the process of initiating dialogues and negotiations on the issues of strengthening regional security and creating a collective security mechanism.

4. To promote cooperation with the United Nations and its specialised agencies, and with international financial and economic organisations, including the International Monetary Fund, the World Bank and the Asian Development Bank.
5. To develop friendly relations with the countries of the former socialist community as well as the newly independent states. When developing relations with these countries, a flexible approach will be adopted, reinforcing the positive legacy of Mongolia's past relations while at the same time taking into account the potential of promoting relations in conformity with the new circumstances. Particular attention will be given to promoting relations with Poland, Hungary and the Czech Republic in Eastern Europe as well as with Kazakhstan, the Ukraine, Belarus, Kyrgyzstan and Uzbekistan.
6. To develop friendly relations with the developing countries and cooperating with them, as much as possible, in the solution of common objectives. Beyond the framework of bilateral relations with these countries, this task will be realised mainly through cooperation within the framework of international organisations and movements, such as the United Nations, the Group of 77 and the Non-Aligned Movement.

Basically, Mongolian policymakers stood by the principle of flexible priorities in the foreign policy implementation with due consideration given to the changes taking place in the international environment because of globalisation.[11] In that sense, since the very beginning, pragmatism seems to have been the core of Mongolia's foreign policy as it has relied on the ongoing international political reality as well as the trends of international economic development. All at once, Mongolia's foreign policy also points to safeguarding the security and prosperity of the country, both internally and externally, by creating with influential countries in the region and in the world a network of relationships based on the interdependence of political, economic and other interests.[12]

Mongolia's Foreign Policy Shift

As the new millennium began, Mongolia felt a need for a paradigm shift in its proactive foreign policy due to the changes witnessed both at the domestic as well as foreign fronts. The changes were more visible in the relations and the balance of power between and among Mongolia's neighbouring powers, which led to the emergence of new non-traditional security threats.[13] Such concerns motivated the Mongolian leadership to rethink about the revision of its existing foreign policy in order to attract foreign partners not only in the politico-strategic field but also in the economic and trade sphere. Hence, the Mongolian Parliament approved an updated National Security Concept in July 2010[14] and a revised Foreign Policy Concept in February 2011.[15] Both the documents redefined the new strategic direction of Mongolia's security and foreign policy. In fact, they aimed at increasing the benefits of external relations and to provide the foreign policy with an economic content in the times of widening foreign relations and cooperation and intensive development of economics. It is to be reiterated that whereas Mongolia's foreign policy for the 1990s was formulated around what Goh (2005) considers as an "omni-enmeshment strategy", its foreign policy from 2000 onwards can best be conceptualised as an "amalgam of omni-enmeshment and balance of influence".[16] Mongolia's new foreign policy strategy, therefore, implicitly identifies China as the country's largest security concern which has been reflected in Ulaanbaatar's post-2000 foreign policy behaviour.

This balance of influence behaviour in Mongolia's foreign policy strategy gave new directions to the whole policy that themselves speak about the security dimension, which are as follows:[17]

1. It elevated Mongolia's third neighbour relations to the same level as relations with China which suggests that Mongolia is interested in forging bilateral relations that can be used as a leverage against China.
2. It specifically mentioned the US as an important partner which suggests that Mongolia wants to limit China strategically.
3. Economic security came into prominence in the foreign policy which suggests that Mongolia realises the need to diversify the foreign actors, especially China, involved in its domestic economic sector.

Overall, the revised foreign policy advocates that the necessity to manage Mongolia's relations with China has become crucial to the country's strategic thinking, and hence the balance of influence approach will provide the bulwark to safeguard the country's overall security, including the economic one. A separate Programme on Enhancing the Economic Orientation of Foreign Relations came into force on March 3, 2010.[18] This Programme has been formulated to create an opportunity for rationalising and developing tangible economic relations with foreign countries taking into account the political and economic benefits from such relations as well as the potential negative impact on the national security, in particular the economic security.[19] There are two-pronged goals of this Programme: (a) to ensure economic benefits through viable foreign relations and (b) intensify foreign policy contribution to the growth of overall economy. These goals have been planned to be achieved by increasing the foreign trade turnover, especially the exports of value-added goods; promoting foreign direct investment; increasing the return from bilateral and multilateral cooperation; ensuring rational utilisation of development loans and aid and promoting Mongolia on the world market.

But, what is important to keep in mind is that Mongolia's economy is almost entirely dependent on China. The Chinese investment in Mongolia over the years has indeed been impressive, and so is China's dominance which is noticeable in the Sino-Mongolian economic and trade cooperation.[20] In 2012, China has been Mongolia's largest trade partner, receiving 91 per cent of its total exports and providing 32 per cent of its imports. China is the largest provider of foreign direct investment (FDI) to Mongolia, providing 51 per cent of the total FDI.[21] Canada and the Netherlands, the second and third largest providers, accounted for just 8 and 6 per cent respectively, while FDI from the United States to Mongolia remains minimal with merely 2.39 per cent.[22] Chinese foreign businesses also dominate Mongolia's domestic sector, officially accounting for 50 per cent of all foreign firms and unofficially accounting for a far larger percentage. Today, over 5,000 Chinese firms operate in Mongolia, with a combined investment of around $2.5 billion, with $1.4 billion invested by Petro China alone.[23] Quite seemingly, China's relations and influence over Mongolia have increased mainly because after the disintegration of the former Soviet Union and the end of the Cold War, Mongolia's trade with Russia declined by 80 per cent.

However, Russia sought to rebuild strong relations with Mongolia, particularly in the late 1990s, to enhance its standing as a regional power. Russia lowered the prices of oil and energy exports to Mongolia and enhanced cross-border trade, apart from writing off 98 per cent of Mongolia's state debt. Today, Russia is being perceived to be an essential partner of Mongolia, particularly in balancing off relations with China, and therefore it appears that Mongolia will continue the policy of developing good-neighbourly relations and mutually beneficial cooperation with Russia on a stable and long-term basis. But unlike the Cold War period, China now cannot be ignored by Mongolia, not only due to geographical reasons but also due to continued relations which have recently been upgraded into a strategic partnership. The visits of the Chinese President Xi Jinping in August 2014 and the Russian President Vladimir Putin in September 2014 only point to the fact that the two neighbours are in the race to confirm that neither of the two would afford to be ignored in Mongolia's foreign policy. On the other hand, Mongolia would play a smart game in maintaining balanced relations with these two neighbours while at the same time trying to ensure its economic security on the basis of the recently concluded mutually advantageous economic and trade ties with both Russia and China. Nevertheless, hungry for Mongolia's coal, metals, and other minerals, China has dominated the Mongolian economy, fuelling fears in Ulaanbaatar of an even greater Chinese control which has resulted in Mongolia imposing strict new laws on foreign investment, especially from foreign sources that have become part of Mongolia's revised foreign policy concept. The security-centric revised foreign policy, therefore, must be seen in the largest interest of safeguarding the Mongolian traditional as well as non-traditional security threat perception.

Relevance for India

Since the very beginning, the main stated theme of the Mongolian foreign policy, as Dierkes emphasises, "has been the so-called 'third neighbour' policy; that is, attempts by successive Mongolian administrations to build closer ties with partners other than Russia and China, its dominant neighbours."[24] But one may ask, why do the Mongols want to have a third partner or a third neighbour? Answers may vary, though the main logic is political realism or Mongolian realpolitik. Mongolia is a case in point when realpolitik is defined. As explained by Porter, "In international politics, *realpolitik* focusses on relations as manifested from national interests instead of driven by ideology."[25] Mongolian academics and policymakers generally agree that because of the lack of a necessary political and economic weight to implement its declared national security policy, Mongolia needs a strong third power as a counterweight to balance its relations with the immediate neighbours. The "third neighbour" policy simply describes the "multipillarity, complexity and openness of Mongolia's foreign policy [which] undoubtedly attracted attention of the regional and world community, and the country's position on the international arena has been strengthened substantially."[26]

However, as the revised new foreign policy suggests, Mongolia hopes its "third neighbour" approach will encourage those external balancers to develop interests in Mongolia who would significantly check the potential Chinese threat to Mongolia's security, both economic as well as strategic. Mongolia relies on the "third neighbours" because of their economic and military power and trusts them because they are geographically distant and do not present the same risks that its immediate neighbours do.[27] The period between 1994 and 2011 was a very successful period for Mongolia's search for a "third neighbour" but now the search seems to have come to an end and among the identified third neighbours India has also occupied a prominent place. India's standing in Mongolia's foreign policy lies to fact that it has been perceived by Mongolia as its third neighbour in both the regional and international contexts, especially given the role that India has been playing in promoting a multipolar security structure in Asia. The Mongolians acknowledge India's positive influence on them through Buddhism since time immemorial. Buddhism not only helped the hitherto scattered and nomadic Mongols to become united and civilised but also facilitated the Mongols to learn about the various dimensions of Indian philosophy and applied knowledge such as astrology, poetry, art, medicine, etc.[28] Such a strong cultural relationship helped the two sides to work towards building a strategic partnership.

It all began in 2009 with the visit of the newly elected Mongolian President Tsakhia Elbegdorj to India that changed the extent and pattern of their bilateral relations into a cooperative partnership. During this visit, both sides signed a civil nuclear treaty for the supply of Mongolian uranium to New Delhi.[29] This comprehensive partnership treaty was to help in developing the Mongolian uranium mining with an MoU on the "peaceful use of radioactive minerals and nuclear energy". Such a deal with India reflects two important considerations: Firstly, Mongolia recognises the need to develop economic ties with a diverse group of countries as outlined in its security and foreign policy concepts and secondly, signing such a pact with India is a direct usage of the third neighbour concept allowing for a continued neutrality between Mongolia and its physical neighbours.[30] Having a mineral wealth of US $1.3 trillion, the Mongolian economy creates wonderful opportunities for further expanding the country's international relations.[31] As India's own demand for imported natural resources multiplies manifold, a cooperative partnership with Mongolia may prove to be beneficial for long-term economic gains. Following the civil nuclear pact, the Jindal Steel and Power Company started doing exploration work for uranium in the Gobi desert. Besides, the Steel Authority of India Limited (SAIL) has been building a three-million tonne steel plant in Mongolia in addition to acquiring a coal mine in order to reduce the costly imports and excessive dependence on Australian coking coal.

The Indian business houses that were taking initiatives to start their operation in Mongolia got a further boost after visit of the then Indian President Pratibha Devisingh Patil to Mongolia in July 2011. During her visit, both sides agreed to encourage cooperation in the fields of nuclear energy, mining, agriculture, culture, education, health and science, in particular information technology and promoting ties in social welfare, natural environment and between local governments. The three key documents signed include the Defence Cooperation agreement, an MoU on Cooperation between Mongolia's Committee for National Development & Reforms and India's Planning Commission and an MoU on Media Exchanges.[32] It needs to be mentioned here that the mining boom that Mongolia is presently experiencing has brought its economy to the extent of becoming one of the fastest growing in the world with a double digit annual GDP growth rate since 2011. The Indian industry houses must take notice of that to exploit the vast opportunities in the mining sector in Mongolia, as the coal, gold, copper and uranium reserves here hold much in store for them. Already, it was noted on March 21, 2013 during the fourth meeting of the India-Mongolia Joint Committee on Cooperation that the Indian companies are interested in playing a larger role in Mongolian mineral processing and mining industry, and that Mongolia has been expected to create a favourable environment for their operations.[33] The New Investment Law of Mongolia, which came into effect on November 1, 2013, makes no distinction between the domestic and foreign private investors, thus eliminating the earlier rules that were perceived as discriminatory against foreigners.[34] This provides a better opportunity for the Indian investors willing to make investments, particularly in the mining sector.

Though the mining boom that Mongolia is presently experiencing is beyond imagination, there are also concerns that a majority of their energy comes from coal-fired plants which is unsustainable over a longer period and creates serious health hazards. Thus, Mongolia has begun considering the need to adopt renewable energy as its primary energy source. India, on its part, came forward and in July 2013 offered to cooperate in developing Mongolia's renewable energy.[35] As regards trade relations, it may be pointed out that Mongolia is landlocked between China and Russia, and therefore, goods have to be shipped through ports in China or Russia which increases freight rates and also delays in the delivery schedule. This has been the primary reason as to why the bilateral trade between India and Mongolia has not developed to the extent it should have been. Even though, the bilateral trade saw a sharp increase during the 2009–2012 period when it touched the figure of US$ 60.2 mn in 2012 from a mere US$12.7 mn in 2009.[36] Despite this growth, the bilateral trade in 2013 again saw the downward trend reaching the figure of just US $ 35 million,[37] thus raising serious concerns if the two sides would be able to enhance their trade in the near future. At the moment, Indian exports to Mongolia include pharmaceutical products, veterinary medicines, mining machinery, automobiles and their parts. The Indian imports from Mongolia mainly include raw wool. India and Mongolia also provide an MFN status to each other in respect of customs duties and all other taxes on imports and exports. Besides, they have been cooperating in IT, Investment Promotion and Protection, Animal Health & Dairy, Technology & Applications, Biotechnology, etc.

Notwithstanding the growing ties between the two countries, the relevance of Mongolia's foreign policy for India is more visible in their defence and military ties. Mongolia is developing an exceptional military strategy that endeavours to balance the conventional and peacekeeping capabilities.[38] This strategy is a well-motivated departure from Mongolia's previous security arrangements with the erstwhile Soviet Union. In accordance with its foreign policy, Mongolia now seeks to facilitate global engagement in the matters of security-related issues, particularly in maintaining its sovereignty, national identity and diplomatic freedom. As such, the defence cooperation between the militaries of Mongolia and India has seen a steady growth over the last decade or so with joint annual exercises being held since 2004. This workout is called "Nomadic Elephant", organised alternatively in India and Mongolia every year. The latest is the tenth such workout which has recently been concluded on February 6, 2015 at the Gwalior Military Cantonment in order to strengthen the bilateral defence ties and to reinforce the commitment to regional security. This exercise has resulted in an increased confidence as also a mutual interoperability which could assist both the armies while undertaking any counter terrorism/insurgency assignments under the United Nations mandate.[39] Since 2006, India has also been participating in the multinational peacekeeping annual exercises in Mongolia called "Khaan Quest" which has now become one of the signature training events for the participating nations.[40] This has, time and again, raised the Chinese concerns that "India is quietly expanding its defence and security links with Mongolia in a bid to monitor China's space and military activities in the region."[41] As opposed to it, India's participation in the multinational military exercises on the Mongolian soil must be viewed in a broad perspective of India's growing collaborative role in East Asia that could give New Delhi a boost for its involvement in the regional cooperation/ integration process.[42] Another development in the Mongolia–India security ties was witnessed in December 2014 when the fourth Director-General level talks between the Border Security Force of India (BSF) and the General Authority for Border Protection of Mongolia (GABP) took place in New Delhi. Since both the countries have a similar terrain at the border and they face similar kinds of challenges on the border, both the GABP and the BSF agreed to help each other in the better management of borders through an exchange of technology, equipment and methodology of border management and to conduct joint exercises in operations, training, technology exchange, etc. besides conducting Joint workshops/seminars on Border Management.[43] Such efforts would essentially go a long way in enhancing the cooperation between the two forces and in improving the Border Management.

As already mentioned elsewhere, the speedy improvement of the Indo-Mongolian security ties found its expression in 2011 itself when both the countries signed a bilateral defence cooperation agreement during President Patil's visit to Mongolia. The pact was not very comprehensive though, as Mongolia remains cautious about getting too cosy with India on defence issues. India, however, seems keen to enhance the defence ties rapidly. The rationale behind this, as Miller puts it, is simple: "New Delhi believes that it will be more competitive in Mongolia's lucrative mining and trade sectors if it diversifies its engagement, morphing from investor to strategic partner."[44] Mongolia also has a significant interest in engaging India's defence expertise which can be attested by the following facts:[45] Firstly, intensified engagement with India complements Mongolia's strategy of drawing attention of the large markets to increase their investments in the country. Mongolia's mineral sector, particularly the substantial reserves of coal, copper, gold and uranium, is crucial to India's principal interest; secondly, regional instability in India's extended neighbourhood of Central Asia remains a major concern for Mongolia which is keen to exploit its reputation of being the most successful democracy among the post-Soviet States and thirdly as well as most importantly, China's continued military dominance in its peripheral countries and all the implications that go along with this require Mongolia's outreach to other stakeholders in Asia, such as India, Japan, South Korea and the United States which are considered as its third neighbours.

In terms of regional cooperation, Mongolia's strategic location as a geographical bridge between Central Asia and Northeast Asia offers a valuable support to Indian interests in the whole region. Though Russia has been a dependable partner ever since India became independent, having more than one strong ally in the region is vital for India. This is especially important for the success of India's "Act East" policy, which aims at strengthening New Delhi's engagement with the Asia-Pacific as a whole. While the Indian foreign policy first through the "Look-East" policy and now through the "Act East" policy seems to be a success story in India's close neighbourhood of Southeast Asia, other regions, especially Northeast Asia, have not received the desired attention, and hence it is high time that India should make its efforts to have its presence in Northeast Asia as the region holds much in terms of economic potential due to the richness in natural resources. Yet, it remains to be seen whether the Mongolia–India synergy would indeed benefit New Delhi in its engagement with Northeast Asia to the extent of becoming a major player in this region in not only containing Chinese activism but also in making its worthy contribution, especially to the integration process.[46] Whatever may be the future scenario, as of now, it appears that Mongolia's proximity with India has been/will be a significant factor to balance off the equation with China, which is in line with the priorities chalked out in Mongolia's revised foreign policy. Perhaps the Indian Prime Minister Narendra Modi's recent visit to Mongolia on May 17, 2015 was influenced by this factor as well, and there is little doubt that the first ever visit to Mongolia by an Indian Prime Minister has left a positive imprint on the Mongolians to feel themselves secured despite living in a complex geostrategic set up.

Conclusion

Going through the revised 2011 Foreign Policy Concept, there is a clear indication that unlike Russia, Mongolia's understanding of its relations with China has changed despite Ulaanbaatar's continued ties with Beijing, especially in the economic and trade fields. While the 1994 Foreign Policy Concept categorises relations with China and Russia as the state's principal foreign policy concern, the 2011 Foreign Policy Concept gives equal priority to Mongolia's relations with its third neighbours, particularly the United States, Japan, India, Turkey, Australia and Canada. This movement away from an unqualified engagement with China towards a robust engagement with it, balanced with a cooperation with the third neighbour partners principally on security issues, provides evidence that Mongolia's foreign policy strategy towards China has changed remarkably. Yet, the ground reality is that China's threat perception is abounding as Beijing still dominates Mongolia at least economically and it will not be an easy task for Ulaanbaatar to replace this southern neighbour outrightly with other powers. The best way for Mongolia is to persuade the third neighbours as alternatives for making investments given the current scenario of the mining boom. This would help reduce Mongolia's economic dependence on China and hence the China threat perception—both economic as well as strategic.

As far as the relevance of the security dimension of Mongolia's foreign policy for India is concerned, New Delhi figures prominently in the specific list of Mongolia's "third neighbours". The relationship between the two sides has now come a long way, i.e., the bilateral relations have turned into a comprehensive partnership which has moved well towards a strategic partnership. In this context, Modi's visit to Mongolia was significant as it witnessed the two sides agreeing to raise the level of comprehensive partnership to a strategic partnership that is conducive to the mutual interests of the two countries. In the future, developing a strategic partnership appears to be a common yet a new objective of their respective foreign policies. This is all the more so because the latest push for boosting Mongolia's relations with India is obligated to Ulaanbaatar's "third neighbour" policy and is driven by strategic concerns. India, on its part, has been patiently expanding its defence and security links with Mongolia as part of an effort to build strategic ties with China's neighbours in line with New Delhi's more action-oriented "Act East" policy; the hitherto "Look East" policy. The increasing understanding that the two countries have in defence and security arenas may prove to be a vantage point for India in expanding its strategic footprint in the backyard of China. Obviously, defence ties between India and Mongolia are gradually developing through joint as well as multilateral military exercises apart from imparting training to the Mongolian defence personnel. For India, Mongolia is important both politically and strategically because it also provides a potential access route to Siberia's untapped resource-rich region and factors importantly into India's Energy, Eurasia, China and Russia policy. Besides, considering India as Mongolia's "spiritual neighbour", using Buddhism as a civilisational resource by New Delhi, will provide a much-needed bulwark to realise India's strategic vision in this part of the world.

NOTES AND REFERENCES

1. Evelyn Goh (2005), "Great Powers and Southeast Asian Regional Security Strategies: Omni-Enmeshment, Balancing and Hierarchical Order", Working

Paper, no. 84, Singapore: Institute of Defence and Strategic Studies, pp. 1-27, URL: https://dr.ntu.edu.sg/bitstream/handle/10220/4481/RSIS-WORK PAPER_84.pdf?sequence=1

2. Evelyn Goh (2007), "Great Power and Hierarchy Order in Southeast Asia: Analysing Regional Security Strategies", *International Security*, vol. 32, no. 3, p. 121.
3. For a more comprehensive analysis of Mongolia's Foreign Policy, see Sharad K. Soni (2015), "The 'Third Neighbour' Approach of Mongolia's Diplomacy of External Relations: Effects on Relations between India and Mongolia", *India Quarterly*, vol. 71, no. 1, pp. 37-52.
4. Sharad K Soni (2006), *Mongolia-China Relations: Modern and Contemporary Times*, New Delhi: Pentagon Press, p. 211.
5. Alicia Campi (2012),"Mongolia's Turn at the Great Game", *Asia-Pacific Bulletin*, no. 184, 1 November, p. 1.
6. Ibid.
7. Sharad K. Soni (2001), "Mongolia's Foreign Policy Priorities", *Himalayan and Central Asian Studies*, vol. 5, no. 1, p. 57.
8. For an understanding of the "Third Neighbour Policy", see Allen Wagner (2012), "Mongolia: Growth, Democracy, and Two Wary Neighbors: An Interview with Alan Wachman", The National Bureau of Asian Research, 3 May, URL: http://www.nbr.org/research/activity.aspx?id=245#.Uic9tzbI1K0; Also see Sharad K. Soni (2012), "Looking beyond Geographic Neighbours : Post-Soviet Mongolia's 'Third Neighbour Policy'" in Suchandana Chatterjee, Anita Sengupta and Sushmita Bhattacharya (eds.), *Eurasia: Twenty Years After*, Delhi: Shipra Publications, pp. 486-503.
9. Ministry of Foreign Affairs (2011), Government of Mongolia, "Concept of Foreign Policy", 21 February, URL: http://www.mfa.gov.mn/en/index.php?option=com_content&view=article&id=79%3Ai-&catid=36%3A2009-12-20-21-52-14&Itemid=55&lang=en
10. Tsedendambyn Batbayar and Sharad K. Soni (2007), *Modern Mongolia: A Concise History*, New Delhi: Pentagon, pp.121ff.
11. M. Durgersuren (1994), "Changing Mongolia in a New Environment," *The Mongolian Journal of International Affairs* (Ulaanbaatar), no. 1, p. 20.
12. Sharad K. Soni (2013), "Evaluating Mongolia's Experience of Democratization: The Post-Soviet Scenario", *The Mongol Journal of International Affairs* (Ulaanbaatar), vol. 18, 2013, p. 39.
13. Ch.Sumiyabazar (2010), "Renewed National Security Concepts of Mongolia Passed", *UB Post* (Ulaanbaatar), 20 July.
14. Government of Mongolia (2010), "National Security Concept of Mongolia", URL: http://www.nsc.gov.mn/?q=node/119
15. Ministry of Foreign Affairs (2011), "Concept of Mongolia's Foreign Policy".
16. An omni-enmeshment strategy is considered to be a strategy of enmeshing all major powers that can influence regional affairs; see Goh (2005), "Great Powers and Southeast Asian Regional Security Strategies", p. 10. Grounded on Goh's analysis, Reeves is of the opinion that Mongolia's revised foreign policy is "an amalgam of omni-enmeshment and balance of influence", see Jeffrey Reeves

(2012), "Mongolia's Evolving Security Strategy: Omni-Enmeshment and Balance of Influence", *The Pacific Review*, vol. 25, no. 5, p. 589.

17. Reeves (2012), "Mongolia's Evolving Security Strategy", pp. 601-602.
18. Ministry of Foreign Affairs (2010), Government of Mongolia, "Programme on Enhancing the Economic Orientation of Foreign Relations of Mongolia", Annex 1 to Government Resolution No. 324 of 2009, 3 March, URL: http://www.mfa.gov.mn/index.php?option=com_content&view=article&id=325&Itemid=103&lang=en
19. Ibid.
20. Sharad K. Soni (2009), "China's Periphery Policy: Implications for Sino-Mongolian Relations", *India Quarterly*, vol. 65, no. 3, p. 262.
21. Alicia Campi (2013), "The New Great Game in Northeast Asia: Potential Impact of Energy Mineral Development In Mongolia on China, Russia, Japan, and Korea", *Asia-Pacific Policy Papers Series*, no. 15, Washington, DC: Edwin O. Reischauer Center for East Asian Studies, Johns Hopkins University-SAIS, p.3.
22. Ibid, pp. 3-4.
23. Ibid.
24. Julian Dierkes (2011), "Mongolia's 'Third Neighbour' Policy and its Impact on Foreign Investment", *East Asia Forum*, 15 February, URL: http://www.eastasiaforum.org/2011/02/15/mongolias-third-neighbour-policy-and-its-impact-on-foreign-investment/
25. Ron A. Porter (2009), "Realpolitik in Mongolia-US Relations", footnote 2, p. 50, URL: http://r-cube.ritsumei.ac.jp/bitstream/10367/947/1/6-RJAPS26_Realpolitik%20in%20Mongolia-US%20Relations.pdf
26. A. Tuvshintugs (2010), "Mongolia's National Security: Past, Present and Future Perspectives" in K. Warikoo and Sharad K. Soni (eds.), *Mongolia in the 21st Century: Society, Culture and International Relations*, New Delhi and London: Pentagon, p. 76.
27. Li Narangoa (2009), "Mongolia and Preventive Diplomacy: Haunted by History and Becoming Cosmopolitan", *Asian Survey*, Vol. 49, Issue 2, p. 376.
28. Sharad K. Soni (2009), "India-Mongolia Relations: Implications for Regional Cooperation in North East Asia", *Mongolian & Tibetan Quarterly* (Taipei), vol.18, no.2, June 2009, p. 52.
29. "India Signs Civil Nuclear Deal with Mongolia", *The Financial Express* (New Delhi), 15 September 2009.
30. Brandon Joseph Miliate (2009), "India's Role in Mongolia's Third Neighbor Policy", SIT Study Abroad: Mongolia, Independent Study Project (ISP) Collection, Paper 802, URL: http://digitalcollections.sit.edu/isp_collection/802
31. Sharad K. Soni (2013), "Evaluating Mongolia's Experience of Democratization: The Post-Soviet Scenario", *The Mongol Journal of International Affairs* (Ulaanbaatar), vol.18, p.43.
32. The Office of the President of Mongolia (2011), "President Elbegdorj and President Patil Participate in Signing Documents on Bilateral Ties and Cooperation", 28 July, URL: http://www.president.mn/eng/newscenter/viewnews.php?newsid=577
33. Ministry of External Affairs (2013), Government of India, "Fourth Meeting of

India-Mongolia Joint Committee on Cooperation", 21 March, URL: http://mea.gov.in/press-releases.htm?dtl/21460/Fourth+meeting+of+INDIA MONGOLIA+Joint+Committee+on+Cooperation

34. Hogan Lovells (2013), "Mongolia Revises its Regulatory Framework for Foreign and Domestic Investment", October, pp. 1-6, URL: http://www.hoganlovells.com/files/Uploads/Documents/13.11.01_F_Mongolia_revises_its_regulatory_framework_for_foreign_and_domestic_investment_October_2013. pdf
35. Press Information Bureau (2013), Government of India, "Dr. Farooq Abdullah Attends Oath Taking Ceremony of Mongolian President; Offers Partnership in Renewable Energy and Human Resource Development", 10 July, URL: http://pib.nic.in/newsite/erelease.aspx?relid=97117
36. Ministry of External Affairs (2013), Government of India, "India-Mongolia Relations", URL: http://www.mea.gov.in/Portal/ForeignRelation/Mongolia_December_2013.pdf
37. Embassy of India, Ulaanbaatar (2015), "India-Mongolia Relations", URL: http://www.eoi.gov.in/ulaanbaatar/?1051?000
38. Christopher Pultz (2014), "The Role of Peacekeeping in Mongolia's Military Strategy: A New Paradigm for Security", *Asia Policy*, no. 17, January, p. 128.
39. "Tenth India-Mongolia Exercise Nomadic Elephant Culminates", 6 February 2015, URL: http://beyondheadlines.in/2015/02/tenth-india-mongolia-exercise-nomadic-elephant-culminates/
40. Started in 2003 by the United States and Mongolia, 'Khan Quest' in 2013 saw 14 nations and over 1,000 officers joining the exercises that included the host Mongolia, the United States, Australia, Canada, France, Germany, Japan, India, Indonesia, Nepal, South Korea, Tajikistan, the United Kingdom and Vietnam. See Jonathan B. Miller (2013), "UN Peacekeeping Exercise 'Khaan Quest' Marks 10 Year Anniversary", *Forbes*, 16 August, URL: http://www.forbes.com/sites/jonathanmiller/2013/08/16/khaan-quest-wraps-up-first-decade/
41. Cited in Soni (2009), "India-Mongolia Relations", pp. 57-58.
42. Ibid, p. 59.
43. "India and Mongolia Strengthen Ties through Director General Level Talk", *Defence and Security of India*, 21 December 2014, http://defencesecurityindia.com/india-mongolia-strengthen-ties-director-general-level-talk/
44. J. Berkshire Miller (2011), "India, Mongolia Cosy Up", *The Diplomat*, 17 September, URL: http://thediplomat.com/2011/09/india-mongolia-cosy-up/
45. Ibid.
46. Sharad K. Soni (2011), "The Importance of Mongolia in India's Engagement with Northeast Asia" in Sudhir Kumar Singh (ed.) *Sino-Indian Relations: Challenges and Opportunities for 21st Century*, New Delhi: Pentagon Press, p. 295.

5

Post-2014 Pakistan's Afghan Policy: Implications for India

Sudhir Singh

ABSTRACT

Pakistan's Afghan policy has always been guided by the parochial prism of keeping it as a client country. In contrast, the Afghans have never accepted the Durand Line demarcated in 1893 by the British which divided the Pathans into two parts. Afghanistan opposed Pakistan's demand of plebiscite in Kashmir on the plea that the same has been denied by Pakistan in the case of the former North-West Frontier Province. In 1979, when the former Soviet Union came to Afghanistan, Pakistan happily became the central element of the United States-sponsored Mujahideen forces. In 1990, the Soviet forces had withdrawn but Pakistan remained busy in trying to stall its puppet regime in Kabul. In 1996, the Pakistan-propelled Taliban took over power in Kabul and Pakistan became the third country along with Saudi Arabia and the United Arab Emirates to recognise it under the norms of international law. After the September 2001 terror attack in New York and Washington, the NATO forces launched "Operation Enduring Freedom" to dismantle the Al Qaeda and the Taliban but surprisingly Pakistan became a focal point of this coalition as well, which is fundamentally contradictory. The elimination of the terror icon, Osama bin Laden, in May 2011 at Abottabad vindicates this assertion. The NATO forces have already withdrawn from Afghanistan since December 2014. In this prevailing scenario what are the policy options for Pakistan?

At this juncture, Pakistan must learn lessons from history that till Afghanistan does not stabilise, Pakistan could not become a stable country. In the 1960s Pakistan's economy was at par with South Korea but today,

South Korea is one of the top ten developed countries and Pakistan is at par with the countries of Sub-Saharan Africa. Since the last one decade Pakistan's economy has been anunder performer and it is under a huge debt burden. More than 65,000 people including 5,500 security forces have been killed in Pakistan since the December 2007 assassination of former PM Benazir Bhutto in terror-related violence. Pakistan needs to transform its Afghan policy to cope with the emerging situations. The Pakistani army is of course the biggest hurdle in this way but the civilian rulers must assert themselves and mend fences with India. That will help to revive the economy and the additionally prevailing trust deficit will reduce. In May 2014, the Pakistani PM Nawaz Sharif visited New Delhi and had a summit level talk with the newly elected Indian PM, Narendra Modi. Pakistan has witnessed the period when the Taliban had ruled over Afghanistan. This radicalisation has Talibanised the entire Pakistani society and converted Pakistan into a battleground of sectarian conflict between Saudi Arabia and Iran. If Pakistan will participate in the Yemen crisis, then this divide is all set to grow further. The NATO withdrawal has provided an ample opportunity to Pakistan to reformulates its policy to cope with the situation. Today, Pakistan is facing an existential threat. If Pakistan will not help out Afghanistan this time to stabilise, then the survival of Pakistan will also be at stake. PM Nawaz Sharif is able to understand this situation but given the prevailing situation it will not be possible for him to implement a reformulated policy.

Keywords: Afghanistan, Pakistan, Taliban, NATO, Haqqani, Karzai, India.

Afghanistan has been geopolitically an extremely important country since the ages. All the northward invasions on India were routed through this country. Before both the World Wars it was an apple of discord between the British and the Russian empires. The British empire divided the Pathans by demarcating the Durand Line in 1893.

After the partition of the subcontinent, Pakistan emerged as a new entity. But, Pakistan and Afghanistan had a bitter relationship till the December 1979 Soviet intervention. In 1989, the Soviets withdrew and a vacuum was created which was filled by the growth of the Taliban, which finally captured power in 1996. Taliban was illegitimately nurtured by Pakistan to pursue its goal of maintaining its strategic depth against India. Since then terror has remained an instrument of Pakistan's foreign policy. The Afghan Jihad was consolidated by the US-led forces during the Soviet intervention but later on emerged as an independent global movement led by Osama bin Laden. After Operation Enduring Freedom (2001), he took shelter in Pakistan and was finally killed by US commandos in May 2011 at Abbotabad. His elimination has vindicated the nexus between the Jihad factory and Pakistan.

Since 2001, India has invested over $ 2 billion dollars in Afghanistan and emerged as the fifth largest global contributor in the reconstruction of this war-torn country. It is an open secret that the NATO withdrawal will create serious questions for India's national security.

During the period of the Taliban rule in Afghanistan (1996–2001), India's internal security was badly hit due to a sustaining cross-border support to terror.

In 1999, an Indian Airlines plane was highjacked from Kathmandu and ended up at Kandahar. This incident dramatically underscores why New Delhi cannot take its eyes off of Afghanistan and the Taliban. The JM quickly became one of the most vicious terrorist groups operating in India—that has had long ties to Afghanistan and the Taliban (it has also enjoyed support from the ISI)—threatening the vital Indian national security interests.[1]

India's engagement with Afghanistan advances its position as an important power beyond South Asia; other interests in Afghanistan specifically advance the regional security concerns localised in Afghanistan and Pakistan. Many of these are tied to the proliferating Islamist militant groups which have terrorised India. Virtually every Islamist militant group operating in and against India (e.g., HUJI, Lashkar-e-Taiba (LeT), Harkat-ul-Mujahideen/Harkat-ul-Ansar, among others) have trained in Afghanistan and Pakistan.

Since 2001, India has upgraded its presence in Afghanistan, particularly in the reconstruction efforts and has built many infrastructure assets. This has enraged Pakistan because it perceives that Afghanistan is its strategic backyard and the Indian presence is a hurdle in sustaining it. Pakistan has provided tacit support to the attacks on the Indian Embassy in Kabul and on other personnel working across Afghanistan.

Since the last two decades, hundreds of terrorist attacks involving LeT militants have occurred throughout India. LeT was implicated in plots like the terrorist attacks in New Delhi in October 2005; in Bangalore in December 2005; in Varanasi in March 2006; in Nagpur in June 2006; in the July 2007 train bombings in Mumbai; the November 2008 Mumbai carnage and Pune in 2013.

India and the Afghanistan Factor and the Concept of Strategic Depth

The Heritage Foundation's Lisa Curtis has cautiously argued that a "transformation of Pakistan-Afghanistan ties can only take place in an overall context of improved Pakistani-Indian relations."[2]

On Afghanistan, India and Pakistan have remained on different pages throughout the last 68 years due to divergences of interests. Some leading pundits of the India–Pakistan relations including the eminent Pakistani writer Ahmed Rashid is of the opinion that till the Kashmir issue is not resolved, the Afghanistan tangle will sustain.

But even in the situation when the Kashmir issue gets be resolved amicably, there would be a gamut of issues beside Afghanistan which will sustain both the countries' relationship in a turbulent manner. According to Ambassador Munir Akram, an eminent Pakistani strategic thinker,

> "The hostility between Pakistan and India has deep historical and popular roots in both countries. Despite cultural, linguistic and ethnic affinities, the mutual hostility between Hindus and Muslims of the sub-continent is real and endemic. It was the *raison d'être* for the creation of Pakistan. The history of last fifty years has, if any thing, further intensified this hostility and given a structural expression in the relationship between the two states. The Kashmir dispute, in essence, is but one expression of this divide and hostility, (Bangladesh relations with India displays the same dynamic). Thus, even if outside issues like Kashmir, are resolved, and some semblance of civility restored between Pakistan and India, their relationship will remain competitive for the foreseeable future. Those who argue that, with goodwill and conflict resolution, peace and harmony can descend on the sub-continent are either ignorant or self-serving."[3]

The eminent Pakistani strategic writer, Ayesha Siddiqa has also argued on the same page in her famous book *Pakistan Military Inc.*

It has happened for the first time in history that the United States has bifurcated its Pakistan policy from its India policy since the last few years. Beside India's rise on the economic front, the changing security architecture in the Asia-Pacific and rise of China as a challenge for US hegemony, the remarkable US shift towards India is a huge dent in the Pakistan–US relations. Rising China is all set to dent the American hegemony in the Asia-Pacific. For Mearsheimer, rising powers tend to seek regional hegemony and China is heading in this direction.[4]

The former Pakistani Prime Minister Yousuf Raza Gilani described the relationship between Pakistan and China as being "higher than mountains, deeper than oceans, stronger than steel and sweeter than honey."[5] Of course, the 2013 moves of Pakistan like the handover of the Gwadar port to China, an all-weather friendship is growing despite the fact that the western Chinese province of Xinjiang is infected with the tentacles of terror and we are aware about the fact that the terror factory is based in Pakistan. But due to geostrategic compulsions, China is undermining those realities. The sustainable rise of India since the last two and half decades has worried the Chinese; therefore, the benefit is bound to go to Pakistan.

Since independence, almost half of the time, Pakistan has been ruled by the military and even under the civilian rule, the military had enjoyed autonomy to pursue its own policies on mainly three fronts: Kashmir, the nuclear issue and Afghanistan.

After the May 2013 election, Sharif again became the PM for a third time. It is a record, given the fragile nature of the Pakistani democracy and the aura of the Pakistani military. Sharif was talking high about the accountability of Kargil (1999) while in opposition but has become ambiguous on the issue recently. He will not like that his relations with the Army should sour. Till date, the Pakistani army is fighting a home-grown insurgency, particularly against the Tehreek-e-Taliban Pakistan (TTP). The NATO forces have already withdrawn. They have kept a small number of soldiers back in Afghanistan. The Afghan National Army (ANA) has been nurtured properly by the NATO forces but still it is an unanswered question that how far it will be able to contain the increasing onslaught of the Taliban. Pakistan has already sustained its nurturing process of the Haqqani network despite many warnings from the United States because it has been proved as an asset to Pakistan.

Pakistan's tacit support to the terror networks operating in Afghanistan has been a bone of contention between Pakistan and the United States. The Quetta Shura, once led by the Taliban's supreme leader Mullah Omar, is considered to be the main insurgent group in Afghanistan. But the latest bogeyman, at least for the US/NATO forces, has become the Haqqani network.[6] It is well connected and has engineered a majority of the attacks against the NATO forces in Afghanistan.

Jalaluddin Haqqani has long since been replaced by his son, Sirajuddin Haqqani, who is known as the khalifah (caliph) among his followers as well among journalists in the tribal region. Now in his mid-thirties, this active operational leader carries a US $ 5 million bounty on his head.[7] The Haqqanis had had close ties with the Arab fighters and the Al Qaeda leaders during the anti-Soviet war and under the Taliban. According to Kathy Gannon, a senior American journalist in the region, "Had he wanted, Haqqani (Jalaluddin) could have hand (ed) over the United States the entire al Qaeda network."[8]

Jalaluddin Haqqani, who went into hiding after the Taliban's collapse, made a rare appearance in a video interview in May 2008 on the Al Jazeera

TV, in which he vowed renewed attacks on what he called "the US and NATO invaders in Afghanistan."[9] The United States has pointed the Haqqani network as its arch-enemy and has pledged to eliminate it. According to Ahmed Rashid,

> "As the US military surge got under way in early 2010 in Helmand and Kandahar provinces, there was increasing US pressure for Pakistan to do more to 'capture or kill' Afghan Taliban leaders. The Army, which was now fully convinced that it had to eliminate the Pakistani Taliban in FATA, and deployed 1,40,000 troops to do so, still refused to go after Haqqanis' base in North Waziristan."[10]

The Pakistani army and the Jehadi factory spearheaded by the Haqqanis have been interlinked since the Soviet intervention era. These so-called non-state actors had been the mastermind for the Mumbai (2008) carnage and a gamut of attacks made against the Indian interests in Afghanistan recently. Some elements of the Jehadi umbrella have inflicted bloodshed in Pakistan also. Some are linked with the sectarian divide as well. Despite all those acts, Pakistan has yet not snapped ties with these groups.

Saudi Arabia has also extended its tacit support to the Haqqani network. The Haqqani network has been extremely detrimental to the NATO forces but according to the Wikileaks, Saudi Arabia has also provided a tacit support to the Haqqani group. The Saudi government has, meanwhile, not acknowledged these cables as authentic and has asked its citizens to ignore them. One of the cables, signed by the former Saudi Ambassador to Pakistan, Abdul Aziz Ibrahim Saleh Al Ghadeer, which is marked 'confidential', narrates his meeting with Nasiruddin Haqqani, one of the sons of the Haqqani-network chief Jalaluddin Haqqani. The meeting between the ambassador and Nasiruddin, who was the emissary and chief financier of the Taliban-linked militant group at the time, took place on Feb 15, 2012. The venue of the meeting has not been mentioned, but the ambassador usually held meetings either at the embassy or his residence, both of which are located in the heavily guarded Diplomatic Enclave and remain under the watchful eyes of the Pakistani intelligence agencies.[11] Given this report, it is entirely impossible that this meeting was held without the tacit approval of the Pakistani intelligence agencies. Besides providing safe havens to the Haqqanis, Pakistan also provided safe haven to the Taliban's former *amir*, Mullah Omar, who virtually ran his exiled government from the Pakistani town of 'Quetta'.

India is also getting increasingly involved in the strategic infrastructure projects in Afghanistan, such as building a transmission line to provide power to Kabul, a hydroelectric project in Herat as well as the Zaranj–Delaram road that connects the Ring Road in Afghanistan to the Iranian port in Chahbahar.[12] It has reduced the Afghan dependence on Pakistan for a sea route. It has been detrimental to the Pakistani interests. Besides this, India has trained the Afghan civilian and military personnel and has provided scholarships to the Afghan students to study in India; the Indian Council for Cultural Relations (ICCR) has offered as many as 500 scholarships a year for the Afghans.[13]

Although the international community generally welcomes the Indian development assistance programmes, it has not embraced India's offers to train Afghanistan's security personnel.[14] But during his December 2013 New Delhi visit, President Karzai requested a defence assistance in addition to a growing number of ANA officers for training in the backdrop of the withdrawal dates of the NATO forces coming closer and the Taliban propelling its violence against the Afghan government, which India accepted. In 2014, India outsourced an arms supply order to Russia for Afghanistan, conceding the outgoing Afghan President's request. But, it was fiercely opposed by Pakistan. It is vindicated from the editorial of a leading Pakistani English newspaper, *Dawn:*

> "The reconciliation process with the Afghan Taliban has stalled not only because of the elections, but more crucially because the key players comprising the Afghan Taliban, Pakistan, the US and Afghanistan have been unable to trust each other. In this unfriendly regional setting, the reported arms agreement between India and Russia is being viewed with misgivings. Initially, reports said, New Delhi would 'source' Russia for the supply of smaller weapons such as light artillery, but eventually this flow of arms paid for by India would include heavy artillery, tanks and helicopters. From India's point of view, such a deal would consolidate the influence New Delhi has already built up in post-Taliban Afghanistan. Hence it would be disastrous if regional states and outside powers were to adopt policies that could once again make Afghanistan an arena for proxy wars."[15]

The US Factor

After the elimination of bin Laden in May 2011, it has become an open secret that Pakistan is playing a double game with the United States. There is a growing anti-Americanism in Pakistan and that has made things extremely tough. But the question remains that does China have the capacity of replacing the US? The answer lies in the future but one thing is clear that despite all the rhetoric, China is unable to replace the US for Pakistan. The growing Indo-US relationship has put China in the trap of the concept of Security Dilemma and the China-India-Pakistan emerging triangular relationship is a classic example.

Another factor of sustainable tension between Pakistan and US has been Afghanistan. Since October 2001, the NATO-led forces operated in Afghanistan and despite its declared pledge, Pakistan has not been cooperating with the US-led NATO forces to eliminate the Taliban and the Al Qaeda. Meanwhile, the United States has poured $ 20 billion as a largesse to Pakistan. There is ample evidence to prove that Pakistan is not cooperating with the US in Afghanistan. It has enhanced the perception that Pakistan is part of the problem in Afghanistan; so how it could be a part of the solution?

Many projections have been made. But only four are worth mentioning. Firstly, the post-Karzai elected government may sustain itself in power. Secondly, it can share power with the Taliban. Thirdly, a division of Afghanistan on the basis of ethnicity between the South and the North is possible and fourthly, the Taliban may take over. The first three scenarios are not suiting Pakistan's interests; therefore, there is hardly any possibility of support of Pakistan to these options. Option four suits Pakistan but it does not suit the US; given all the scenarios, it is extremely tough for the US too to maximise its national interests. The India factor in Afghanistan is also important and Pakistan has kept demanding the reduction of the growing Indian imprint in the reconstruction of Afghanistan.

Pakistan has been pursuing the doctrine of strategic depth since independence in Afghanistan against India. In the Pakistani context, strategic depth is an outcome of national insecurity with regard to India. In order to curtail the Indian influence, Pakistan has long supported anti-India proxies in the form of various militant groups. Other people believe that the Pakistani army uses militant proxies on the pretext of strategic depth not only to pursue its strategic designs in the neighbouring countries but also to obtain foreign aid.[16] By virtue of Operation Enduring Freedom, India is back in Afghanistan and since October 2001 has been proactive. According to Ahmed Rashid,

> "The India factor has now returned with vengeance for the Pakistan army. When India did return to Pakistan after 9/11 it found its non-Pashtun allies within the government as it had aided the Northern Alliance in the civil war. It also found many allies among secular and educated Pashtuns, who rejected the Taliban and were sick of ISI manipulation. India swiftly developed an extremely well

conceived aid program investing approximately US $1.2 billion that speared Indian projects and largesse across all ethnic groups, built key infrastructure projects, set up the transport system in Kabul and contributed to important social programs like health. Unlike western aid agencies, 80 per cent of Indian money was actually spent on projects as Indian NGOs had low expenditures."[17]

Pakistan has paid a heavy price for supporting the Taliban. Despite paying a high price for following this policy, Pakistan's military establishment still seems stuck to it, meaning that it continues to rely on the Afghan Taliban groups as proxies for its so-called strategic interest. But this has proven to be an unrealistic approach, for despite the unprecedented sacrifices made by its people in hosting millions of Afghan refugees since the 1980s, today Pakistan is one of the most hated countries in Afghanistan.[18] This hostility is no longer confined to the Northern Alliance or elements in the Afghan government, but now runs so deep that most Afghans have stopped differentiating between Pakistan's military and the general population.[19]

Nexus between the Pakistani Army and the Jehad Factory

In the eyes of Pakistan's security establishment, strategic depth is a genuine requirement for the country's security and survival, for it is now a security state being increasingly encircled by "enemies." The "strategic partnership" agreement signed between Afghanistan and India in 2013 once again sends the wrong signal at a critical time, for all it does is reinforce the Pakistani paranoia and, perhaps, it might push the country to provide even more support to its proxies.[20]

Pakistan's Policy Options

India has tried in some measure to protect its key personnel in Afghanistan. For example, to protect civilians with the Border Roads Organization (BRO) which were building the southern portion of the Ring Road, India deployed the Indo-Tibetan Police Force (ITPF) as well as a small number of army commandos. After the Embassy and other attacks, India expanded the ITPF presence in Afghanistan to protect the key Indian installations.[21] These measures have infuriated Pakistan. It should be noted that some of these attacks have been linked to the ISI.[22]

In the backdrop of the Soviet withdrawal from Afghanistan in 1989, the Jehadi elements became a consolidated force. The establishment of the Taliban regime further emboldened their firepower. The danger is equally great, and perhaps more urgent within Pakistan itself, as it becomes increasingly uncertain whether its leadership is "master or victim"[23] of the militant fundamentalism it fuelled for its campaign against the Russian presence in Afghanistan throughout the 1980s, and continues to stoke in pursuit of its strategic ambitions in Kashmir. Ahmed Rashid notes the devastating potential of Pakistan's flirtations with "fundamentalist" mass mobilisation:

> "In the late 1990s the repercussions were much more pervasive, undermining all the institutions of the state ... law and order broke down as Islamic militants enacted their own laws and a new breed of anti-Shia Islamic radicals, who were given sanctuary by the Taliban, killed hundreds of Pakistani Shias between 1996 and 1999. This sectarian bloodshed is now fueling a much wider rift between Pakistan's Sunni majority and Shia minority and undermining relations between Pakistan and Iran. At the same time, over 80,000 Pakistani Islamic militants have trained and fought with the Taliban since 1994. They form a hard core of Islamic activists, ever ready to carry out a similar Taliban-style Islamic revolution in Pakistan".[24]

Pakistan, despite being a partner of NATO in its global war against terror in Afghanistan, has never really cooperated with the NATO. It is merely because terror has remained an instrument of Pakistan's foreign policy since the last two decades and one of the most powerful tools of the Army's dominance over the entire system. According to a book *Duty: Memories of a Secretary at War* written by the former US Defense Secretary Robert Gates, the author has commented, "I gave him a list of specific actions we wanted Pakistan to take. The US also instructed Musharraf to disrupt certain major infiltration routes across the border; enhance intelligence cooperation and streamline Pakistani decision making on targeting. Musharraf kept a straight face and pretended to take all this seriously."[25] In her book, *The Wrong Enemy: America in Afghanistan 2001-2004*, senior American journalist Carlotta Gall who has spent ten years in Afghanistan has concluded that "The embassy bombing was on operation by rouge ISI agents acting on their own. It was sanctioned and monitored by the most senior officials in Pakistani intelligence." The evidence was so damning that the Bush administration dispatched the deputy chief of the CIA, Stephen Kappes, to Islamabad to remonstrate with the Pakistanis. The bomber struck before Kappes could reach Islamabad. Gall writes, "Investigators found the bomber's cell phone in the wreckage of his exploded car. They tracked down his collaborator in Kabul, the man who had provided the logistics for the attack. The facilitator, an Afghan, had been in direct contact with Pakistan by telephone."[26] According to Gall, as the Afghan government investigated the attack, they became convinced that "the ISI was working with al Qaeda, the Taliban, the Haqqanis, and Pakistani groups such as Lashkar-e-Taiba." Gall concludes, "At the core of Pakistan's thinking was an obsessive desire to dominate Afghanistan in order to protect its own rear flank from India. In that way of thinking, the Taliban were guarantors of Pakistan's national strategic interests."[27]

Pakistan has kept up these nefarious activities against the Indian assets in Afghanistan and post-2014 NATO withdrawal, it is bound to propel them further.

Pakistan is not ready to allow Afghanistan to stabilise and its biggest fear is India. The NATO forces according to the Department of Defense have identified 2,274 American service members who have died as a part of the Afghan war and related operations till November 5, 2013.[28] There are casualties in three digits for the NATO minus US forces as well.

The June 2011 Pew Research poll showed that most Pakistanis see the United States as an enemy and a potential threat to their country's security.[29] On the one hand, since joining hands in late 2001, Washington has been praising Islamabad for its commitment and sacrifice of more than 5,500 military personnel and as many as 65,000 Pakistani civilians in the "war on terror." In 2011, soon after the killing of Osama bin Laden inside Pakistan, President Barack Obama said, "We have been able to kill more terrorists on Pakistani soil than just about anyplace else. We could not have done that without Pakistani cooperation."[30] On the other hand, American officials have suspected and often accused the Pakistani military of supporting militant groups, particularly the Afghan Taliban. Although Washington and Islamabad have never been on the same page since 9/11, both sides have always made an effort to maintain their ties. This scenario has developed a status which could be termed as 'trust deficit' between both. In its one decade experience, the US has realised that Pakistan is part of the problem and not the part of the solution in Afghanistan. The parochial prism of the Pakistani army about Afghanistan is still dominant in the power corridor despite the eight years of the recent post-military democratic governance. In the scenario of the backdrop of the withdrawal of the NATO forces, the Afghan people and the international community are anxious about the post-withdrawal security situation. Nawaz Sharif is in power and it has given much anxiety to the Afghan people. Interestingly, many Afghans are also uncomfortable with the return of Nawaz Sharif as Pakistan's premier. One of Nawaz Sharif's 1993 election campaign slogans (targeting the Pakistan People's Party at the time) was 'you gave up Dhaka, we took Kabul'. Till today, these words are recalled with dismay by the Afghans.[31]

Pakistan has also not contained the anti-Americanism by the Islamists. There has been a rapidly growing and widespread leverage that is being gained by the intolerant religious and sectarian groups such as the Difa-e Pakistan Council (DPC) or the Defense Council of Pakistan—a group of more than 40 religious parties and Islamists—whose main focus is to prevent the Pakistani state from improving relations with the United States and India.[32] The US has declared a reward of $ 5 million dollar on Hafeez Saeed and India has also accused him as the mastermind of the November 2008 Mumbai attack. But, Pakistan has not done anything against him and he is living openly in Lahore and addressing rallies throughout the country. This attitude has proved the allegation that Pakistan has been using terror as an instrument of foreign policy.

9/11 again became a turning point for its relationship with the US but due to Pakistani non-cooperation on the containment of terror and the killing of bin Laden near Pakistan's military academy, the relationship got dented. The security of the nuclear arsenals in Pakistan is also one of the nightmares for the United States in the backdrop of a series of terror attacks on Pakistan's security establishments. High stakes are involved in Afghanistan, particularly in the post-2014 scenario. The United States has understood that Pakistan is part of the problem in Afghanistan and does not want a stable Afghanistan. This issue has sustained the estranged relationship between Pakistan and the United States. An eminent American scholar on Pakistani issues, Stephen Cohen, has also argued that the US has many Pakistan policies due to the complex situation prevailing in Pakistan. This has put the Americans in a security dilemma. According to a US Congressman, Dana Rohrabacher, "Things have changed in last 20 years....We have now an ally in India and an enemy in Pakistan."[33]

What are the policy options for Pakistan? It has to understand that the 2015 Afghanistan is different from 1990. A stable Afghanistan will only stabilise Pakistan. The Afghan people do not like Pakistan despite the fact that Pakistan has given shelter to millions of Afghans since the last three decades and even today the top Taliban leadership has been given safe haven by Pakistan. Since the last one decade, the Afghan people have seen a relative peace and have aspired to make their country as an abode of peace and development. "Today, the verdict from Afghanistan is loud and clear—the Afghans want to be left alone. They do not want international and regional powers to once again turn their country into a battle ground for their short-lived tactical gains. Their steaming anger, the highest it has ever been, should caution Pakistan as the scenario today is starkly different to what it was in the 90s."[34] The 2014 Presidential election has vindicated this the fact because over 70 per cent people voted despite a gamut of threats from the Taliban.

Pakistan is facing a turbulent time since the last one decade. Devastation on a massive scale is going on. Already, the TTP has been threatening the writ of the state since the last many years and intends to sustain the process till the rule of the Prophet (*Nizam-e-Mustafa*) does not get established. Although, the military's professional reputation has been dented by the sustainability of terror, it has been able to safeguard its interests. Sectarian violence is also on the rampage and more than 10,000 people have been killed. The health of the economy has also been critical and needs special treatment at an urgent basis. The situation in Baluchistan is also critical and is threatening the unity of the country. The situation in the financial hub Karachi is not much better and in the year 2012 alone, more than 2,000 people have been killed.[35] It is time when Pakistan should learn some inherent lessons from history that till peace and development do not prevail in Afghanistan, Pakistan could not remain in peace. The last three decades of gradual Pakistani intervention has converted Afghanistan into the world's most deadly places after Syria and Iraq. Pakistan has a unique geostrategic status and it must be utilised for the sustainable development of the country instead of creating turbulences in neighbourhood. It is vindicated by the following statement of Mr Haqqani, the former Pakistani Ambassador to the United States,

> "The Policy tripod I wrote about has become less sustainable. Among the factors that have changed is the stress within Pakistan. The issue of India as an eternal enemy has come under a lot of strain. Before the Bin Laden raid, Pakistan was a subject discussed only among American foreign policy experts. Now Pakistan has become part of the American pop culture. Pakistan's elite should embrace a new liberal paradigm. There is no eternal enemy of Pakistan, there is no existential threat to Pakistan, it should maintain an effective military, it should maintain a minimum nuclear deterrent, and after that it should focus on educating its people. Put our 48 per cent children who do not go to school into schools, open up the economy, organize agriculture, create jobs, take advantage of being at the centre of trade ties from India to Central Asia, from Iran to India, from the Middle East to India and China. For the last 66 years, the elite have thought that Pakistan is strategically important because it sits at the crossroads of conflict. I say that Pakistan should now look at itself as sitting at the crossroads of opportunity."[36]

But given the prevailing situation in the power corridor in Islamabad at the middle of 2015, it is amply clear that Islamabad has not learnt any lessons from its past mistakes. Islamabad is still hell-bent to use terror as an instrument of its foreign policy. On January 26, 2014, an outlawed militant group, the Jaish-e-Muhammad (JeM), held a rally of militants at Muzaffarabad.

Maulana Masood Azhar, commander of the JeM, declared "Kashmir is part of Pakistan and unless Kashmiri Muslims get their rights, there cannot be any friendship with India," he declared.[37]

In April 2014, Presidential elections started in Afghanistan. In the wake of this crucial election, the Taliban stepped up its attacks. President Karzai had pointed his accusations at Pakistan directly as the sponsor of these attacks. In a phone call with the US Secretary of State John Kerry, Hamid Karzai accused Pakistan of being behind the March 2014 series of attacks and of blocking his government from striking a peace deal with the Taliban.[38] Pakistan is dedicated to the bleeding India at a thousand places. It has been revealed by Riyaz Bhatkal that Pakistan's ISI has given Rs 26 crore to the Indian Mujahideen in the last three years for anti-India operations.[39] On May 23, 2014 the Indian Consulate in Herat was attacked and again the needle of suspicion tilted towards the military–Jehadi nexus in Pakistan. It is opined that this attack was an attempt to derail the goodwill created by the invitation of the then Indian PM-designate Narendra Modi to the Pakistani PM, Nawaz Sharif.[40] PM Sharif finally attended the swearing-in ceremony and had a meeting with the new Indian PM Modi. In this prevailing situation, the demand of the times is that India must prepare itself for containing the propelling incidents of cross-border terror. We have to face this situation as an essential reality. At the same time, we must sustain our efforts to ensure peace and development in Afghanistan. 2015's Afghanistan is different and the people of Afghanistan are hell-bent on sustaining peace. Since the last one decade, they have experienced relative peace. The over 70 per cent of the voting in the Presidential election despite an all-round violent threat by the Taliban has vindicated the courage and dedication of the Afghan people and their urge to bring peace and participatory democracy. India must ensure close cooperation with Iran, Russia and the Central Asian Republics as they had done during the Taliban rule in Afghanistan. The Chinese support must be also solicited.

Concluding Remarks

An eminent Indian security analyst, C. Raja Mohan, has rightly stated in November 2013,

> "Any nuclear deal between Washington and Tehran will immediately bring down oil prices, relieve the current macroeconomic pressures on India, and improve Delhi's energy security calculus over the longer term. US–Iran rapprochement will help to strengthen Afghanistan against the Taliban and Pakistan and expand India's room for regional maneuver after 2014."[41]

The interim deal between Washington and Tehran has already been concluded and finally will be inked in the first half of July 2015 and it is time when the Indian diplomacy must burn the extra oil to bring Iran and the United States on the same page to ensure peace and stability in Afghanistan. Iran could be an important player to contain the Islamic State, which is gradually getting a foothold in Afghanistan. Iran is an important player and it had been part and parcel of the Indian efforts along with Russia and the Central Asian Republics to contain the Taliban and form the Northern Alliance to combat it. (1996–2001).

The newly elected President Ashraf Ghani visited Islamabad in September 2014 and convinced Pakistan's security 'establishment' to change its strategic approach to Afghanistan. Pakistani PM Sharif and Chief of the Army Staff, General Rahil Sharif have also visited Kabul. Far from a regime entrenched in hostility and resentment towards Pakistan, Islamabad found a leader who acknowledged the vital and symbiotic nature of the Pakistan–Afghan relations and understood Pakistan's concerns regarding India's role in Afghanistan. All the doors of economic and security cooperation between the two countries have been opened. Most significantly, Kabul has extended active cooperation to combat the TTP and Islamabad has committed to prevent the cross-border attacks against Afghanistan and to promote the reconciliation with the Taliban.

Just after President Ghani's first visit to Islamabad in September 2014, the Foreign Policy Adviser to Pakistan's PM stated that fighting with the Afghan Taliban is not the duty of Pakistan because they have done nothing wrong against Pakistan. Aziz's statement is self-explanatory which proves that Pakistan is part of the Afghan problem and despite the all-round global efforts it cannot be the part of the solution. The killing of Osama bin Laden despite the thousands of denials by Pakistan in May 2011 proves that since the launching of "Operation Enduring Freedom" Pakistan has played a double game. As President Ghani has rightly stated in his March 2015 Washington visit that the durability of any insurgency is not possible till sanctuary is not provided by a neighbour. Since the last four decades, Pakistan has perceived the terrorists as an asset and has used them as an instrument of its foreign policy in all the cases. It is also an open secret that Mullah Omar resided at Quetta and supervised the insurgency in Afghanistan with the tacit understanding of the Pakistani security establishment. The military–mullah alliance is still hopeful that Afghanistan could be a model country where the sharia could be imposed. They have equally intended to use Afghanistan as a rear base against India because of a lack of hinterland in the Pakistani geostrategic ambience.

Kabul's posture towards the US is also visibly different. During his March 2015 US visit, Ghani was effusive in his gratitude for The US's military support and sacrifices and insistent in requesting its continued security and economic support. The US has consequently agreed to keep just under 10,000 troops and two military bases in Afghanistan in place for the present and continue its financial support to Kabul.

President Ghani has shown some flexibility towards Pakistan in comparison with his predecessor, President Karzai and after the December 2014 Peshawar school attack, both countries have pledged to work together. Speaking at the Council of Foreign Relations in New York on March 26, he said that he thought, "Pakistan is integral to peace efforts with the Taliban".[42] However, in the veiled attack on Pakistan he stated that both countries were working to end 13 years of hostilities; he believes that improved relations with Pakistan are key to denying support for the Afghan Taliban insurgents.

"Without sanctuary, a long-term rebellion is impossible. When sanctuaries end, peace breaks out. That is what happened in Central America and Latin America, that is what has happened in Africa," he said.[43]

In contrast, historically, the Afghanistan–India relations have been cordial. Due to its dual policy, Pakistan has become extremely unpopular and due to its huge investment of over $ 2 billion, India is well respected among all sections of the Afghans. According to former Pakistani NSA, Mahmud Ali Durrani, "Hamid Karzai mistrusted us, I blame Pervez Musharraf also. Once I told Musharraf, you should invite him here, but he disagreed. He said he is a third class chap. The Afghan people, by and large, have far greater respect for India than they have for us."[44]

The NDA II government has multiple challenges on this front. We have witnessed since 1999 till date that whenever we are proposing high-profile peace talks with Pakistan, it has been reciprocated by Kargil/Mumbai/Jammu, etc. Pakistan is still trying to create new turbulence in Kashmir particularly in the backdrop of the formation of the BJP–PDP government there. India must sustain its reconstruction activities in Afghanistan and in the meanwhile must sustain its dialogue with Pakistan but at a low-key level beside the periodical summit level talks in international foras. This front is one of the most turbulent challenges for the Modi government.

The civil–political relations in Pakistan have been always tilted towards the Army. Former PM Gilani had stated in 2012 that while he was the PM, "Pakistani military is not within the Pakistani state but Pakistani state is within the Pakistani army." It is important to mention here that he was leading the Pakistan People's Party coalition; his assertion is self-contradictory and proves that the military is all-powerful in Pakistan. But, it is the only super power when the issues related to India, Afghanistan and the nuclear one come. The Pakistani Army has portrayed India as the permanent foe and has nursed certain terror outfits to sustain its anti-India megalomania. When Benazir Bhutto took oath as the first woman PM of Pakistan in 1988, the then Chief of Army Staff, General Aslam Beg took three assurances from her that she will not intervene in India, Afghanistan and on the nuclear issue and decisions will be formulated by the army on these affairs. The evidence is that she sustained the General Zia era Foreign Minister, Shebzada Yakub Khan, as her FM also. Here it is significant to mention that Khan had fought the 1988 election on an IJI ticket and got elected against Benazir's PPP.[45] In February 1999, PM Vajpayee rode on a bus to Lahore and inked the historic 'Lahore Declaration'. It was reciprocated by the Army and its terror stooges through Kargil. PM Manmohan Singh had started engaging Pakistan in his first term but that was reciprocated by the Mumbai terror attack in 2008. PM Modi called all SAARC leaders including the Pakistani PM to witness his swearing-in ceremony. This gesture was also reciprocated by the March 2015 Jammu attack. The former Pakistani NSA stressed that "The political classes, by and large, wants peace. Where the difference comes in is the religious political classes. But the biggest monster is the army. The army has always felt that India is a very serious threat to us. Every military of the world has to have an enemy, a threat to point their guns at."[46]

In the last week of June 2015, the Afghan Parliament complex was attacked by suicide terrorists. The Afghan intelligence services spokesman Hassib Sediqqi stated that the officers in the Inter-Services Intelligence had helped the Haqqani network carry out the attack outside the Parliament in Kabul, which killed two people and wounded more than 30 as the lawmakers were meeting inside.[47] Almost a month ago, ISI and the Aghan intelligence agency—National Directorate of Security (NDS)—had signed a landmark deal aimed at bolstering the fight against terrorism.[48] The nexus between the Haqqani network and ISI is well known. This attack vindicates the fact that despite the many recent deals and reconciliation efforts by President Ghani, ISI is not going to allow peace in Afghanistan.

India must revive the 'Northern Alliance' spirit among Russia, Iran, the Central Asian Republics and China to contain a takeover of the Taliban or the IS in Afghanistan. Although China has thorny relations with India and an all-round friendship with Pakistan, it knows that Pakistan has also used terror in its insurgent-infested western region of Xinjiang. Needless to say that if the Modi government will take these steps effectively it will not only minimise the terror incidents but also consolidate the country's all-round development. Peace is must for development and the Modi government must take these steps to ensure peace. We should not forget that the headquarters of international terrorism is still based in Pakistan and Afghanistan. The terror network in India also originates from here and the in-built anti-India megalomania in the mullah–military alliance in Pakistan has further enhanced these threats. The threats of terror are looming large in the backdrop of the withdrawal of the NATO troops. The Modi government through implementing the above steps can push away the terror threats and ensure a sustainable development.

The Afghan President Ashraf Ghani had visited New Delhi in April 2015 and pledged to sustain deep engagements with India. His urge to cooperate with Pakistan has been duly reciprocated by it. Increasing incidents of violence are proving this assertion. We have to understand that the Pakistani army is formulating and implementing Pakistan's Afghan policy since 1979. It seems that it has not changed it even today. Pakistan, despite global persuasion, is not going to abandon its old Afghan policy. The civilian regime has been in power since 2008 till date but it has no teeth in the formulation of the foreign policy particularly on the Afghanistan and India fronts and this is likely to be sustainable in the foreseeable future. Needless to say, the situation in Afghanistan will determine the security architecture of India and South-West Asia and will make an imprint on global peace as well. India must take all possible steps to ensure peace and stability with a tacit understanding with the like-minded countries in Afghanistan. It has emerged as the utmost challenge for the Modi government.

NOTES AND REFERENCES

1. Praveen Swami "Terrorism in Jammu and Kashmir in Theory and Practice", *India Review*, 2, no. 3 (July 2003), pp. 55-88.
2. Lisa Curtis, "Afghanistan and Pakistan: Understanding and Engaging Regional Stakeholders", Testimony before the Committee on Oversight and Government Reform, Subcommittee on National Security and Foreign Affairs, U.S. House of Representatives, March 31, 2009, http://www.heritage.org/research/asiaandthepacific/tst040209a.cfm.

3. Munir Akram, "Reversing Strategic Shrinkage" in Maleeha Lodhi (ed.) *Pakistan: Beyond the 'Crisis State'*, Columbia University Press, New York, 2011, pp. 287-288.
4. Mearsheimer, John J., "China's Unpeaceful Rise", *Current History*, 2006, 105 (690), p. 161.
5. The statement was made during the visit of the Chinese Public Security Minister, Meng Jianzho, to Pakistan in September 2011. "Ties with China Hailed: Gilani Cautions US on Negative Messaging", *Dawn*, Karachi, 28 September 2011.
6. For more details on the Haqqani Network see Don Rassler and Wahid Brown, "The Haqqanis Nexus and the Evolution of Al Qaeda", Combatting Terrorism Center, West Point. July 13, 2011.
7. Bill Roggio, "US Places Bounty on Senior Taliban and Al Qaeda Leaders", *Long Wars Journal*, March 25, 2009.
8. Kathy Gannon, "I for Infidel, From Holy War to Holy Terror: 18 Years Inside Afghanistan", *Public Affairs*, New York, 2005, p 94.
9. "Taliban Leader Vows Renewed Attacks", *Al-Jazeera*, March 22, 2008.
10. Op. cit., No. 3, p. 311.
11. Baqir Sajjad Syed, *"Cables Detail Saudi Diplomat's Meeting with Haqqani's Son"*, *Dawn*, Karachi, 28 June 2015.
12. For a detailed account of Indian assistance, see the Indian Embassy (Kabul), "India's Assistance Programme for Afghanistan's Reconstruction", http://meakabul.nic.in/; also see V.K. Shashikumar, "The India Factor in Afghanistan", *Indian Defence Review* 23, no. 3 (July-September 2008), http://www.indiandefencereview.com/2009/05/the-india-factor-in-afghanistan.html.
13. For details see the various annual reports of India's Ministry of External Affairs, http:// meaindia.nic.in/mystart.php?id_2702.
14. "India's Developmental Efforts in Afghanistan get US Endorsement", *Economic Times*, April 20, 2010, http://economictimes.indiatimes.com/news/politics/nation/Indiasdevelopmental-efforts-in-Afghanistan-get-US-endorsement/articleshow/5834076.cms.
15. "Indian Arms for Kabul", Editorial, *Dawn*, Karachi, 2 May 2014.
16. S. Akbar Zaidi, "Who Benefits from Aid to Pakistan", The News on Sunday, *The News*, Islamabad, October 16, 2011.
17. Op. cit, No. 3, p. 315.
18. Dr Pervez Hoodbhoy, "What Pakistan should do in Afghanistan?" *Express Tribune*, Lahore, March 18, 2012.
19. "Helmand Despatch: 'Pakistan is the True Enemy", *Daily Telegraph*, London. August 1, 2010.
20. "Afghanistan and India Sign 'Strategic Partnership", *BBC News*, October 4, 2011.
21. See "India to send more ITBP troops to Afghanistan", *Rediff.com*, March 12, 2010, http://news.rediff.com/report/2010/mar/12/india-to-send-more-itbp-troops-to-afghanistan.htm.
22. See Mark Mazzetti and Eric Schmitt, "Pakistanis Aided Attack in Kabul, US Officials Say", *New York Times*, New York, August 1, 2008, http://www.nytimes.com/2008/08/01/world/asia/01pstan.html?_r_2.

23. Also see "Master or Victim: Pakistan's Afghan War" in Ahmed Rashid, *Taliban: Islam, Oil and the New Great Game in Central Asia* (London & New York: I.B. Tauris Publishers, 2001), pp. 183-195. Jessica Stern refers to this as a typical "principal–agent" problem, observing that the interests of the state (principal) and those of the militant groups (the agent) are not fully aligned. See "Pakistan's Jihad Culture", *Foreign Affairs*, November-December 2000 at <http://www.foreignaffairs.org/issues/0011/stern.html>.
24. Ibid, p. 194.
25. "Musharraff Refused to Act against Al-Qaeda, Taliban: US Ex-Defense Secretary", PTI, *The Indian Express*, New Delhi, p. 12, January 12, 2014.
26. Lalit K. Jha, "ISI Executed Kabul Indian Embassy Attack, US Couldn't Stop It", *The Indian Express*, New Delhi, March 24, 2014.
27. Ibid.
28. *New York Times*, New York, November 6, 2013.
29. "U.S. Image in Pakistan Falls No Further Following bin Laden Killing".
30. "Obama: U.S., Pakistan Can Find Ways To Improve Cooperation", May 8, 2011.
31. Hina Baloch, "Afghans and Pakistanis; Friends Turned Foes?", *Dawn*, Karachi, 28 January 2014.
32. Arif Rafiq, "The Emergence of Difa-e-Pakistan Islamist Coalition", Combating Terrorism Center Sentinel, *West Point*, March 22, 2012.
33. *The Times of India*, New Delhi, March 25, 2013, p.20.
34. Op. cit, No.27.
35. Singh, Sudhir, "Limits of Electoral Mandate in Pakistan", *Politico*, Vol. 1, No. 1, 2013, p. 79.
36. "The Idea Exchange", *Indian Express*, New Delhi, October 20, 2013.
37. Tariq, "Banned Group Holds Rally in Muzaffarabad", *Dawn*, 27 January 2014.
38. "AP: Karzai Steps Up Pakistan Accusations", *Dawn*, Karachi, 30 March 2014.
39. Neeraj Chauhan, "ISI gave Rs 26 cr for Anti-India Ops", *The Times of India*, New Delhi, March 31, 2014.
40. *Times of India*, New Delhi, 24 May 2014.
41. C. Raja Mohan, "The Great Game Folio", *The Indian Express*, New Delhi, 20 November 2013.
42. Masood Haider, "Pakistan Integral to Peace Efforts, Says Ghani", *Dawn*, Karachi, 28 March, 2015.
43. Ibid.
44. "Idea Exchange, Mahmud Ali Durrani", *The Indian Express*, March 22, 2015, p. 12.
45. Rizvi, Hasan Aksari, *Military, State & Society in Pakistan*, St Martin Press, London, 2000, p.43.
46. Ibid., Op. cit. No. 43.
47. Irfan Haider, "ISI Officer Involved in Kabul Parliament Attack, Claims Afghan Intelligence", *Dawn*, Karachi, 25 June 2015.
48. Ibid.

PART II

Human Security and Violence Against Women

6

Violence against Women: A Case Study of Domestic Violence among Married Women in India

Anuradha Banerjee and Koyel Sarkar

ABSTRACT

Acts of violence in society stand against the fundamental rights of human beings and curbs the freedom of leading a long and healthy life of dignity and integrity. Gendered aspects of such violence are often targeted towards women in every phase of her life starting from infancy to elderly in many countries. India has been ranked to have one of the worst situations with respect to women in a recent G-20 survey. Accordingly, National Family Health Survey 3 (NFHS 3; 2005-06) data reveals that 1 in every 5 women face domestic violence from their husbands and The National Crime Record Bureau (2007) reports crime against women has increased by 12.5 percent from 2006 along with a 6.2 percent increase in rates of cases filed under "dowry deaths". Women experiencing abuse are 1.5 times more likely to have a sexually transmitted infection (STI); HIV and twice as likely to have an abortion. Violence against women is thus a major public health concern and more importantly, a violation of women's human rights. In this context, the present study tries to explore the trends and patterns of domestic violence in India. Furthermore, an attempt has been made to analyse the relationship of socio-economic factors with domestic violence and its impact on women's health. Finally, an attempt has been made to critically analyse the legal provisions backing prevention of domestic violence along with policy imperatives in the Indian context. The study has been based on secondary data sources from NFHS 3 covering a sample of 66,658 of ever married women, aged 15 to 49 years.

The main findings reveals that acts of domestic violence among women are more prevalent in urban than rural areas. Women with least education and poor family background are more prone to become a victim to domestic violence. Like other studies, education seems to be the black box in having the propensity to pull women towards betterment and away from being a subject to violence. Paradoxically, women who enjoy more autonomy, (financial, mobility and decision making) show higher prevalence of domestic violence. This calls for a need to change the outlook of the male members in the society to accept women as their equal counterparts and therefore it is important to stop treating women as subordinates as in a patriarchal set up. Also, women whose husbands suffer from substance abuse, primarily alcohol, are the ones who suffer more violence. The health burden also increases among women suffering from domestic violence and they are most likely to experience pregnancy as well as post-partum complications, STD and RTI, high anaemia level and low BMI (Body Mass Index). The study thus brings to the fore the cause and effect syndrome of domestic violence among married women in India. Women being the primary care givers in most Indian societies should be treated with utmost care not only for her dignity, but for the welfare of the entire family and society at large.

Keywords: Domestic violence, human right, health, autonomy, anaemia, post-partum.

Introduction

The stage of a civilisation progressing towards maturity cannot be defined through limited benchmarks of a handful of scientific innovations and other development indicators. It is but a broader scenario where humanity is seen blossoming in an evolutionary manner in every stage as compared to its previous stages, growing with perfection and learning beyond defects. However, modernism has brought along several illicit facets of grave concern to the civil society. With a growing burden on earth along with increasing ecological footprints, which questions the very existence of humankind in the far future, we have successfully generated even greater causes to live beyond solidarity and cohesion. Human conflict and violence is one such aspect of the modern world which questions the very idea of development. Resulting from a growing hierarchical structure of the society in terms of all categories like gender, race, religion, caste and community, the differences seem to keep expanding in leaps and bounds. The growing conflict in human nature resulting in violence and outrageous acts inflicted upon individuals has led to secularism, fraternity and peace occupying mere spaces in the dictionary. These acts of violence not only reveal the shunned aspects of the civil society but their ever-increasing kind—both in numbers as well as nature—which have made every step of advancement of humankind falter.

However, imperfection being mortal and knowing that it is not an indefinite inadequacy we can always strive to live wiser, finer and in a superior way with every experience. On this line, this study has been taken to critically analyse a very important aspect—domestic violence. Violence can be defined as the intention of hurting another person or group, physically or mentally, with the use of force or power, without considering the outcome it produces. Domestic violence thus, involves the act of abuse of one partner against another in an intimate relationship such as marriage, cohabitation or within the family. It is mostly a gender-specific violence where the victims are always women, expressly because of the fact that they are women or as a result of the norms of a patriarchal society.

The UN Declaration on the Elimination of Violence against Women states that *"violence against women is a manifestation of historically unequal power relations between men and women"* and that *"violence against women is one of the crucial social mechanisms by which women are forced into a subordinate position compared with men"*. The United Nations has thus defined Violence against Women as, *"Any act of gender-based violence that results in or is likely to result in physical, sexual, or psychological harm or suffering to women, including threats of such acts, coercion or arbitrary deprivation of liberty, whether occurring in public or private life"*.

Violence against women in every phase of life starting from infancy to old age, constitutes the reality of most girls and women living in India. Physical, sexual, emotional and economic violence based on gender discrimination manifested in the preference for a son, unequal resource distribution and decision-making power (in both private and public spaces), caste discrimination (especially towards women from specific castes), communal violence against women, etc. comprise most of the types of violence practiced against women.

India has been ranked as the worst place to be a woman according to a recent G-20 survey. According to the NFHS 3 survey, 1 in every 5 women faces domestic violence from her husband. The National Crimes Record Bureau (2007) reveals that the total crime against women has increased by 12.5 per cent from 2006 along with a 6.2 per cent increase in the rates of cases filed under dowry "deaths". Under-reporting of the acts of violence against women in India as well as across the globe is a matter of great concern.

Table 1.1: Types of Violence Experienced by Women according to the Phases of their Lives

Phase	Type of Violence
Prenatal and postnatal	Sex-selective abortion, Female infanticide
Childhood	Child marriage; female genital mutilation; physical, sexual and psychological abuse; child prostitution and pornography
Adolescence and adulthood	Acid attack; molestation; sexual abuse; rape; forced prostitution and pornography; trafficking; partner violence; marital rape; dowry abuse and murders; partner homicide; psychological abuse; forced pregnancy
Elderly	Forced "suicide" or homicide of widows; sexual, physical and psychological abuse

Source: "Violence against Women: Definition and Scope of the Problem", *World Health Organisation*, July, 1997.

According to the NFHS 3, domestic violence has been recognised and categorised under three types—physical, emotional and sexual. Of these, at an all-India level, 35 per cent of married women have experienced physical spousal violence; 16 per cent and 10 per cent have encountered emotional and sexual violence respectively. The 2013 analysis found that women who had been physically or sexually abused were 1.5 times more likely to have a sexually transmitted infection and—in some regions, HIV—compared to the women who had not experienced partner violence. They are also twice as likely to have an abortion. Violence against women is thus a major public health problem and more importantly, a violation of women's human rights.

Rationale of the Study

Factors associated with domestic violence usually occur within individual behavioural characteristics generated by families, communities and society. These risk factors include lower levels of education, the witnessing of family violence, antisocial personality disorder, excessive use of alcohol, suspicion, insecurity, multiple partners, attitudes of acceptance of violence and gender inequality, past history of violence, marital discord and dissatisfaction, desire for sex selective children and various others.

Domestic violence usually results in serious short- and long-term physical, mental, sexual and reproductive health problems for survivors and for their children. The results can be fatal at times, like homicide or suicide. It can lead to injuries, unintended pregnancies, induced abortions,

Table 3.1: Conceptual Framework

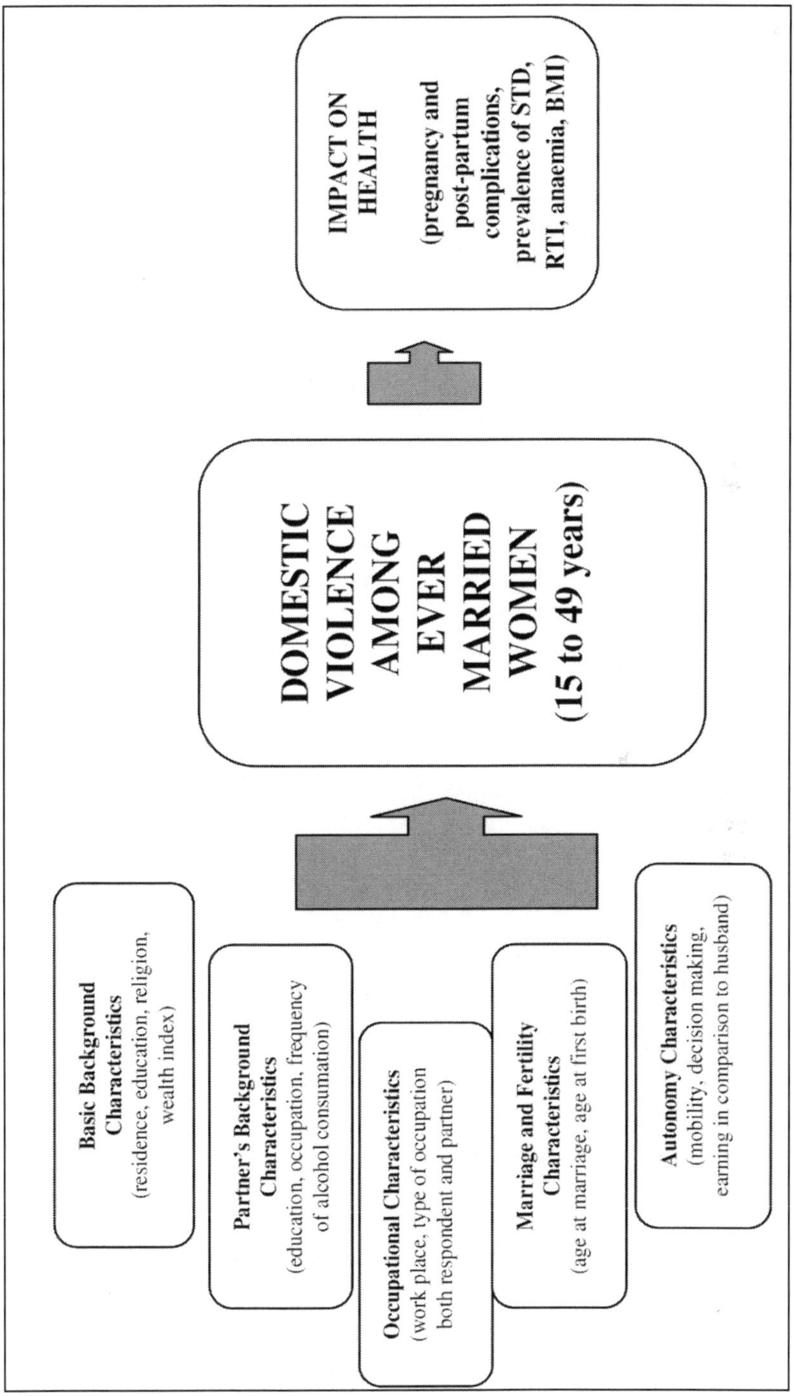

miscarriage, stillbirth, gynaecological problems, STDs including HIV, pre-term delivery and low birth weight babies. Domestic violence leads to depression, post-traumatic stress and suicide attempts. Children who grow up in families where there is violence may suffer a range of behavioural and emotional disturbances. Health effects include headaches, back pain, abdominal pain and poor overall health. Risky lifestyle practices like increased smoking, drug and alcohol misuse, risky sexual behaviours, etc. are also associated with domestic violence.

The factors associated with domestic violence and its impact on women's health, children and society as cited above clearly explain the aggravated situation of women in the society as a human right concern. Women are the primary caretakers of household health but the decisions regarding their health at most times depend on the male (son/partner/husband) members in the family; thus, their health remains to be one of the most highly neglected areas in the society. However, in spite of the various legal provisions, violence on women continues unabated and domestic violence remains a neglected area since most of the cases are not reported or remain suppressed as part of the cultural norms of Indian women. This explains why the incidence of such violence should be further researched particularly in the context of the overall impact on women's health.

Conceptual Framework

This study has looked into the interlinkages of the various socio-economic characteristics like how the selected individual background characteristics (place of residence, education level, religion, wealth index), occupational characteristics (occupation type, work place, earning in comparison to partner), marriage and fertility characteristics (age at marriage, age at first birth), autonomy characteristics (media exposure, mobility and decision-making autonomy) and husband's characteristics (education level, occupation type, alcohol consumption and frequency) have affected the prevalence of domestic among married women and what is its impact on women's overall health (pregnancy and post-partum complications, prevalence of STD, RTI, anaemia and BMI).

Objectives

- To study the trends and patterns of domestic violence in India
- To study the relationship of socio-economic and cultural background factors on domestic violence

- To study the impact of domestic violence and women's health
- Critically analyse the legal provisions backing the prevention of domestic violence against women in India along with suggestions for policy imperatives regarding domestic violence in the Indian context.

Data and Methods

The National Family Health Survey (NFHS) in its third round during 2005–06 has collected information on different forms of spousal violence experienced by married women between the ages of 15–49 years (66,658) belonging to all states and union territories of India. Making use of this data from its all-India report in this paper, an attempt has been made to reach the target objectives. The paper employs both qualitative as well as quantitative analyses; however, certain specific methodology has been applied according to the need of the study, for example, cross-tabulation and correlation matrix subjected to chi square tests, binary logistic regression, simple frequency, etc., to understand the distribution, relationship and impact between the target variables.

Discussions

Domestic violence prevalence and trends vary widely within countries, across cultures and affect people from all stratas of the society. While some countries outlaw domestic violence and consider it as an intolerable behaviour, few others still partially accept domestic violence in the name of the disciplinary need that a husband has on his wife and children unless he leaves any physical mark on their body.[1] Social acceptability of domestic violence also varies widely among countries. While some consider the husband beating his wife as unacceptable, some African, Latin American and Middle East countries consider it acceptable under certain circumstances.[2] However, modern attention to domestic violence was given only around the late 1990s with the growing concern of feminism and women's human rights.

In spite of the widely disputed records, a study has found that the global prevalence of abuse by an intimate partner as reported by women varies form10 to 69 per cent.[3] Globally on an average, 30 per cent of women who have been in a relationship report that they have experienced some form of physical or sexual violence by their partner. Nationally, the north–south divide cannot be placed in equal terms in case of domestic violence

Table 6.1: Ranking of States with a Prevalence of Domestic Violence:

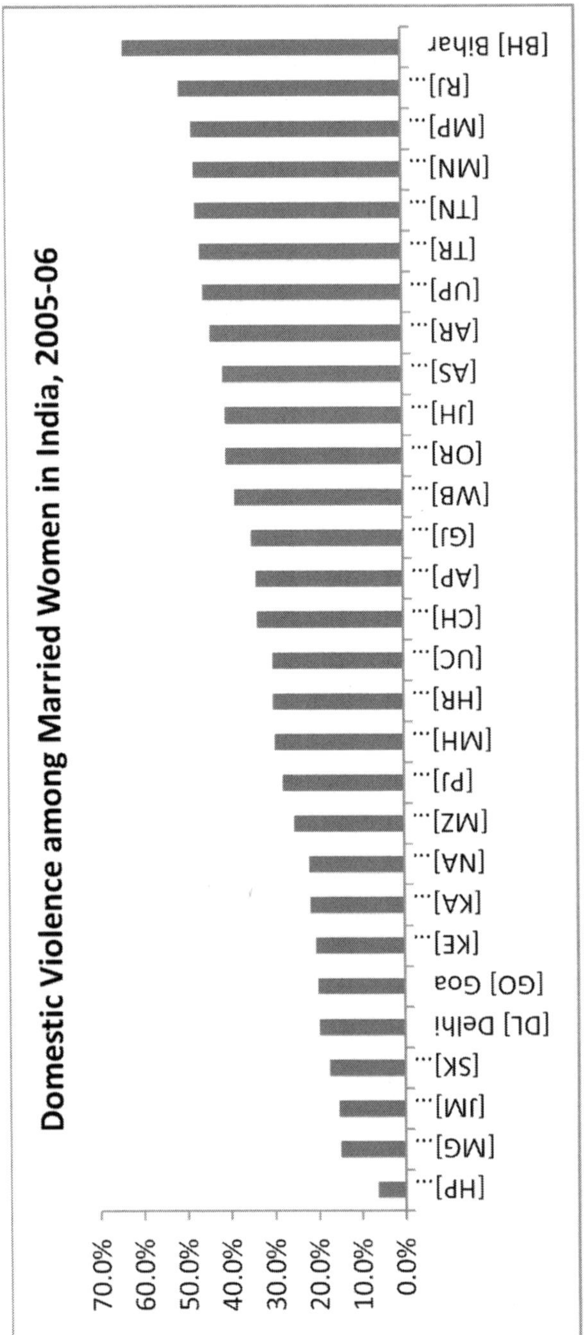

Source: Computed from NFHS 3, 2005-06.

Table 6.2: Prevalence of Domestic Violence among Women according to its Types:

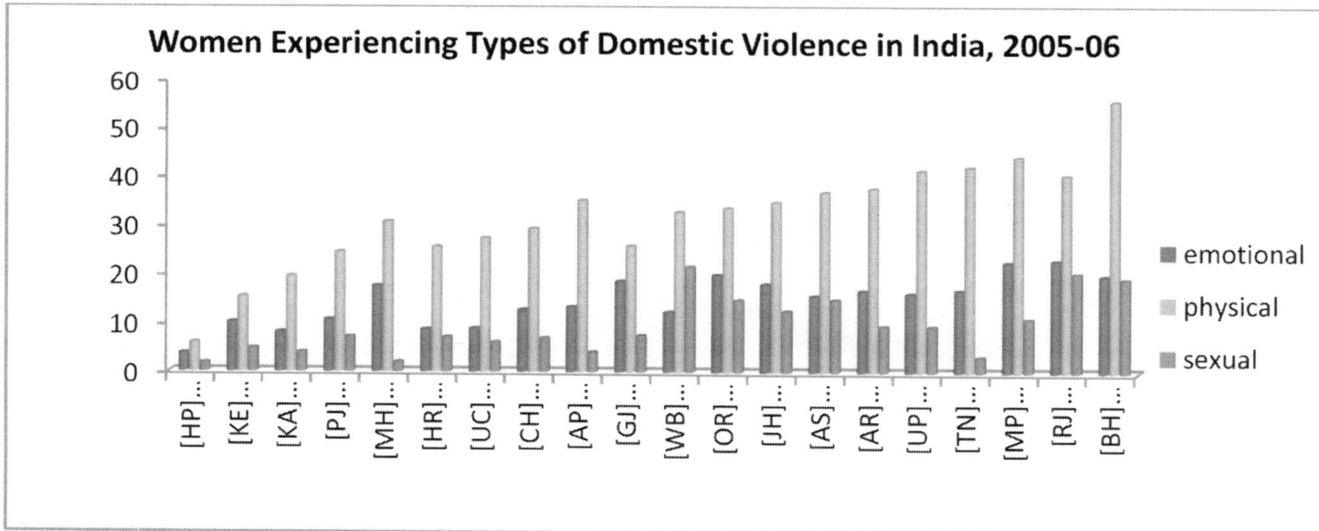

Source: Computed from NFHS 3, 2005-06

in India due to a host of socio-cultural differences that lead to a number of behavioural differences among the people.

Trends and Pattern

The states showing high prevalence of domestic violence among married women aged 15 to 49 years in India are the BIMARU states (Bihar, Madhya Pradesh, Rajasthan and Uttar Pradesh) along with West Bengal, Orissa, Jharkhand; north-eastern states like Assam, Arunachal Pradesh, Manipur, Tripura and contrastingly a South Indian state too, i.e., Tamil Nadu. This distribution gives a preliminary backdrop to the incidence of domestic violence in India, which seems to explain that it is more of a behavioural collision among individual characteristics rather than an outcome of developmental factors.

Physical violence (categorised in NFHS as "pushed her", "shook her", "threw something at her", "slapped her", "twisted her arm or pulled her hair", "punched her with his fist or with something that could hurt her", "kicked her", "dragged her", "beat her up", "tried to choke her or burn her won purpose", "threatened her or attacked her with a knife, gun, or any other weapon") is highly prevalent and comprise the maximum percentage in all three types of domestic violence in all states. Following this, the other type of domestic violence widely prevalent is emotional violence (categorised in NFHS as "said or did something to humiliate her in front of others", "threatened to hurt or harm her or someone close to her", "insulted her or made her feel bad about herself") and lastly sexual violence (categorised in NFHS as "physically forced her to have sexual intercourse with him even when she did not want to", "forced her to perform any sexual acts which she did not want to").

On studying the types of violence, 8 per cent of married women have been subjected to sexual violence—31 per cent of whom have been subjected to "less severe" physical abuse, while 10 per cent show "severe domestic violence". With regard to emotional abuse, 14 per cent of Indian women have experienced this at some point in their lives. However, the incidence of such violence varies considerably at a regional level and also across all kinds of cultural and background characteristics. Maximum injuries from physical violence have been reported by married women in Tripura (31 per cent), followed by Bihar (20 per cent), Assam (19 per cent) and Uttarakhand (15 per cent). Domestic violence is more reported in Tamil Nadu and Andhra Pradesh as well as in Arunachal Pradesh and Manipur. "Severe" domestic violence is reported maximum in the states of Bihar, Tamil Nadu, Uttar Pradesh, Madhya Pradesh, Rajasthan, Tripura,

Arunachal Pradesh, Jharkhand, Orissa, West Bengal and Andhra Pradesh. Also, the same states show the maximum instances of sexual violence except Andhra Pradesh and Tamil Nadu but including Manipur and Assam.

Socio-Economic Determinants of Domestic Violence

From the study of the prevalence of domestic violence with background characteristics, it is seen than it is mostly aimed at women who have less education, come from poor families, work in agricultural sector or are manual labours; marry at a lower age along with a low age at first birth. Women who earn more than their husbands or have husbands who do not earn at all or who work as manual labours or consume alcohol very often, are also the ones who show a high prevalence of the domestic violence experience.

However, this distribution even though subjected to the chi square tests, does not reveal the exact behavioural pattern as it does not control the effect of other variables while computing. Hence, we have used a binary logistic regression where the prevalence of domestic violence among women aged 15 to 49 years has been studied under either 'yes' or 'no' with imposing a controller on the effect of other variables (or background characteristics) while computing. Thus, the regression results show that domestic violence among women is more prone in urban areas than rural areas. The reason for such can be cited as the cosmopolitan culture in urban areas, increasing insecurity among the urban males, stressed lives, etc. Women with the least education and poor family backgrounds are more prone to domestic violence while the prevalence reduces with an increase in education and wealth. At most times, knowledge, wisdom and financial security hold the ground for females enabling them to cope with difficult situations and also prevent them from being a burden to others. Thus, like other studies, education seems to act like a black box which alone has the propensity to pull the women's ground towards betterment and also taking it away from their being subject to violence. Muslim women and women who marry at early ages are more susceptible to domestic violence as compared to the others.

A very contrasting result gets revealed on the empowerment side. Women, who enjoy more autonomy, in terms of earning more than their husbands (or who are the sole earning members of the family and whose husbands do not earn at all) and enjoying mobility and a decision-making autonomy, show a higher prevalence of domestic violence than women who are less autonomous. This clearly reveals the fact that it is the more conservative families which do not believe in women empowerment that are the ones involved in the practices of domestic violence. This calls for a need to change the outlook of the male members in the society to accept women as their equal counterparts and that it is important to stop treating women as submissive characters in the society.

Again, in terms of the husband's characteristics, it is seen that women whose husbands consume alcohol more often and are less educated are the ones who suffer from domestic violence more than any other women.

Impact of Domestic Violence on Women's Health

The impact of domestic violence on women's health reveals that women who experience any kind of domestic violence (emotional, less severe, severe and sexual violence) are the ones who exhibit a high prevalence of pregnancy complications and anaemia. A significant proportion of women who experience domestic violence are also subjected to post-partum complications. However, domestic violence also results in low BMI, i.e., chronic energy deficiency syndrome and acute undernutrition, among women.

The correlation matrix of domestic violence and other health indicators reveals that it has a strong relationship with women's health. Women who suffer from any kind of domestic violence (emotional, less severe, severe and sexual violence) are highly prone to pregnancy as well as post-partum complications, STD and RTI, high anaemia level and low BMI. Pregnancy and post-partum complications as a result of domestic violence lead to a high prevalence of anaemia and a low BMI among women.

Policy Imperatives

Laws in India on the violence against women were promulgated during the colonial period. The British did not want to interfere in the local religious rules and customs and therefore accepted a legal framework which gave sanction to the patriarchal society that existed in spite of the fact that they opposed some of the more heinous activities like Sati. Section 498A of Indian Penal Code (1860) made cruelty to women in marriage by her husband or other relatives a crime but this failed to specifically detail the domestic violence and its scope. However, the country continued to follow the same laws. The many reasons for this can be referred to the facts that the legislatures in most of the states as well as the national Parliament are dominated by men who are believed to be less sensitive to the cause of women; competitive politics plays another role in preventing the legislature to take a modern view of the old regressive and outdated laws. This explains why little work has been done in Independent India to change the personal laws in tune with the modern times and thinking. Most laws supporting women are made only after pressure by the public or support groups and there has been little initiative on the part of government to act on its own to better the lives of women in a patriarchal society.

Several enactments by the government were, however made, like the Dowry Prohibition Act that legally barred any property or valuable (direct or indirect) given before, at or after the marriage; Section 304B recognised the death of a woman within 7 years of her marriage as a crime on the in-laws' side; Section 498A where the husband or his family subjects the woman to cruelty ("intentional" behaviour that causes serious injury or harassment for dowry); Section 376 implemented the first rape law; Section 294 was the law against obscene acts and songs and Section 354 where any intention to outrage a woman's modesty was recognised as a serious crime.

However, the final rectification came in 2005 when the Parliament passed the Protection of Women from Domestic Violence Act (PWDVA) in 2005 which was brought into force by the Indian government from October 26, 2006. This has been the first law in the country to define domestic violence in a comprehensive way and has advocated the right of every woman to live with dignity. Of about 8,000 criminal cases registered all over India under this act, Rajasthan had 3440 cases; Kerala had 1,028, while Punjab had 172 cases registered.

While the law has been passed, its implementation remains a problem. Entrenched beliefs, customs and socio-economic situations discourage women to report domestic violence. As such, only a fraction of the actual crimes taking place in India are reported. Social taboo and acceptance of the actions of male members of the family is deep-rooted and few women want to damage their "married life" by reporting the crime. They prefer to remain in unhappy marriages rather than risk going to the police. Unsympathetic police officials make it even more difficult for women to report the crimes, as reporting of more crimes will mean that the police is not effectively doing its job. At the same time, a lack of women police officers denies the aggrieved females a sympathetic ear. The perception that nothing can or will be achieved by going to the police except shameful publicity of private issues is further strengthened due to a lack of prosecution in the courts. The Indian courts are overburdened and it is not uncommon for cases to go on for 10 or 20 years. Also, it is difficult to prove the domestic violence which is perpetrated within the confines of the family walls. In such a scenario, the victim feels it is wiser to suffer the crime than to report it.

Conclusions

The study thus succeeds in recognising the ill-effects of violence against women as a threat to modern-day civilisation and the propensity of any crime against women to pull down the development goals achieved so far. Clearly, health as a basic right for every human is grounded on women's health alone as she being the primary caretaker of the household health needs to be taken utmost care of. Her dependence on the male counterpart reveals the importance of men's role in stopping the crime against women. The women's mind-set of being the weaker sex, aggravated by apparent superiority of men displayed at workplaces as well as at home is some of the challenges that need to be addressed. An increased involvement by men in parenting and an awareness of human rights need to be done through gender sensitisation workshops, state, civil society organisations as well as the public at large, joint campaigns on violence against women along with an increase in women's participation at all levels (social, economic and political).

NOTES AND REFERENCES

1. UAE Court Ruling. 2010, Articles.cnn.com. Retrieved on 2014-01-24.
2. "Statistics by Area: Attitudes towards Wife-Beating – Statistical Table", Childinfo.org. Retrieved 2013-09-08.
3. Heise, Lori, Ellsberg, Mary, Gottemoeller, Megan (1999), "Ending Violence Against Women", Population Reports, Series L. No. 11.

Chaudhary, Sudha, "Domestic Violence In India", *Journal of Indian Research*, Vol. 1, No. 2, Pages 146-152, April-June 2013.

Ghosh Biswajit and Choudhuri Tanima, "Legal Protection against Domestic Violence in India: Scope and Limitations", *Springer Science, Business and Media*, Vol. 26, Pages 319-330, 29 March 2011.

Jaising Indira, "Mapping Violence against Women", 13th March 2012.

Kavitha V. R. S., "Spousal Domestic Violence of Married Women in India", *Journal of Sociology and Social Anthropology*, Volume 3, No. 1, Page 7-13, 2012.

National Family Health Survey, 2005-06, India, *Indian Institute of Population Sciences*, Vol. 1, September 2007.

National Family Health Survey, 1998-99, India, *Indian Institute of Population Sciences*, October 2000.

Neuman, Sandra, "The Issue of Sexual Violence against Women in Contemporary

India", Master Thesis, Linnaeus University, School of Social Sciences, *Department of Peace and Development Studies*, June 7, 2013.

Saravanan, Sheela, "Violence against Women in India: A Literature Review", *Institute of Social Studies Trust*, March 2000.

Tiwari, KN "Violence against Women in India: Suffering Continues Despite Progress All Over", *Disha Social Organization*.

Tjaden, Patricia and Thoennes, Nancy, "Extent, Nature, and Consequences of Intimate Partner Violence: Findings from the National Violence against Women Survey", National Institute of Justice, Centres for Disease Control and Prevention, *U.S. Department of Justice*; April 1998.

Uma, Saumaya and Grover, Vrinda, "Addressing Domestic Violence through the Law: *A Guide to The Protection of Women—Domestic Violence Act*",2005.

"Violence against Women: Chapter 6—"The World's Women". *UNITE; UN Department of Public Information*, 127-139, November 2009.

"Violence against Women: Definition and Scope of the Problem", *World Health Organisation*, July, 1997.

ANNEXURES

Table 6.3: Distribution of Women Suffering from Domestic Violence according to their Background Characteristics

Background Variables		*Domestic Violence*		*Chi Square*	*Background Variables*		*Domestic Violence*		*Chi Square*
		No	*Yes*				*No*	*Yes*	
Type of place of residence	Urban	20956 68.7%	9538 31.3%	0.000	Media exposure	no	39338 63.1%	23007 36.9%	0.000
	Rural	24009 61.7%	14906 38.3%			yes	5627 79.7%	1437 20.3%	
Highest educational level	No education	14924 54.2%	12595 45.8%	0.000	Mobility	no	25328 64.0%	14247 36.0%	0.000
	Primary	6377 59.4%	4355 40.6%			yes	19637 65.8%	10197 34.2%	
	Secondary	18368 73.1%	6757 26.9%		Decision-making	no	24968 62.4%	15035 37.6%	0.000
	Higher	5292 87.8%	736 12.2%			yes	19997 68.0%	9409 32.0%	
Wealth index	Poorest	4808 49.5%	4913 50.5%	0.000	Partner's occupation	professional	14846 74.8%	4991 25.2%	0.000
	Poorer	5955 53.6%	5154 46.4%			agricultural	10305 58.7%	7254 41.3%	
	Middle	8182 60.5%	5352 39.5%			manual	18931 62.0%	11625 38.0%	
	Richer	10604 66.1%	5430 33.9%		Respondent's occupation	professional	3646 72.9%	1355 27.1%	0.000
	Richest	15416 81.1%	3595 18.9%			agricultural	8338 55.5%	6689 44.5%	

(Contd.)

Table 6.3 Continued

Background Variables		*Domestic Violence*		*Chi Square*	*Background Variables*		*Domestic Violence*		*Chi Square*
		No	*Yes*				*No*	*Yes*	
Respondent works at home or away	At home	3738 58.7%	2625 41.3%	0.105		manual	4966 53.5%	4315 46.5%	
	Away	13329 57.6%	9806 42.4%		Husband's education	No education	8494 53.5%	7371 46.5%	0.000
Partner drinks alcohol	No	31605 72.7%	11874 27.3%	0.000		Primary	6014 55.9%	4751 44.1%	
	Yes	13322 51.5%	12564 48.5%			Secondary	22155 68.2%	10314 31.8%	
Times partner gets drunk	Never	2583 58.8%	1807 41.2%	0.000		Higher	7970 82.2%	1721 17.8%	
	Often	1660 31.3%	3637 68.7%		Earns more than the partner	more than him	1113 55.2%	902 44.8%	0.000
	Sometimes	9061 56.1%	7087 43.9%			less than him	7696 58.2%	5533 41.8%	
Religion	Hindu	33165 64.3%	18437 35.7%	0.000		same	1311 62.5%	788 37.5%	
	Muslim	5210 60.6%	3381 39.4%			partner doesn't bring money	201 47.3%	224 52.7%	
	Christian	4204 73.7%	1504 26.3%		Age at first birth	20 and less	23254 59.1%	16116 40.9%	0.000
	Others	2386 68.0%	1122 32.0%			21 to 25 years	12788 70.1%	5457 29.9%	
Age at marriage	Less than 18 years	25182 58.8%	17632 41.2%	0.000		above 26 years	4330 76.9%	1298 23.1%	
	19 to 29 years	19139 74.3%	6620 25.7%						
	above 30 years	644 77.0%	192 23.0%						

Source: Computed from NFHS 3, 2005-06.

Table 6.4: Binary Logistic Regression to Show the Relationship between Background Variables and Prevalence of Domestic Violence

Background Variables		*Exp (B)*	*Background Variables*		*Exp (B)*
Type of place of residence	Urban		Media exposure	no	
	Rural	0.7129***		yes	1.226**
Highest educational level	No education		Mobility	no	
	Primary	1.133*		yes	1.146***
	Secondary	.992	Decision-making	no	
	Higher	0.644***		yes	.977
Wealth index	Poorest		Husband's occupation	professional	
	Poorer	.973		agricultural	1.004
	Middle	0.757***		manual	1.077
	Richer	0.683***	Respondent's occupation	professional	
	Richest	0.425***		agricultural	1.155
Respondent work place	At home			manual	1.038
	Away	.957	Husband's education	No education	
Partner drinks alcohol	No			Primary	1.262***
	Yes	2.172*		Secondary	1.030
Times partner gets drunk	Never			Higher	0.784*
	Often	2.683***	Earns more than partner	more than him	
	Sometimes	1.104		less than him	0.833**
Religion	Hindu			same	0.782**
	Muslim	1.553***		partner doesn't bring money	1.373***
	Christian	0.623***	Age at first birth	20 and less	
	Others	1.022		21 to 25 years	.979
Age at marriage	Less than 18 years			above 26 years	.846
	19 to 29 years	0.853**			
	above 30 years	.951			

Source: Computed from NFHS 3, 2005-06.

Table 6.5: Frequency Distribution showing Health Outcomes among Women Suffering from Domestic Violence

Health Indicators		*Pregnancy Complications*		*Post-Partum Complications*		*Prevalence of STD, RTI*		*Anaemic*		*Body Mass Index*		
Prevalence		*no*	*yes*	*no*	*yes*	*no*	*yes*	*no*	*yes*	*< 18.5*	*18.5–25*	*> 25*
Domestic Violence	No	46.9%	53.1%	83.8%	16.2%	93.1%	6.9%	47.3%	52.7%	25.2%	54.2%	20.6%
		87270	98985	156333	30172	418354	30989	193581	215486	113758	244961	93096
	Yes	37.2%	62.8%	74.7%	25.3%	84.3%	15.7%	42.7%	57.3%	34.1%	52.8%	13.1%
		41548	70286	83620	28360	214171	39768	102837	137889	87092	134954	33609

Source: Computed from NFHS 3, 2005-06.

Table 6.6: Correlation Matrix Showing the Inter-Relationship Between Domestic Violence and Other Health Outcomes

	Domestic Violence	*Pregnancy Complications*	*Post-partum Complications*	*Prevalence of STD and RTI*	*Anaemia*	*BMI*
DomesticViolence	1	.095**	.112**	.140**	.045**	-.117**
Pregnancy Complications	.095**	1	.210**	.115	.026**	-.006**
Post-partum Complications	.112**	.210	1	.114	.032**	-.054**
Prevalence of STD and RTI	.140**	.115**	.114**	1	.019	-.038
Anaemia	.045**	.026	.032	.019	1	-.102**
BMI	-.117**	-.006	-.054	-.038	-.102	1

Source: Computed from NFHS 3, 2005-06.

7

Rural Women and Food Security in India: Contribution and Constraints

Haseena Hashia

ABSTRACT

The concept of food security has undergone enormous changes during the past few decades. The availability and stability of food stocks in adequate measures do not necessarily ensure food security. As such, conditions of hunger, starvation and undernutrition of a sizeable section of population co-exist despite a surplus of food stocks. It is a well-documented phenomenon that most poor families spend 80% of their total income on foodgrains. Despite a good economic performance, over 200 million people are food insecure, with India being home to the largest number of hungry people in the world. The Global Hunger Index (GHI) 2009 ranks India at the bottom at the 65th position (out of 84 countries) with a GHI of 29.90. In the Global Gender Gap Index, India occupies the 113th position out of 130 countries. The sex Ratio, including the juvenile sex ratio, has shown an alarming reduction over the years. It reflects a deep-rooted gender bias in the society.

India is predominantly an agricultural country where about 70 per cent of the total population lives in the rural areas. Patriarchy and other factors force women to keep the hearth, especially among the poor. Almost all agricultural operations are performed by women. According to the Food Security Atlas of India, there are a sufficient number of food insecure districts in India. While doing some pilot survey in one such district, a shocking situation was experienced that food insecurity had led to trafficking among women and young girls which makes them vulnerable to HIV/AIDS and other sexually transmitted diseases. There is a positive linkage between agriculture and rural empowerment. The present paper attempts to explore and highlight the food insecure regions of India, vulnerability and struggle of the Indian rural women for food, nutrition security and the constraints which they come across and also identify the future strategies for improvement. The paper is based on primary data from various parts of rural India.

Key Words: Food security, Global Hunger Index, patriarchy, coexistence, vulnerability, nutritional security, availability and stability of food products.

Introduction

The concept of food security has undergone an enormous change over the past few decades. Availability and stability of food stocks in adequate measures do not necessarily ensure food security. As such, a condition of hunger, starvation and undernutrition of a sizeable section of population coexists despite the availability of food stocks. It is a well-documented fact that poor families spend 80% of their total income on foodgrains. Further, people often fail to eat enough food only because they do not have sufficient purchasing power. The Nobel Laureate, Amartya Sen, stated that the causes of hunger in India are currently due to a wide prevalence of poverty and the inability of a large section of the population to buy food or to establish entitlement over an adequate amount of food. Despite a good economic performance and with over 200 million people who are food insecure, India happens to be home to the largest number of hungry people in the world. The International Food Policy Research Institute has alerted the acute situation of Indian hunger. The Global Hunger Index (GHI) 2009 ranks India at the bottom with a rank of 65 (out of 84 countries) with a GHI of 29.90.

The survey is based on child malnutrition, child death rate and under-calorie intake. India's position is lower than Bangladesh and Sub-Saharan nations. Dr M.S. Swaminathan, Chairman of the National Commission on Farmers, explains that sustainable food security depends on the availability of foodgrains in the market, accessibility of the general public in procuring these from the market and absorption of food in the body that is determined by access to safe drinking water, environmental hygiene and primary health care.

Food is the most basic need of a person. The inability of a person to eat enough, stay active and lead a healthy life comes under the purview of food insecurity. Availability of sufficient food, either through production or through import, is only a part of the story. The full story of food insecurity is related to poverty, illiteracy, discrimination and neglect. It is also related to unhygienic living, lack of basic amenities and healthcare. Ultimately it is a story of failed governance at all levels—local, national and global. Micronutrient deficiencies are widespread in India and the most critically affected are the women and children (NFHS-2, 1998-99).

Despite years of development efforts and various programmes targeted at eliminating hunger and deprivation, millions of people are still consuming diets deficient in calories. As per the National Sample Survey data (NSS, 1993-94; fiftieth round survey), the percentage of population consuming less than 1890 Kcal per day per consumer unit, stood at 13.4 per cent of the rural population and 16.4 per cent of the urban population. The percentage of population consuming less than 2160 Kcal constituted 26.4 per cent of the rural population and 31.9 per cent of the urban population. Those consuming less than 2400 Kcal constitute 42 per cent of the rural population and 48.8 per cent of the urban population.

The present paper attempts to document and highlight the struggle of the Indian rural women for food security and nutrition. The paper analyses the major hurdles faced by the women and suggests the appropriate measures and options to overcome them.

Area of Study

Although India occupies only 2.4% of the world's land area, it supports over 15% of the world's population. India is predominantly an agricultural country where about 70% of the total population lives in rural areas. This 70% population lives in more than 550,000 villages, and the remainder in more than 200 towns and cities. India's ranking in the Global Gender Gap Index is 113/130, taking into consideration the ranks for political empowerment (25), Educational Attainment (116), Health and Survival (128).

India's ranking in terms of the Human Development Index 2009 (which incorporates life-expectancy, adult literacy, school enrolment and per capita Income) is 134 out of 182 countries. The sex ratio, including juvenile sex ratio, has shown an alarming reduction over the years. It reflects a deep-rooted gender bias in the society.

India is home to several hundred million undernourished people which form more than 25 per cent of the national population who are constantly trying to move out in search of livelihood options. The Planning Commission as the Government's nodal agency estimates the incidence of poverty at the national and state levels on the basis of the

National Sample Survey (NSS) on household consumer expenditure conducted every year. Those people whose per capita consumption at 2004 prices is below Rs 368 per month in rural areas and below Rs 559 per month in the urban areas, are considered as people below the poverty line. More than 25 per cent of the total population of India lives below the poverty line. The main causes of poverty are fast population growth, illiteracy and inappropriate polices of the Government since 1947. The spatial poverty pattern in India according to the 2007–08 estimates is given in Figure 1.

Figure 1 clearly depicts that acute poverty prevails in Orissa (46.4%), Bihar (41.4%) and Jharkhand (40.3%). The lowest level of poverty exists in Goa (8%), Punjab (8.4%), Jammu & Kashmir (9%), Himachal Pradesh (10%), Kerala (15%) and Gujarat (16.8%). The incidence of poverty is higher than the national average of 27.5% in the states of Orissa, Bihar, Jharkhand, Chhattisgarh, Madhya Pradesh, Maharashtra, Uttarakhand and Uttar Pradesh.

Food Insecurity in India

The report on the state of food insecurity in rural India has been jointly prepared by the United Nations World Food Programme and the M.S. Swaminathan Research Foundation (MSSRF). Some of the states for which data was available by the MSSRF has been depicted in Figure 2.Further, the "State of Food Insecurity in the World" (2008) released by the FAO, estimates that India is home to more than 230 million undernourished people, which is about 25 per cent of the national population. The Dietary Energy Supply (DES) for India has been estimated to be 2,360 kcal per capita per day. The "India State Hunger Index", released by the International Food Policy Research Institute (IFPRI), measures calorie undernourishment by taking a cut-off of 1,632 kcal per capita per day. The "Report on the State of Food Insecurity in Rural India" prepared jointly by the WFP and MSSRF uses a cut-off point of 1,890 kcal per consumer unit per day, based on the NSS-recommended threshold of 70 per cent of the international norm of 2700 kcal per consumer unit per day.

On the composite index of food insecurity of rural India, states like Jharkhand and Chhattisgarh are found in the 'very high' level of food insecurity, followed by Madhya Pradesh, Bihar and Gujarat. The better performers include Himachal Pradesh, Kerala, Punjab and Jammu and Kashmir, all of which report an Index value below 0.5. Andhra Pradesh, Madhya Pradesh, Bihar, Gujarat, Karnataka, Orissa and Maharashtra perform poorly. Even economically developed states like Gujarat,

Figure 1: Population Percentages below the Poverty Line in Rural India

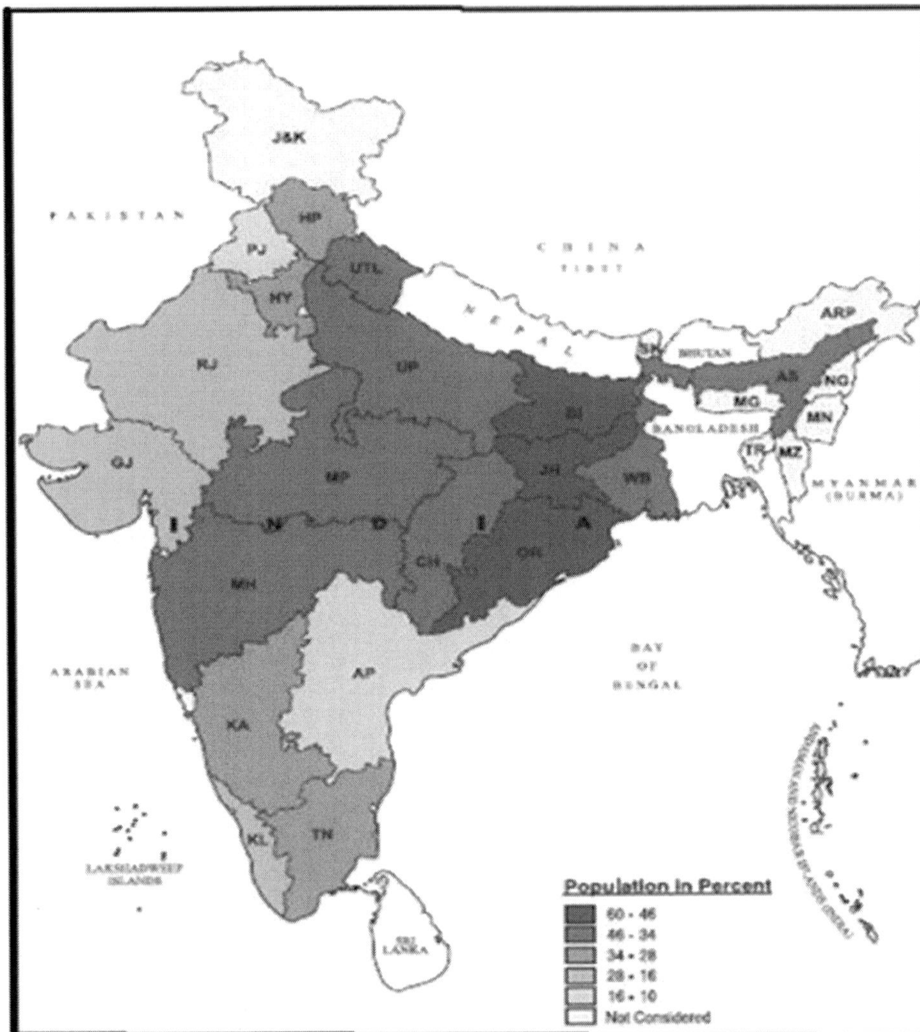

Figure 2: Levels of Food Insecurity in India (2008)

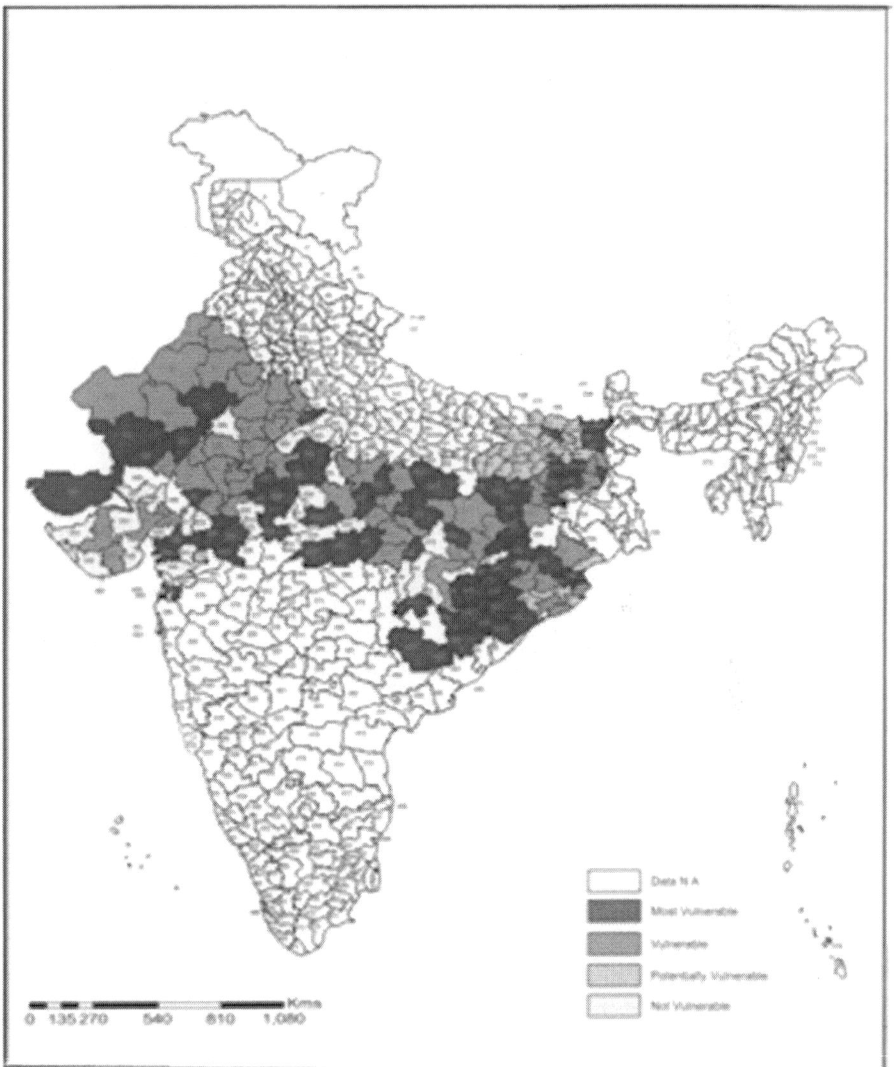

Source: Dutta Mondira, *UN Women*, 2011.

Figure 3: State of Food Insecurity in Rural India

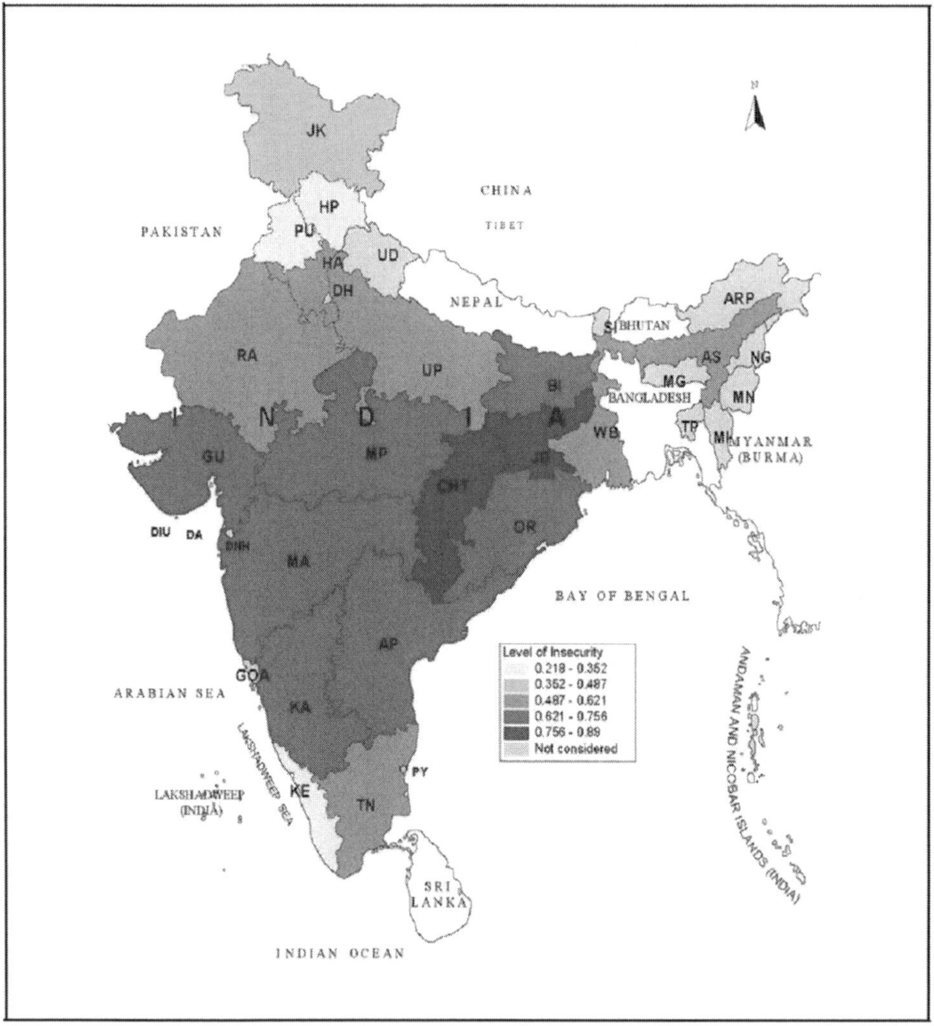

Note: A higher Index Value represents a higher level of Food Insecurity

Maharashtra, Andhra Pradesh and Karnataka find themselves in the category of high food insecurity—a reflection perhaps of the manifestation of the agrarian crisis in the states and its consequent negative impact on the health and well-being of the rural population.

Role of Women and Food Insecurity

Women are the poorest of the poor in the developing and underdeveloped countries. In a patriarchal society like India, women are regarded as a dependent class, and described as the "Second Sex" and the "Second Creature", who live on surplus with their very existence being parasitic on men, who rule them. Sexual difference represents a social distinction of the highest rank. Women are "burdened" with cumulative inequalities as a result of socio-cultural and economic discriminatory practices which until recently have been taken for granted as though they are part of the immutable scheme of things established by nature.

The structural subordination of women to men becomes more manifested when the phenomenon is considered in the context of rural women. The rural women are an ineviable lot. They are the unsung heroines, born to die in the backyard of human civilisation, carrying on the burden of humanity for a mere pittance. They work in the scorching heat, pouring rain and snow. They earn on their own or supplement the family income to keep off starvation. They cook and look after the children in addition to almost everything that men do, go around to fetch water and collect fuelwood to keep the fire of the hearth glowing. They sow the seeds, transplant and harvest the crops. They pluck fruits and help in their packing. There are numerous other indoor and outdoor activities also, which are exclusively or largely performed by the women in India.

The 2001 Census indicates that in the rural sector, women constitute about 35 per cent of the workforce. They work on their own fields and also work as landless labourers. A field survey was conducted in the four northern states of India (Jammu & Kashmir, Himachal Pradesh, Haryana and Uttar Pradesh) to know the participation of women in various agricultural operations of farm households as well as landless households. Three villages were selected from each state and 4 per cent households were taken as sample in each village. The women's participation in various agricultural operations is given in Table 1.

Table 1: Women's Participation in Various Agricultural Operations (Selected Villages)

S. No	*Crop-Raising Operations*	*Level of Female Participation*	
		Main Role	*Helping Role*
1	Transportation of farm inputs of fields	35.7	64.3
2	Preparation of fields		
	(a) Ploughing	28.3	71.7
	(b) Breaking of clumps, levelling, etc.	68	32
3	Sowing/Transplantation	63.80	36.2
4	Application of manures/fertilisers to crops	27	73
5	Weeding/inter-culture	40.5	59.5
6	Harvesting of crops	68.7	31.3
7	Transporting of crops	62.6	37.4
8	Storage of farm produce	70.2	29.8
9	Processing of farm produce	73.2	26.8

Source: Field work by the author (2010).

Figure 4: Women's Participation in Agricultural Activities

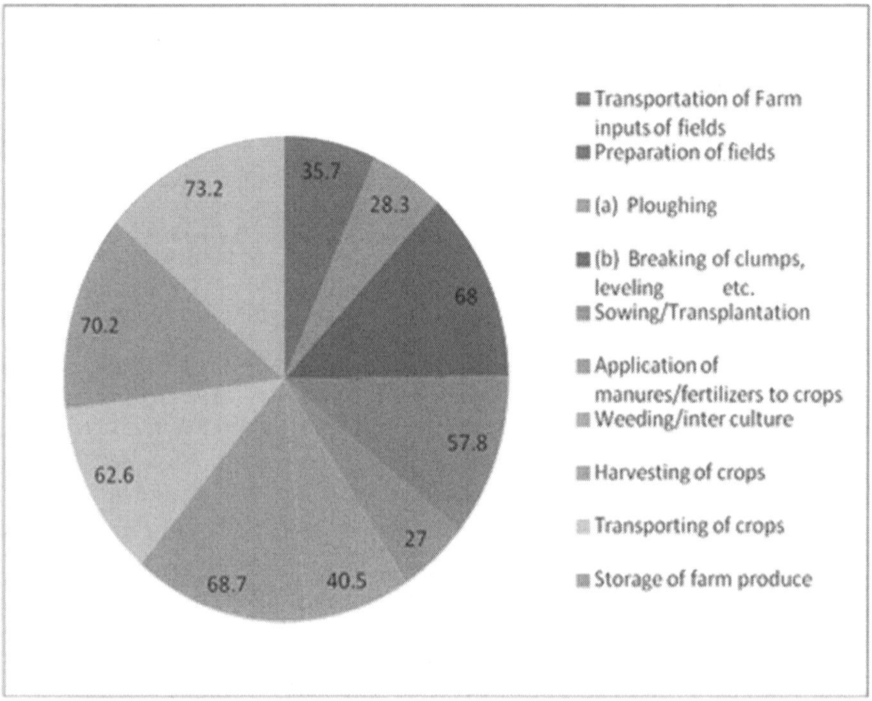

Source: Field work undertaken by the author (2010).

An examination of Table 1 shows that women are playing a very vital role in almost all agricultural operations. From collection and transportation of manures to the storage of farm produce and marketing, women are responsible for every phase of the food cycle. In the farm households, this is regarded as a routine, unpaid housework rather than productive work. The care and management of livestock is another important activity that is associated with farm households. Poultry and maintaining of kitchen gardens for growing vegetables is also performed by women.

Most micro studies show that women do at least 75 per cent of the work in livestock production. In dairy keeping, women perform intensive labour and supervisory work. Men, whose work is marginal compared to that of women, are the key controlling authorities in the crucial sphere of marketing and collection of income as well as sale and purchase of livestock. Women are equally engaged in the fishing activities in the coastal states of India, but commercial fishing is mainly done by menfolk. While conducting a field survey in Kerala (2009), it was found that fishing is a very common activity of women in the coastal areas. Women catch fish for local consumption. They sell it in the local market either to support their families fully or to enhance the family income. Thus, women are more concerned towards the food security of their families and for the society. Their active participation in various agricultural operations, livestock rearing, processing of fruits, vegetables and animal products are sufficient testimony of their role in the food security system. Scientific achievements and modernisation have yet to make an impact on them. Their implements are traditional and their work back-breaking and full of drudgery. Yet, they are remarkable human machines for work with a high level of endurance, patience and efficiency. However, they are not visible as participants, rather as beneficiaries of developmental programmes.

It is thus evident that women are food providers but starve themselves and remain hungry and malnourished for the sake of their family. A study by S. Mishra et al (2008) shows that farmwomen are involved in the supply of green leaves which provide vitamin A to the family. They also provide vegetables and fruits which are rich sources of carotene, vitamin C, folic acid, calcium and iron. Their role is for providing milk, the source of calcium and riboflavin and animal protein, source of B-complex vitamins, vitamin A, calcium and iodine. They also play a great role in the preparation of food which primarily supplies energy to the body. For the poor, mushrooms and meat which are high in protein value, are supplied to the family through collection. Thus, the rural women play a predominant role in food security.

Constraints

- Work done by women within a given occupation (whether in agriculture, cottage industries or in any casual work as wage labourers) is considered inferior and subordinate. Accordingly, women's overall earnings from the job done are less than that of the men. Gender-based wage discrimination continues even for identical tasks performed by men and women. A lower average rate of remuneration combined with a shorter period of employment over the year is likely to push a typical woman agricultural labourer way below the poverty line.
- The labour market favours men over women and the division of labour within the occupation is sex-biased.
- Poor women are usually illiterate; so, with illiteracy and ignorance, a higher level of exploitation takes place at every step.
- The inheritance rights are gender discriminatory in the majority of the South Asian countries and also in India. This amounts greatly to the lower status of women in the household.
- The household farm work, household duties, childcare, care of elderly people and other family members, etc. are invisible, unpaid, and unproductive. Also, with wage employment, women are supposed to complete all the household and social duties. This overwork affects the health of women adversely. The overwork, lack of proper food and hygienic conditions affect the women's health. Anaemia and iron and calcium deficiencies are common. These conditions in turn affect the coming generations because pregnant women give birth to stunted and abnormal children, who do not survive more and child mortality increases.
- Women are responsible for the food security of their families. A mother can sleep hungry but cannot bear that her children go to bed hungry. To keep the hearth burning and to save the family from starvation, poor women are forced into the flesh trade. A survey conducted in the hunger-prone districts of India (2010) reveals the tragic truth that in these districts human trafficking is common. This fact was also conformed during the pilot survey in the district of Madhya Pradesh where about 15 households were surveyed.

Measures and Options

1. Efforts should be made to realise the right to food including the steps to promote conditions for everyone to be free from hunger and the possibility of enjoying fully the right to food. The State is an important actor in maintaining food and nutritional security as many of the requirements for sustaining a food and nutritionally secure population are directly under state control, such as provision of safe drinking water, healthcare, sanitation, sewage facilities, etc. With the provision of public investment, the State should develop infrastructure and ensure the physical and economic access to food for the vulnerable population.
2. Effective Public Distribution System (PDS): The PDS was introduced in 1997 by identifying the 'poor' and 'non-poor' households on the basis of income–poverty criterion. The households were identified as BPL and APL but there is a problem in this type of distinction as no estimate exists regarding the actual income of the households. The competence of the officials deciding the inclusion of households in one category or the other is doubtful. This system should be improved so that the vulnerable section may benefit.
3. Setting up of food buffers at the Gram Panchayat and Gram Sabha levels so that the supply to the needy could be ensured at the right time. Such food buffers should be used for the beneficiaries as part of their wages in different rural employment programmes. The maintenance of food banks and food buffers should be kept with the Panchayats under the supervision of a central agency.
4. Though the government has implemented various poverty alleviation programmes, there is not much success stories among women. The major failure for poverty alleviation programmes is due to the wrong identification of beneficiaries and the selection of activities. Therefore, poverty alleviation programmes should focus on savings, credit and assets for poor women, meeting their social needs and indulging them in income-generating activities.
5. The nutritional security schemes of the government should focus more on pregnant women, adolescent girls and infants.
6. The immediate focus should be on agriculture, nutrition, health and livelihood through endowment of land and non-land assets and generating opportunities for women.
7. The concept of self-help groups should be strengthened and

universalised because it will not only create work for the needy but will also increase the income level of the participants, thus increasing their purchasing power. Thus, all steps should be taken for enhancing the purchasing power of the poor households by introducing employment-guarantee programmes. Food security for all requires a combination of policies, a well-functioning PDS system, employment-guarantee programmes and special food programmes for groups within the population with special needs.

8. The fact that the key to the family and individual food and nutritional security lies in the women's hands, is yet to be acknowledged. Empowering women through ownership rights, proper opportunities of employment, equal wages and education are essential for universal food security.

NOTES AND REFERENCES

1. Dreze, Jean, and Sen, Amartya (1995), "Introduction to The Political Economy of Hunger" in *Political Economy of Hunger* Dreze, Jean, Sen, Amartya and Hussain, Athar (eds.), Clarendon Press, Oxford.
2. Dutta, Mondira (2011), "Mapping Vulnerability of Women & Girls to Trafficking in India", *UN Women*.
3. FAO (2008), "Assessment of the World Food Security and Nutrition Situation", Committee on World Food Security, 34th Session, Rome 14th-17th, Oct.
4. National Family Health Survey (NFHS-2) (1998-99), International Institute for Population Sciences (IIPS) and ORC Macro, India, Mumbai.
5. National Sample Survey Organisation (NSSO), 50th Round, Vol. I, "Quantity of Consumption of all Food Items", (1993/1994), (Rural).
6. "Report on the State of Food Insecurity in Rural India" (2008), M.S. Swaminathan Foundation and World Food Programme, United Nations, December 2008.
7. Swaminathan, M. (2004), "Ending Endemic Hunger", *Social Scientist*, 32, (7-8 August).

8

Legal Framework to Combat Human Trafficking in the European Union: Relevance for South Asia

Sideek Mohamed Seyad

ABSTRACT

The underlying objective of the European Union (EU) is to establish a single market where goods, services, persons and capital could move freely across the borders. These economic freedoms have also been subject to abuse by criminals who operate across the borders.

One of the major challenges confronting the EU is the problem of human trafficking which has assumed critical proportions in recent times. There are several factors which could be identified for the explosion of this serious crime and until recently the EU had to persuade its Member States to deal with this problem unilaterally. After the Lisbon Treaty came into force, the EU has acquired the competence to make laws in the field of criminal justice.

This paper will examine two specific legal instruments adopted to confront the crime of human trafficking. In this context, it is proposed to examine the extent to which the EU's approaches in dealing with human trafficking could be applicable in the context of South Asia.

Keywords: European Union, SAARC, SAPTA, South Asia, single market, Lisbon Treaty, human trafficking, smuggling, legal instruments, criminal justice.

Introduction

The European Union (EU) has its roots on the European Coal and Steel Community set up by the Treaty of Paris 1952 with six founder member states. It was initially launched as a peace project and to achieve this objective its members decided to jointly exploit the natural resources such as coal and steel strictly for peaceful purposes.

As this experiment of coexistence proved to be a successful project, the same six member states decided to extend this cooperation to a wider field of economic cooperation. The next major step forward in this regional cooperation was the establishment of the European Economic Community by ratifying the Treaty of Rome, 1958. The primary objective of this Community is to establish a common market in goods, persons, services and capital. In terms of this legally binding agreement, all member states agreed to remove the legal and other barriers to the free movement of goods, persons, services and capital within the common market.

Since the economic cooperation within the framework of the common market was a success story, the member states decided to extend their coexistence beyond the traditional field of economic cooperation. The ratification of the Maastricht Treaty on European Union 1993 was a major departure in the political, economic and monetary environment of the EU. It provided for the development of common policies not only in relation to economic activities but also laid the foundation for the development of a common policy in police and judicial cooperation and a common foreign and security policy.

The benefits of the widening and deepening of the integration of the EU no doubt outweigh the costs of regional integration. There are, however, various forms of costs of such an economic integration achieved by the liberalisation of the free movement of goods, services, persons and capital. Some of the economic freedoms have been subject to abuse by criminals who operate across the borders.

The paper will examine one of the negative outcomes of regional integration. The problem of human trafficking is one of the two major evils which are demeaning the sanctity of the single market. The paper will critically examine the adequacy of the **EU legal instruments adopted to confront this serious crime in terms of their scope and effectiveness**. It will also examine the extent of the EU approach in dealing with human trafficking that could be applicable in the context of South Asia.

An Overview of the EU's Single Market

The legal foundation of the single market of the EU is based on four economic freedoms. The first freedom, known in the EU's legal jargon as the free movement of goods, prohibits member states of the EU to impose any customs duty or quantitative restrictions on the movement of goods within the single market. The EU law also provides legal protection to its citizens to move freely across the borders and to search and take up employment subject to the same rights and obligations as they apply to the nationals based in the host country. The individuals and companies located within the EU have the freedom to set up their own business or provide their services as guaranteed by the EU rules on the right of establishment and freedom to provide cross-border services. The fourth and the last economic freedom on which the single market is based is the free movement of capital which enables citizens and companies to freely move their legally earned money across the borders for any legal purposes such as to move residence, start up a business or simply to deposit their money or invest in the stock exchange in another member state.

Since the launch of the internal market in 1993, the cross-border movement of goods, persons, services and capital intensified as the legal and technical barriers to free movement were dismantled. At the same time, there had been also correspondingly an increase in the criminalisation of these economic freedoms. The problem of smuggling of goods such as alcohol and cigarettes from third countries into the EU is one such abuse of the liberal rules on the free movement of goods. The criminals launder their dirty money which has been facilitated not only by the removal of the obstacles to the free movement of capital but also by the integration of the EU's financial market as a consequence of the liberalisation of the free movement of services. The liberal regime on the free movement of people has been also abused by criminals to commit serious crimes such as human trafficking.

The EU Legal Instruments to Combat Cross-Border Crimes

For more than three decades since the launching of the EU, it did not have a specific competence to deal with the problem associated with the criminalisation of the economic freedoms. It was only after the Maastricht Treaty that came into force in 1993 that there was some degree of recognition of the EU's competence in the field of criminal law. This major Treaty amendment created a three-pillar structure which included Justice and Home Affairs (JHA) as one of the pillars. The lawmaking in the sphere of criminal justice was however subject to intergovernmental cooperation. Some progress was made by the Amsterdam Treaty, which sub divided the JHA into two spheres. All matters relating to asylum, immigration and related issues were moved to the so-called Community pillar and matters relating to criminal justice remained in the JHA pillar. The difference between the Community and the JHA pillars was that lawmaking was much easier under the Community pillar.

Despite the lack of specific competence in the field of criminal law, the EU did adopt certain legal instruments to combat crimes associated with the four economic freedoms. There are also various bodies and agencies that have been established to combat these crimes.

The European Police College began operations on January 1, 2001.[1] It is a network of national police training institutes and its main aim is to train the police and other law enforcement personnel to work and operate in a European context. It aims to develop a joint approach to the main problems encountered in the fight against crime and crime prevention through training courses and seminars aimed at qualified police officers.

The Eurojust is an agency of the European Union dealing with judicial cooperation in criminal matters.[2] It is a network of national prosecutors, magistrates and police officers drawn from each member state. It was established in 2002 to improve the combat of serious cross-border and organised crime. The means to achieve this objective is by coordinating the work of the investigative and prosecutorial agencies of the member states. It is composed of judges, prosecutors or police officers drawn from all member states.

The Europol is the law enforcement agency of the EU.[3] It acts as a middleman between the member states and assists them with the supply of criminal intelligence. It also actively helps them to combat serious organised crime.

The other tasks of the Europol include the collection, storage and exchange of information with other member states and third countries and to coordinate and implement investigative and operational action carried out jointly with the member states.

The aim of introducing the European Arrest Warrant (EAW) is to simplify the judicial procedures in relation to the surrender of people for the purpose of conducting a criminal prosecution or for executing a custodial sentence or detention.[4] The basic objective of this legal instrument is to provide a mechanism for faster and simpler surrender procedures between the member states. It imposes a legal obligation on the member states to surrender even their own nationals to another member state who have committed a serious crime or are suspected of having committed such a crime within the Union.

Criminal Justice in the EU

The Union did not have specific competence in the field of criminal law until the Lisbon Treaty came into force in 2009. There had been some form of direct and indirect forms of competence in the field of criminal law but they were not only incomprehensive and inconsistent but also very much limited in scope.

Before the Maastricht Treaty came into force, all matters relating to crime were subject to intergovernmental cooperation between the member states of the EU. Such cooperation extended to criminal law issues relating to the free movement of persons, customs and judicial cooperation. The Maastricht Treaty made tremendous changes to the objectives of the EU and laid the foundation for a new legal framework to achieve some of those new objectives such as the creation of the economic and monetary union which paved the way for the introduction of the euro as the single currency of the majority of the member states of the EU.

The Maastricht Treaty introduced a three-pillar structure with each structure determining the level of competence of the EU. The first pillar was known as the Community pillar which covers wide areas such as the internal market and the EU had almost exclusive competence within this pillar. The second pillar dealt with a common foreign and security policy and the decisions in this sector were subject to intergovernmental cooperation. The third pillar dealt with justice and home affairs which were initially subject to intergovernmental cooperation leaving intact the veto rights of the member states when it came to lawmaking in the field of criminal law.

The Lisbon Treaty brought about radical changes to the lawmaking system in the field of criminal law. The Treaty establishes a new title known as an Area of Freedom, Security and Justice recognising the specific competence of the EU in the field of criminal law. The EU now has competence in lawmaking in the fields of criminal and civil law and provides for closer police cooperation between the member states. The aim of this programme is to protect and strengthen the internal security of the EU. It provides the Union's citizens a high level of protection which is to be achieved by preventing and combating crimes, terrorism, etc. The means to achieve this goal is by way of close cooperation between the police, customs and judicial officers of the member states.

Under the new legal environment created by the Lisbon Treaty, the EU has the power to adopt directives on the definition of criminal offences and sanctions. Judicial cooperation in criminal matters will be based on the cooperation between relevant authorities in the member states. Such judicial cooperation shall be based on the principle of mutual recognition of judgements and judicial decisions. It is now possible to establish rules by ordinary legislative procedure to facilitate a mutual admissibility of evidence between the member states, define the rights of individuals in a criminal procedure and the rights of victims of crimes. When laws are made by means of an ordinary legislative procedure, it deprives the veto rights of the member states in the field of criminal justice.

The Lisbon Treaty also gives competence to the EU to define offences and sanctions. Such competence specifically covers offences such as drug and women trafficking, money laundering, corruption, computer crime and organised crime.

A major innovation in the Lisbon Treaty 2009 is that it provides a clear and precise competence to the EU in the field of criminal law.[5] Simplified lawmaking in this field has been introduced for the first time in the history of the EU. The legal measures may be adopted by means of ordinary legislative procedure and the Treaty prescribes the use of regulations, directives and decisions for this purpose. It no longer requires a unanimity voting in the Council, which had been one of the major obstacles for the adoption of any legal measures in the field of criminal law.

Another distinct feature in the Lisbon Treaty relevant to the combating of trafficking is that it provides for the establishment of a European Public Prosecutor. This body has to be created by unanimity voting in the Council. The Commission proposed a regulation on the establishment of a European Prosecutor's office based on Article 86 TFEU.[6] This law enforcement agency shall have the competence to investigate and prosecute all offences against the EU's financial interests. It shall cooperate with the Europol, which has as one of its tasks the assistance of member states in their war on trafficking.

The Lisbon Treaty provides for a judicial cooperation in criminal matters based on the principle of the mutual recognition of judgements. The European Parliament and Council shall set out more specifically the areas of competence. The Treaty also facilitates the adoption of legislation for the purposes of mutual admissibility of evidence between the member states. The protection of the rights of individuals in the criminal procedure and the rights of the victims of crimes has been given primary importance in the Treaty.

The Treaty authorises the European Parliament and Council to establish minimum rules for the definition of offences and sanctions. It also sets out a list of crimes such as terrorism, trafficking in human beings and sexual exploitation of women and children, illicit drug trafficking, illicit arms trafficking, money laundering, corruption, counterfeiting of means of payment, computer crime and organised crime.

Human Trafficking and Human Smuggling

Trafficking in human beings may be described as modern-day slavery. This human problem is not confined to a particular country or a region but has spread its tentacles globally. The victims of this trade are children, men, women who are subject to forced labour, sexual exploitation or organ trafficking or a combination of them.[7] The explosion of illegal migration in the European and South Asian context has correspondingly created a wider space and opportunity for the trafficking in persons.

There is a tendency often to erroneously assume that trafficking and human smuggling are synonymous. There are major legal distinctions between these crimes that are associated with the movement of human beings.

Trafficking in General

In the context of human trafficking, human beings are moved from one location to another for the sole purpose of some kind of exploitation. The human traffickers may use force or deceive or coerce their innocent victims to engage in exploitative employment, sex work, organ removal, etc. The consent of the victims is often extracted by way of deception, fraud, coercion or other illegal means.[8]

According to the UN Convention on Organized Crime,[9] trafficking in persons is defined as the recruitment, transportation, transfer, harbouring or receipt of persons, by means of the threat or use of force or other forms of coercion, of abduction, of fraud, of deception, of the abuse of power or of a position of vulnerability or of the giving or receiving of payments or benefits to achieve the consent of a person having control over another person, for the purpose of exploitation. It also explains what constitutes exploitation. The Convention declares that it shall include as exploitation the prostitution of others or other forms of sexual exploitation, forced labour or services, slavery, servitude or the removal of organs.

Types of Trafficking

The aim of trafficking is for different criminal purposes. The legal formulations of such different forms of trafficking, their definitions and the nature of punishment for such crimes are not the same.

Sex Trafficking

What attracts the public very often are the crimes associated with sex trafficking. Such an offence involves the trafficking in persons for the purpose of commercial sexual exploitation. It occurs when people are forced or coerced into the commercial sex trade against their consent. The legal definition of sex trafficking often includes terms such as recruitment, harbouring, transportation, provision or obtaining of a person for the purpose of a commercial sexual act.

In the context of the EU, there are hardly any border controls when crossing to another member state. Even in the South Asian context, the rigidities of border control have been relaxed in recent times. For example, countries like Indian and Sri Lanka have taken the lead in relaxing visa rules and issuing such visas on arrival at the airports. With the relaxation of cross-border travel and the growth of the sex industry, there is also a greater demand for sexual services. Very often than not, such a demand is catered to by the victims of human trafficking.

Trafficking for Forced Labour

Forced labour is another form of human trafficking. The victims of forced labour could be men, women and children.[10] According to the United Nations Global Initiative to Fight Human Trafficking (UN-GIFT) the movement of people for the purpose of forced labour and services usually involves an agent or recruiter, a transporter, and a final employer, who will derive a profit from the exploitation of the trafficked person.[11]

Elements of Human Trafficking

According to definition given in the Trafficking in Persons Protocol, the trafficking in persons has three constituent elements involving the Act, Means and Purpose. **The Act** or what is done broadly covers recruitment, transportation, transfer, harbouring or receipt of persons. **The Means** or how it is done may for legal purposes constitute a threat or use of force, coercion, abduction, fraud, deception, abuse of power or vulnerability, or in giving payments or benefits to a person in control of the victim. Finally, the **Purpose** or why it is done has to be for exploitation, which includes exploiting the prostitution of others, sexual exploitation, forced labour, slavery or similar practices and the removal of organs.

Organ Trafficking

Apart from commercial sexual exploitation and forced labour, another objective of trafficking is for the trade in human organs. It occurs when the victims are trafficked so that traffickers can sell their organs for use in transplants.

Unlike sex trafficking, organ trafficking is not always illegal. If it is done against the will of the donor, then it is obviously illegal. There are often cases where family members, close relatives, neighbours or others who voluntarily agree to donate their organs to a patient for the purposes of legal transplantation.

The problem with organ trafficking is the criminals who prey upon the poor forcing them to part with their organs. Poverty is one of the major factors for the trade in organs. They may be forced to give their consent for a minimum financial consideration as a means to write off their debts. This is a major problem which is found in many developing and underdeveloped countries. Such involuntary donation of organs may occur internally or across the borders.

Human Smuggling

As highlighted, human smuggling and trafficking are often but erroneously used synonymously. It is useful and relevant to at least very briefly highlight the distinction between what constitute human smuggling and trafficking. From a legal perspective, there are major differences between these illegal activities. In the case of human smuggling, people voluntarily use a people smuggler to move from one place to another, very often from one country or continent to another, such as overloaded and unsafe vessels carrying potential refugees from Africa to enter the EU, especially via Italy.

Smuggling involves an illegal entry into another country and it is always across the borders. This definition has to be qualified in the context of countries where there is no border control such as within the European Union. The people who carry out smuggling only facilitate the cross border transport. It is also done with the consent of the potential migrant.

Sometimes, the distinction between smuggling and trafficking is too thin to distinguish between. There are several thousands of innocent people from Syria, Iraq and some other countries in this region who are desperately seeking to get out of their countries due to an endless bloodshed, death and destruction of property and people. Their ultimate goal is to reach the European Union, especially countries like Germany and Sweden, which are considered to be more tolerant, receptive and relatively generous to refugees. Most of them have no possibility to legally escape from this inhuman situation in their respective countries to such safer places. In desperation, they look for the services of criminals who engage in moving people across the borders paying large sums of money. In this context, both the smuggler and smuggled who once cross into another sovereign state without an entry visa or other legal documents are guilty of the immigration rules of the recipient country.

Trafficking in the European Union

There are several men, women and children who are trafficked within and into the EU for prostitution and menial labour. According to a report published by the European Commission, 30,146 people had been registered as victims of human trafficking across the Union during the period 2010–2013. The report says that 80% of the victims were women and 69% of all those trafficked were victims of sexual exploitation. More than 1,000 child victims were trafficked for sexual exploitation. Two-thirds of the victims were EU citizens. Nigeria and China were the main non-EU countries of origin.

According to a report by the EU justice agency, Eurojust, published in 2012 gives some positive outcome of its work in combating trafficking. It assists member states in their fight on human trafficking and the report highlights some cases in which the suspects were identified through a joint cross-border police work. The report gives some information about the case of Bulgarian criminals who trafficked pregnant Bulgarian women to Greece. The mothers were forced to give up their new-borns for adoption to Greek couples. In another case, a joint Polish-UK police work uncovered a Polish criminal group that was trafficking people to the UK. The report also speaks about a case involving a Czech gang based in the UK which had lured Czech women to the UK and made them work as prostitutes. In all these cases, the Eurojust had assisted the national prosecutors to secure a conviction.

Criminalisation of the Free Movement of People

The free movement of people is one of the fundamental freedoms recognised by EU law. The free movement of workers covers not only their right to move to another member state but also to earn a living there. This freedom had been further widened and strengthened by judicial intervention especially after the creation of the concept of European Citizenship by the Maastricht Treaty.

The free movement of people also includes various other rights. It covers the right to take up employment in another member state, the right to move and reside and to claim social rights such as access to medical benefits. It also includes political and consular rights which give the European citizens the right to vote in local elections in other member states if resident for a specific period of time. They have the right to secure consular help from their embassies outside the Union if they belong to another member state.

All these positive features have made the EU a source of attraction to people from outside the EU. It has also created an excellent environment for the criminals to indulge in trafficking into the safe and prosperous zone. Due to a mixture or reasons such as poverty, civil war, discrimination and the desire to search a more prosperous life, there is no shortage of potential clients for traffickers.

Factors Contributing to the Upsurge in Human Trafficking in the EU

One of the major challenges confronting the EU is the problem of human trafficking. There are several factors which could be identified for the explosion of this serious crime.

The integration of the EU by the removal of all barriers to the free movement of people also facilitates the free movement of criminals. Since there is hardly any border control within the EU, especially within the Schengen region, which consists of all member states of the EU and countries belonging to the European Free Trade Agreement except the UK and Ireland, the criminals have a wide and open geographical area to carry out their criminal operations in.

Another factor that has contributed to the increase in human smuggling is due to the various economic and political conditions prevailing in some countries outside the EU. The problem of economic impoverishment and poverty in some countries such as those in Africa and political instability in the Middle East, North Africa and Central Asia also have contributed to the problem of trafficking in the EU. There are many human beings who wish to leave their home countries due to economic and political considerations and they become easy prey to criminal groups who on a professional basis promise to find an illegal passage into the EU.

Legal Framework to Combat Human Trafficking

An important piece of legislation adopted by the EU before the Lisbon

Treaty to combat trafficking was the Council Framework Decision 2002/629/JHA of July 19, 2002. The Lisbon Treaty repealed legal acts such as the Framework Decision. After the Lisbon Treaty came into force, it had to replace all the legal acts based on the Framework Decision as they had legally ceased to exist.

The first legal act adopted by the Union after the Lisbon Treaty in the field of criminal law was the replacement of the Framework Decision on trafficking.[12] It adopted a directive as envisaged in the Lisbon Treaty on trafficking and it came into force in April 2013. The United Kingdom and Denmark which have Treaty derogation on matters relating to criminal law decided to opt out of this legal instrument.

After the Lisbon Treaty, the EU has stepped up its efforts to combat human trafficking by way of adopting new laws and strengthening their focus on the prevention and protection of victims. The Directive on Trafficking is the latest piece of EU legislation in this field.

The aim of this legal instrument is to bring together the substantive criminal law and the criminal procedural rules of the member states on combating trafficking in human beings. The centrepiece of this legislation is to offer a regime focusing on the defence of human rights, implementing the victims' protection and assistance mechanisms and in preventing and suppressing crime.

Since the problem of human trafficking is a global problem, the relevant EU law was also influenced in its drafting by other international legal instruments dealing with this heinous crime. It follows for example, the global approach which is the prevention of crime, the protection of victims and the criminal persecution of offenders.

Definition of Trafficking

The directive establishes minimum rules concerning the definition of trafficking in human beings and the corresponding sanctions. The directive has only set the minimum rules allowing the member states the right to transpose the law even more strictly. Trafficking has been defined very broadly in the directive. It declares that the recruitment, transportation, transfer, harbouring or reception of persons, including the exchange or transfer of control over those persons, by means of the threat or use of force or other forms of coercion, of abduction, of fraud, of deception, of the abuse of power or of a position of vulnerability or of the giving or receiving of payments or benefits to achieve the consent of a person having control over another person, for the purpose of exploitation.

The directive emphasis on exploitation which is broadly defined as exploitation of the prostitution of others or other forms of sexual exploitation, forced labour or services including begging, slavery or practices similar to slavery, servitude or the exploitation of criminal activities or the removal of organs. It also covers labour exploitation such as construction work, farming or domestic services. The defence of consent is of no value if the person had been subject to any of these inhuman treatments by threat or use of force.

The penalties that the member states are required to impose for trafficking are prescribed in the directive. The member states shall impose a penalty of at least five years of imprisonment. The punishment shall be increased to ten years imprisonment if the victim is a child or the crime was accompanied by the use of serious violence or committed within the framework of a criminal organisation. The directive also provides for the confiscation of the proceeds of the crime.

The criminal procedure prescribed in the directive is also quite unique. It provides that the investigation into or prosecution is not dependent on reporting or accusation by a victim. Criminal proceedings may continue even if the victim has withdrawn his or her statement.

Assistance for Victims

The directive provides for assistance and support for the victims of trafficking in human beings. It mandates the member states to take the necessary measures to ensure that assistance and support are provided to the victims before and for a limited period of time after the conclusion of the criminal proceedings. The member states are also required to attend to the victims with special needs, to see whether they are pregnant, to their health, to a disability, to a mental or psychological disorder that they may have or to a serious form of psychological, physical or sexual violence that they may have suffered.

Protection of Victims

Another important feature in the directive is that it provides for a special protection of the victims of trafficking in human beings. The member states shall ensure they have access without delay to legal counselling and in accordance with the role of victims in the relevant justice system, to legal representation including for the purpose of claiming compensation. Legal counselling and legal representation shall be free of charge where the victim does not have the sufficient financial resources.

The member states should ensure that the victims of trafficking receive the appropriate protection on the basis of an individual risk assessment inter alia by having access to witness protection programmes or to other similar measures. They are also required to ensure that the victims of trafficking receive a specific treatment aimed at preventing secondary victimisation such as unnecessary repetition of interviews during investigation and prosecution, the giving of evidence in open court and unnecessary questioning concerning the victim's private life.

Support to Child Victims

Another distinctive feature in the directive is the obligation imposed on the member states to take the necessary measures to ensure specific actions related to physical and psycho-social recovery in order to assist and support the child victims of trafficking in human beings. The member states should take due account of the child's views, needs and concerns with a view to finding a durable solution for the child.

Protection of Child Victims in Criminal Investigations and Proceedings

There is an additional protection envisaged in the directive for the child victim both at the investigative and prosecutorial stages. The member states are required to appoint a representative for a child victim of trafficking in human beings whereby the national law the holders of parental responsibility are precluded from representing the child as a result of a conflict of interest between them and the child victim.

Anti-Trafficking Coordinator

This is a position created within the European Commission. The post of the EU Anti-Trafficking Coordinator was initially foreseen in the Stockholm Programme and elaborated in the EU Anti-Trafficking Directive 2011/36/EU.

The EU Anti-Trafficking Coordinator is responsible for improving the coordination and coherence among the EU institutions, EU agencies, member states and international actors and in developing the existing and new EU policies to address trafficking in human beings. The Coordinator shall monitor the implementation of the Union strategy towards the eradication of trafficking.

Residence Permits for Victims of Trafficking

Another piece of EU legislation which has a direct bearing on the combat of human trafficking is the directive relating to the victims of trafficking.[13] The aim of this legislation is to extend protection to the victims who are non-EU nationals but are living illegally within the Union. It provides for granting various kinds of benefits to such victims provided they cooperate with the EU law enforcement agencies.

The victims are required to cooperate with the law enforcement agencies even though they are living illegally within the territory of the EU. They are given a reflection period to decide whether or not to cooperate with the police and other relevant agencies. Such cooperation is based on a voluntary basis without any direct or indirect pressure from the law enforcement agencies.

The directive provides for various forms of inducements to such victims to cooperate with the police. If they cooperate, the victims are entitled to free medical treatment in the relevant member state where they are illegally resident. They also have the right to obtain residence permit for a certain length of time. There are also other benefits that shall accrue to a victim who is granted a residence permit such as access to the labour market, vocational training and education according to the national legislation of the country of residence of the victim. However, according to the Commission, member states are underusing this law and are hesitant to issue temporary residence permits to the non-EU victims of trafficking who are cooperating with the authorities.[14]

An Overview of the South Asian Association for Regional Cooperation (SAARC)

In the South Asian context, a gradual and cautious start was given towards the end of 1985 as an initial step towards regionalism by the establishment of the South Asian Association for Regional Cooperation, known as SAARC.[15] It is one of the most populous regions in the world where the population exceeds 1.6 billion people. Like many other regional groupings such as the European Union, economic cooperation was not the fundamental reason for the creation of SAARC.

The initial problems in the establishment of SAARC are also not something which was unique to this organisation. The success or failure of the establishment and the maintenance of a regional body largely depends upon the political environment of the region. The motivations for regional integration or their lack can be attributable to the nature of the prevailing international, regional and national political climate.

The political situation in the SAARC region had been a great divisive force for regional cooperation. It must be appreciated that despite the existence of such serious bilateral political animosities,[16] the South Asian nations succeeded in creating the SAARC which may be considered to be a remarkable achievement of regional diplomacy. The stability and further development of SAARC depends largely on the resolution of some of these long-standing political disputes.[17] The common fear of the region's smaller nations of domination by the larger neighbours, different political ideologies, the sharp differences in the sizes and resources of these countries and different levels of development are some other factors which have not been conducive to regional integration.

SAARC Charter: A Minimalistic Approach

The SAARC Charter was negotiated at a time when the bilateral political relationship of some of the member states was at its lowest ebb. The political distrust which was prevailing at this time is clearly reflected in the SAARC Charter which excluded the areas of cooperation that can have any political ramifications.

Some of the areas identified for cooperation among the states are Agriculture, Rural Development, Telecommunications, Meteorology, Health and Transport. The headquarters of each of these services are located in different member states which was a political compromise to avoid any allegations of concentration of most of their services in one particular member state.

Another area of cooperation which deserves mention here is the establishment of an emergency food security reserve which may be utilised by any of the member states in times of food scarcity. This is a welcome humanitarian gesture which not only has the potential to reduce the tensions but also to promote and strengthen the unity among the member states.

South Asian Preferential Trade Arrangement (SAPTA)

It was to the credit of Sri Lanka's initiative that at the summit meeting of the Heads of States held in Dhaka in March 1993, the leaders agreed to lower or abolish tariffs on intra-regional trade. A general framework called the South Asian Preferential Trade Arrangement (SAPTA) was signed by the Foreign Ministers of the SAARC countries.

It only sets out a framework for action and all the other minute details such as the products to be included, the rate of reduction of tariff and the time limit for such initiatives have to be worked out in greater detail. The agreement was carefully worded so as not to stipulate any preconditions for reciprocity or uniformity. A member state can unilaterally reduce its tariffs on imports from all the other member states or it may extend tariff privileges only to selected countries.[18]

The signing of the SAPTA has given SAARC an economic content which is a great success for those member states which advocate the idea of extending SAARC to cover the areas of closer economic cooperation. There are several areas which could be identified for intra-regional trade expansion such as the movement of goods and services. Learning from the experience of other economic integration schemes, the range of products should be of a less comprehensive character in which the areas of cooperation with the greatest potential for conflict could be completely excluded. It would be better to adopt a product-by-product approach, like the Association for South East Asian Nation (ASEAN), to reduce or eliminate tariff. There are certain products such as tea, jute and textiles which are politically and economically sensitive to any form of liberalisation but it has been suggested that the member states could pool their resources to develop this sector by securing new markets and also to provide transport services such as shipping.[19]

Neither the SAARC charter nor any subsequent annual summit declarations have given much thought to the feasibility of at least partially liberalising the financial and the other services sector. The liberalisation of financial services such as banking and insurance is fundamental to the building up of a liberal market economy. The foreign investment policies of a majority of the SAARC member states have been highly restrictive. Some countries like Sri Lanka and India have greatly liberalised their economies, removed much of the foreign exchange controls and have enacted foreign investment protection laws, whose cumulative effect should be to boost the intra-SAARC trade and industry. These voluntary initiatives of some of the member states should be reciprocated by the others by which a foundation may be laid for a future common market in the financial services.

Some of the member states have relaxed the restrictions in the movement of professionals such as businesspeople, lawyers and doctors. There is also free movement for parliamentarians and senior judicial officers. Tourism is another services sector where the member states could work together. All the member states have the potential and the infrastructure to develop tourism and they can pool their resources to develop the tourist industry at a regional level.

As far as the movement of workers and capital is concerned, it is advisable to move in this direction cautiously. These factors of production which are of a highly mobile character have to be liberalised restrictively. Even the most advanced and highly developed single market still retains a certain control over the movement of persons and capital. All the SAARC countries face similar development problems such as growing unemployment and underemployment and rapidly increasing populations and any attempt to liberalise the labour movement can aggravate this situation. The free movement of labour carries with it other related issues such as access to healthcare, education and housing. The SAARC countries are still struggling to provide these basic amenities to their own nationals and an influx of foreigners will not only frustrate their efforts in finding a solution but can also lead to a political, economic and social crisis in the region. Capital movements should be liberalised to the extent that the free movement of goods and services can be liberalised. In recent times, Sri Lanka has greatly relaxed the foreign exchange rules and India has floated its currency and made it freely convertible which is a boost for free trade.

Human Trafficking in South Asia in General

The problem of human trafficking is both global and as old as humanity in the context of South Asia; its strategic location close to the Silk Road which linked the East and the West has attracted human traffickers from time immemorial.

Since the 1970s, many South Asia countries have been exposed to a new type of trafficking in the form of migrant labour workers. There are several thousand of people, mostly young girls, who seek employment as housemaids in the Middle East, Far East, etc. Unfortunately, some of them have become victims of traffickers who sell them for illegal purposes such as prostitution, slavery, etc. According to reliable reports, in South Asia alone, some 150,000 persons are trafficked every year.

In most of the South Asian economies, remittances of migrant workers form a substantial source of foreign exchange earnings. In these countries, human trafficking operations are carried out in different forms. They are sometimes disguised as reputed licensed agents of foreign employment with modern and attractive offices set up in the big cities. In order to reach out to their potential victims in the villages, they outsource their activities to so-called sub agents who operate in such areas.

Furthermore, these so-called employment agencies are well connected with their counterparts in the final destinations or intermediary countries in the process of human trafficking. There is much evidence to show that international human trafficking is closely aligned to international organised crime networks which engage in different forms of illegal activities ranging from arms and drug smuggling to money laundering and terror networks.

SAARC is not only one of the most populous regions in the world but also has a high level of poverty and porous borders between the member states. This is an attractive environment for human smuggling and trafficking. Ironically, the reduction in poverty in this region has not minimised the problem of human smuggling and trafficking. Most of the countries have moved from being least developed countries to the rank of lower middle income countries.[20]

There is a marked upsurge in economic growth in some of the SAARC countries. There is a growing demand for labour in the various sectors of their economy and this has also enhanced the opportunity for trafficking to supply cheap labur. With the emergence of a middle class, there is also a clear tendency of the growth of the sex tourism sector. It is a combination of economic hardships, globalisation and the desire for creating and enhancing wealth that has created a lucrative environment for human traffickers in the SAARC region.

Is the EU Model of Legal and Judicial Cooperation Feasible in South Asia?

The problem of human trafficking is not confined to any particular country, region or a continent. It is a global problem and as such a harmonious, cooperative and coordinated global assault on this crime is desirable. It is in this spirit that that the individual countries and regional organisations need to cooperate with each other and learn from their good practices in their war on trafficking. Most of the countries in South Asia have signed up for various international Conventions to combat human trafficking but they are as not effective as those found in the EU.

The United Nations Convention on Transnational Organized Crime was adopted in 2003. This legal instrument also includes specific protocols on how to prevent and control human trafficking and migrant smuggling. The Convention and its protocols provide universally accepted definitions of what constitutes trafficking in human beings and define measures that the signatories should take such as prosecution, protection of the victims and prevention. With regard to the prosecution of these crimes, the international cooperation measures such as extradition, mutual legal assistance and confiscation of assets are of special importance. Unfortunately, not all of the countries have international cooperation mechanisms in place that allow the expedition of mutual legal assistance requests or extraditions.

The EU model however cannot be transplanted in its totality to any other part of the world; not least to the South Asian region or vice versa. In the EU context, its 28 member states are much more integrated than those of any other regional organisations in existence. There are strict and binding requirements on all its member states to fully and effectively transpose the EU law into domestic law and these directives on trafficking are not an exception. If a member state fails to do so, the European Commission in its role as the guardian of EU law shall bring infringement proceedings against any member state which is in breach of EU Law. Such a binding and enforcement mechanism does not exist in the South Asian context.

The level of regional integration achieved in the Asian context is insufficient to follow the EU model to combat human trafficking but there are certain features which may be relevant and useful to the South Asian countries. As highlighted earlier, there is however some commonalities with the global and multilateral approach to combat human trafficking and as such it is desirable to develop a closer cooperation between the EU and the South Asian countries in this context.

Concluding Remarks

The EU has a clear and effective legal mechanism to combat human trafficking by means of prevention, prosecution and punishment. Such an effective legal framework was necessitated by the removal of all barriers to the free movement of goods, persons, services and capital within its single market.

The EU legal framework dealing with human trafficking is not perfect. Human trafficking is often associated with prostitution. The EU does not have a common law which prohibits such activity. In some member states such as Holland and Germany, prostitution is not a crime. In some other member states such as Sweden, prostitution has been made a crime. The relevant Swedish law has been formulated in a manner which makes prostitution services not as a direct crime but the receipt of such services is treated as a crime. The Swedish law does not ban prostitutes but only their customers. Thus, a legal paradox is created where in the latter situation a prostitute would be considered as a normal worker, especially as a self-employer.

The Court of Justice, the judicial arm of the European Union, had declared that the pursuit of an activity as an employed person or the provision of services for remuneration must be regarded as an economic activity within the meaning of Article 3 TEU and Article 119 TFEU, provided the work performed is genuine and effective and not such as to be regarded as purely marginal and ancillary.[21] The relevant case involved two women from the Czech Republic and Poland who before joining the EU had been charged with engaging in prostitution in the Netherlands. In terms of a free-trade agreement between the EU and these countries, the freedom to provide services was covered by this agreement. Based on this agreement, the Court of Justice declared that these women were engaged in an economic activity and that the Netherlands was in breach of EU law.

The problem of human trafficking in the EU is largely a product of external developments. The source country of the victims of human trafficking and even the traffickers are largely based outside the EU. This creates a problem of competence for the EU to deal with criminal elements operating outside EU. There are various agreements on legal cooperation signed by the EU with third countries but they are of limited scope and effectiveness. There are cases where the state agencies in certain countries directly or indirectly cooperate with the criminal groups engaged in human trafficking. The EU has the power, for example, to impose economic sanctions on third countries if they violate the fundamental rights of the minorities or suppress the political rights, freedom of expression, etc. If there is clear evidence of state involvement in human trafficking, the EU should seriously consider imposing an economic sanction action against such countries.

The EU method of combating trafficking cannot be fully transplanted in the South Asian context. The adoption of such rules and practices should take into consideration the local conditions such as the legal system, cultures, level of economic development, social environment, etc.

However there are certain provisions in the EU directives which are universally applicable. The prohibition of trafficking in human beings, special and additional rights to children and people with disabilities and the EU rules on these issues are relevant globally. The countries within South Asia should also move towards closer legal and judicial cooperation like in the EU to combat cross-border human trafficking in this part of the world. There should be potentially less political resistance for the SAARC countries in collectively fighting the war on trafficking.

NOTES AND REFERENCES

1. Council Decision of 22 December 2000 establishing a European Police College [Official Journal L 336 of 30.12.2000].
2. Council Decision 2009/426/JHA of 16 December 2008 on the strengthening of Eurojust and amending Decision 2002/187/JHA setting up Eurojust with a view to reinforcing the fight against serious crime.
3. Council Decision of 6 April 2009 establishing the European Police Office (Europol) (2009/371/JHA).
4. Council Framework Decision of 13 June 2002 on the European arrest warrant and the surrender procedures between Member States (2002/584/JHA).
5. It provides for the creation of an Area of Freedom, Security and Justice in Title V, TFEU. It consists of 5 chapters dealing with general provisions (Articles 67–76); Chapter 2 on border checks, asylum and immigration (Articles 77–80); Chapter 3 on judicial cooperation in civil matters (Article) 81; Chapter 4 on judicial cooperation in criminal matters (Article 82–86) and Chapter 5 on police cooperation (Articles 87–89).
6. Proposal for a Council Regulation on the establishment of the European Public Prosecutor's Office, COM/2013/0534 final - 2013/0255.
7. According to an International Labor Organization report in 2012, there were 20.9 million people who had been held against their will in various forms of forced labour around the world. The majority of these labourers were women at 55% and males at 45%. The annual profits from industries specialising in forced labour averaged 44.3 billion dollars in 2005.
8. Report of the International Labor Office, 2012.
9. The Protocol to Prevent, Suppress and Punish Trafficking in Persons Especially Women and Children, supplementing the United Nations Convention against Transnational Organized Crime (also referred to as the Trafficking Protocol or UN TIP Protocol) is a protocol to the Convention against Transnational Organized Crime (Adopted and opened for signature, ratification and accession by the General Assembly Resolution 55/25 of 15 November 2000).
10. According to an NGO report released in 2009, 48% of the returnee Sri Lankan domestic workers had been assaulted by a member of their employer's household, 52% had not been paid the salary promised to them and 84% had not been paid for their overtime work; abuses that may indicate forced labour.
11. The UN-GIFT is a multi-stakeholder initiative providing global access to expertise, knowledge and innovative partnerships to combat human trafficking. Its mission is to fight human trafficking. It mobilises State and non-State actors to eradicate human trafficking by reducing both the vulnerability of potential victims and the demand for exploitation in all its forms, to ensure adequate protection and support to those who do fall victim and supporting the efficient prosecution of the criminals involved.

12. Directive 2011/36/EU of the European Parliament and of the Council of 5 April 2011 on the prevention and combat of trafficking in human beings and protection of its victims.
13. Council Directive 2004/81 on the residence permit issued to third country nationals who are victims of trafficking.
14. In 2012, the EU countries granted 1,124 permits. registered was 2,171.
15. Bangladesh, Bhutan, India, Maldive Islands, Nepal, Pakistan and Sri Lanka are the founding members of the SAARC.
16. For example, the Indo-Pakistan problem over Kashmir and the Sikh separatist issue, the Indo-Lanka problem over the Tamil issue, etc.
17. On more than one occasion, the summit meetings of the Heads of States and Governments had to be suddenly postponed due to disagreements amongst themselves.
18. *Far Eastern Economic Review*, 22 April 1993.
19. Praveen Bhalla, "Regional Groupings in Asia: Should SAARC Follow the ASEAN Model?" *Journal of International Development*, Vol. 2, No. 3, July 1990, page 285-301.
20. According to an OECD report, Bangladesh, Bhutan and Nepal are classified as least developed countries whereas India, Pakistan and Sri Lanka fall into the category of lower middle income countries.
21. ECJ, 20.11.2001, Case C-268/99, Aldona Malgorzata Jany and Others v Staatssecretaris van Justitie.

9

Understanding Maldives in the Context of Human Trafficking

Mondira Dutta

ABSTRACT

The present paper attempts to study the situational analysis of Maldives with regard to trafficking of men and boys who get exploited almost at par with slavery and forced labour. The area of study is the Maldives which happens to be the smallest Asian country in terms of both population and land area. The country had been devastated during the Tsunami and had to be reconstructed with the help of migrant labourers mainly from Bangladesh, Sri Lanka and India. Most of such workers get trafficked through unscrupulous agents and are exploited in the Maldives. An estimated more than 70,000 foreign employees live in the country in addition to another 33,000 illegal immigrants, attributing to more than one-third of the Maldivian population. An estimated number of 85,000 migrant workers were registered in 2008, out of which 28,000 happened to be Indians. However, Bangladesh tops the list in terms of expatriates followed by Indians. In all, there may be more than 50 per cent of the workers who are illegal. Many of them who arrive in the Maldives are not even aware as to which country they have come to or who their agents are. The migrant labour population contributes significantly towards the Gross Domestic Product of the Maldivian economy and constitutes one of the largest groups in terms of being the country's menial job providers.

The Maldives has been placed in the 'Tier 2 Watch List' and has been identified as primarily a destination country among the migrant workers who are often trafficked into forced labour and, to a lesser degree, for the purpose of commercial sexual exploitation. Efforts towards developing the anti-human trafficking law enforcement machinery remain weak and there exists no law on human trafficking. Although the Constitution of the Maldives Government prohibits forced labour and slavery, the only prescribed penalty for the labour trafficking offence is a mere fine.

This paper attempts to study the conditions and situation in Maldives with regard to the trafficked victims and highlights the current status of their plight. The issue of human trafficking remains undefined and under-acknowledged within the country. Such a term is new and unknown to a majority of the local Maldivians. It is in this context that the present study attempts to undertake a deeper understanding of the issue of vulnerability to trafficking among the labour migrants in South Asia who have migrated to Maldives in search of livelihood options.

Keywords: Human trafficking in Maldives, labour traffickers, illegal migrants, expatriates in Maldives, trafficked victims in Maldives, trafficking of men and boys.

Background

Human trafficking is one of the world's most shameful crimes that affect the lives of millions of people whose dignity is robbed from them. While the best-known form of human trafficking is for the purpose of sexual exploitation, it goes much beyond that covering a wide gambit of the social canvas such as 'forced' marriages, bonded labour, agricultural plantation workers, organ trade, entertainment industry, begging and domestic servitude. The human traffickers consider people as commodities and goods that can be exploited and traded for financial gains. The largest segment of trafficking is for sexual exploitation followed by forced labour according to a study undertaken by the UNODC in 2010.[1] It is quite common to find that some national laws tend to recognise only the victims of trafficking for sexual exploitation. Even if the law provides for other forms of trafficking, the sexually exploited women and children get prioritised for enforcement and assistance; hence, the data collected tends to be biased towards the sexually exploited victims rather than for those victimised by all forms of trafficking.

Studies on trafficking for the purpose of forced labour appear to be concentrated and focussed on the conditions of work and not so much about the fact that the victims have been trapped by means of deception and fraud into the world of the so-called dirty, dangerous or demeaning jobs. Today, in a globalised world with established public welfare protections, a lesser number of people are willing or able to take on these menial jobs at an internationally competitive wage, thus generating the demand for labour. The coercion of labour thus becomes rampant and more profitable. Besides the many other factors that make the source country vulnerable to human trafficking, poverty emerges as the major one. But, poverty is not the only factor as there are many poor countries that do not seem to produce a large number of trafficked victims. The presence of organised crime in the destination countries and the siaspora population are some of the other factors that could be attributed as consequential in the trafficking of men and boys.[2] Recruitment is often carried out by the nationals of the same country in order to gain the trust of potential victims. The victims' trust is also needed at the destination to reduce the risk of escape. Hence, it is usually found that the nationality of the victims and the traffickers are the same. The traffickers may also belong to the nationality of the destination countries as well.

The present paper attempts to cover this aspect of trafficking among the men and boys who get exploited and end up in a situation of slavery and forced labour. The paper studies the situational analysis of Maldives which is the smallest Asian country in terms of both population and land area. Maldives happens to be one of the most incongruent countries in the world. Situated in South Asia in the Indian Ocean, it consists of more than a thousand coral islands located in the shape of a double chain. The Maldives government have grouped the islands into twenty-one administrative divisions including the city of Male[3]. Gan is the largest island in Maldives.

Area of Study

The census of 1905 shows that the population of the country was around 100,000 and remained as such for the next sixty years. After independence in 1965, the population growth rate rose due to an improved health status doubling by 1978 and the growth rate peaked at 3.4% in 1985. By 2007, the population had reached 300,000 despite a decline in the population growth rate by 1.9% as depicted through the 2000 Census. The life expectancy at birth grew from 46 years in 1978 to the current figure of 72 years. Infant mortality declined drastically from 127 per thousand in 1977 to 12 per thousand today and adult literacy recorded a high of 99%. The combined school enrolment record also shows in the high 90s.

Although the social parameters tend to suggest an enhancement in the lives of the people, according to the records of 2008, more than 70,000 foreign employees live in the country in addition to another 33,000 illegal immigrants, attributing to more than one third of the Maldivian population. They mainly hail from the neighbouring South Asian countries of Bangladesh, India, Sri Lanka and Nepal[4] besides Philippines and a few other countries. The migrant population contributes significantly towards the Gross Domestic Product of the Maldivian economy and constitutes one of the largest groups in terms of the country's menial job providers.

On many occasions, these migrant workers do not receive a salary for months together. They have a long duration of working hours, often being subjected to arduous inhuman living conditions. It is also a common sight to find fighting and violence escalating between the fellow inmates belonging to different countries. Without a law in place, there is simply no mechanism to address such an issue. Research studies towards this have been scanty and domestic legislations addressing issues on human trafficking in the Maldives are yet to be developed.

Context

The Maldives has been placed in the 'Tier 2 Watch List'[5] and has been identified as primarily a destination country for migrant workers often being trafficked into forced labour and, to a lesser degree, for the purpose of commercial sexual exploitation. The movement of women and children from one island to another for educational, employment and medical purposes has been a common practice. They run the risk of becoming victims to various forms of exploitation in the new environment. The efforts towards developing the anti-human trafficking law enforcement machinery have been weak. Although the constitution of the Maldives Government prohibits forced labour and slavery, the only prescribed penalty for the labour trafficking offence is a mere fine. There hardly exists any documentation reflecting the magnitude of the trafficked victims. An initial investigation has revealed that there is a stream of regular migrant workers travelling to the country in search of livelihood options. Most of the regular migrant workers are engaged in the construction sector, in the domestic services and as nurses, doctors, teachers, etc. At the same time, there is another substantial lot which is also moving into the country through unscrupulous elements who are not registered employers either in the Maldives or in any of the countries concerned. It is estimated according to the 2008 records that there exists a sum total of 85,000 migrant workers out of which 28,000 are Indians. The deportation data shows that the main reason for deportation is 'illegally working'. Bangladesh tops the list in terms of deportation.

Fig. 1: Main Reason for Deportation, Jan-Jun 2010

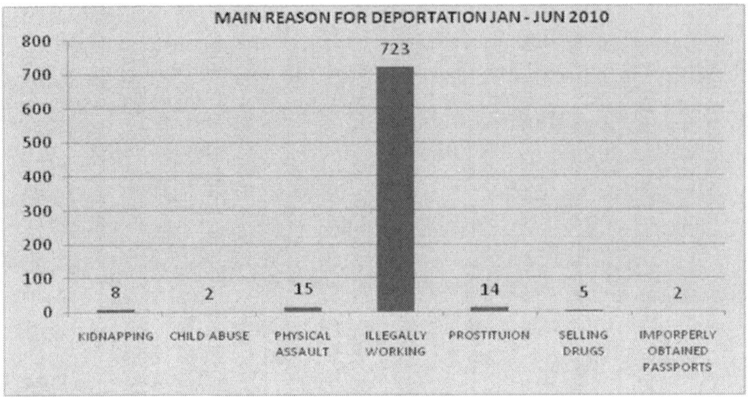

There are more than 50 per cent of the workers who are illegal. They are illiterate and belong to the poorest of the poor from the developing parts of the world. Many of them who arrive in the Maldives are not even aware as to which country they have come to or who their agents are.[6] Being illiterate and unaware they are extremely vulnerable and become an easy prey to fraudulent recruitment practices. These illegal migrants are often exploited by being forced to work in situations which do not comply with the domestic and international labour standards[7] and do not match the job profile that is stated in the work permit. Another common practice is that upon arrival the passports of the migrant workers are taken away by their employers.[8] This makes them even more insecure and vulnerable. Those who were employed have complained about this practice as they were unable to leave the country urgently in the event of a death in the family or to meet an emergency—more so if this happens to be a Friday or Saturday which is a weekend in Maldives.

Fig. 2: Deportation by Nationality, Jan-Jun 2010

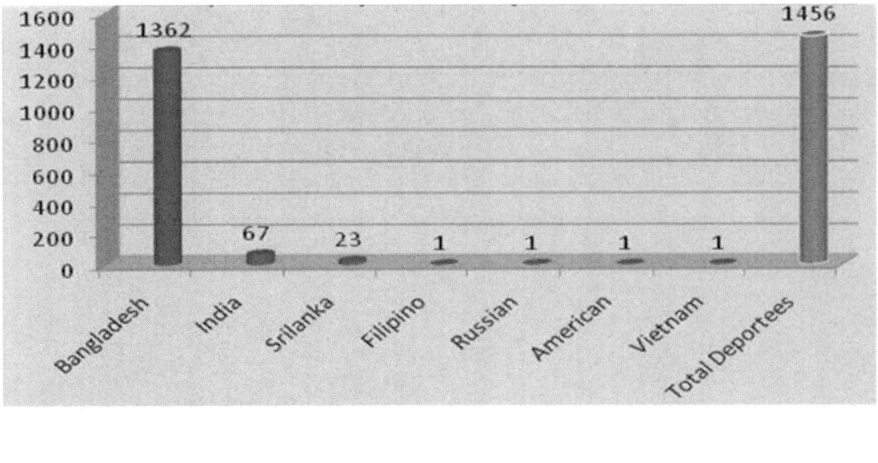

Field Visit Experiences

An interview with the various stakeholders revealed that on many occasions these migrant workers do not receive their salaries for several months. They have long duration of working hours, often being subjected to arduous inhuman living conditions.[9] It is also a common sight to find fighting and violence escalating between fellow inmates belonging to different countries. It has been frequently observed that out of sheer desperation, the migrant workers quit their present job and simply opt for other menial jobs which provide them with at least a regular wage. Thus, they end up entailing a cancellation of their job permit by the employers and are simply declared illegal. Their passports which were retained by the employers are put on hold and they are unable to escape from the country. The passport is retained as a security measure against the expatriate in case he/she runs away before the contract is over. There are cases where the migrant workers have been working silently in the country's islands for more than five years[10] without a job permit or a passport. A focussed group discussion with the irregular migrant workers from India and Bangladesh revealed that most of them had put their land and property at stake in order to be able to generate the requisite deposit[11] that they were to pay to the agents. They come with just a phone number of some agent which may not even exist.

In terms of magnitude, this is a massive number which becomes a huge burden on the Maldivian government. Without a law in place, there is simply no mechanism to address such an issue. Research studies towards this have been scanty and domestic legislations addressing issues on human trafficking in the Maldives are yet to be developed. The issue of human trafficking remains undefined and under-acknowledged within the country. Such a term is new and unknown to a majority of the local Maldivians.

Data Base and Methodology

The study comprises of both primary and secondary sources of information. A desk review of relevant literature comprises reports on the Trafficking in Persons (TIP), Tier Placements, Human Rights Commission of Maldives, UNFPA 2010, Statistical Yearbook of Maldives 2010, Media Reporting and News Articles, Strategic Action Plans, International Conventions ratified and action taken, Conventions on Regional Cooperation, Joint Collaborations with IOM, ILO, the Australian government and others.

A primary survey of 15 days was undertaken in May 2011 at Male. A questionnaire was designed and a list of stakeholders was listed. The identification of important stakeholders was made with the help of secondary sources of information. The field visit undertaken consisted of interviews and focused group discussions among the target group and the stakeholders. The data collected was validated through the triangulation of data with the concerned stakeholders. The data was analysed with the help of simple table and graphs and the narratives were used for an understanding of the situational analysis.

The important stakeholders interviewed in the field included the trafficked victims from Bangladesh, India and Nepal besides the members of the Human Rights Commission of the Maldives, UNFPA, UNDP, the Indian High Commission, Bangladesh High Commission, Maldives Port Limited, Department of Labour, Employment Agencies, some of the survivor victims, NGOs, Ministries of Tourism, Foreign Affairs and Education, Maldives Police Services, Employment Tribunal, Department of Immigration and Emigration, Prosecutor General's Office, Ministry of Health, Department of Gender and Family, the ADK Hospital Staff, media and several others. During the course of the interviews, it was attested to by most that ultimately it was the Ministry of Human Resources which records all information and takes the decision for the migrants. And, the final authority to declare the verdict for the convicts is declared through the Attorney General's Office. So, in addition to the above, a special interview with the Ministry of Human Resources and the Attorney General's Office was also undertaken. An interview with the former Foreign Minister, Dr Shahid, was also undertaken. He was the first to have recognised that human trafficking is taking place in the Maldives and stated, "Human Trafficking is there. Let's address it".

In the absence of secondary sources of information, an initial interview, FGD and discussion with the help of a structured questionnaire were utilised for generating the necessary information that was made available from the various departments. A record of all the interviews based on questionnaires and field notes was carefully documented.

Magnitude and Conditions of the Trafficked Labour Migrants

The city of Male is full of expatriates (legal and illegal) who throng the city park in the evenings and on weekends. It is a common sight to find several of the labour migrants loitering in the city killing their time. Most of them are either from Bangladesh, followed by the Indians and others. The data provided from the secondary sources in the year 2004 to 2008 shows the dominating source of expatriates.

Table 1: Source of Expatriate Employment by Citizenship, 2004–2008

Year	*Major Countries*					*Others*	*Total*
	Sri Lanka	*India*	*Bangladesh*	*Nepal*	*Indonesia*		
2004	8320	16657	9337	802	544	2753	38413
2005	7430	19430	13537	934	563	2951	44845
2006	7517	20582	20414	1450	572	3366	53901
2007	8728	23496	29409	2514	1116	4812	70075
2008	9575	23032	38952	2879	1412	4989	80839
Total (2004-08)	41570	103197	111649	8579	4207	18871	288073

Source: Ministry of Human Resources, Youth and Sports, Govt of Maldives

Table 1 shows that a majority of the expatriates are from Bangladesh, followed by India and Sri Lanka. This also shows that the trend of the expatriate community in Maldivies is expanding at a fast pace. In 2008, the volume of expatriates working in Maldives had exceeded up to 80,000. The country from which Maldives imports the highest number of labourers was Bangladesh (nearly half). It is possible that the sustenance of the Maldivian economy is greatly dependent upon foreign workers. In fact, the limited number of active local manual workers existing in Maldives may be inadequate for the survival of the economy and social life. The sector that is the most apparent to experience a further worsening of circumstances is the employment sector. Some professionals such as teachers and doctors, however, believe that the professional group also faces similar exploitation at times. The skilled-service providers, in particular those providing personnel services such as those offered in spa facilities, also face an increased risk of exploitation, compared to other groups.

The primary survey undertaken in May 2011, revealed that the expatriates from Bangladesh, India, Sri Lanka and other countries sometimes lived in the same room of a guest house. The guest houses itself consisted of only one room. A few of the tourism resorts in the islands were also visited in order to assess the proportion of the illegal workers employed. A discussion with one of the tourists from South Africa revealed that most of the workers are housed in the centre of the island while the tourist resorts are located closer to the waters and these have no access to the common public or workers without prior permission. A tourist books literally the whole island and not just the resort where no common person is allowed to visit. Despite such restrictions, the expatriate worker sometimes manages to run off to one of these islands and lives on his own by ploughing the land and growing watermelons and vegetables. Such workers automatically become illegal migrants and have no way to escape the country as their passports are in the custody of the authorities. During the field visit many instances were quoted about men who have been staying in this way for more than twenty-two years.

One of the guest houses located in the city of Male was owned by a Bangladeshi national. The place was rented from a local and was being operated by the Bangladeshi national. He charged 50 Rufaiya per day and 1200 Rufaiya per month inclusive of two meals per day. The meals mainly consisted of rice and beef or fish. All the inmates (about 30–35) lived in a tiny room partitioned into three parts; the space barely enough for washing, cleaning, a kitchen with no open outlets, a space hardly 8′x6′ in dimension full of bunk beds without any ventilation. The top-most bunk almost touched the ceiling. There was a foul stink everywhere. One single fan was at the entrance of the door. It is a marvel as to how 35 to 40 people were kept cramped up in such a tiny accommodation, just like a tin of sardines! The owner of the so-called 'guest house' revealed that he felt sorry for his countryfolk and allowed them to stay but now the agents themselves bring the people for him to accommodate. The owner of course worked nowhere and ran the guest house and that was his business. Possibilities of his being involved and in league with the agents seemed suspicious. He even beat up the inmates and injured them badly. One of them was being taken to the hospital.

The young men who arrived at Male had to pay a huge sum to the agents in order to come to Maldives. They were given a rosy picture of a job where they would earn at least 300 USD per month in addition to the food and shelter being free. Some of them, who were employed, earned a meagre 100–120 USD per month. This was hardly enough for them to live on and also send the money back home for the loans to be paid to the moneylenders. Several of them broke down while narrating their story. A man from Rajasthan stated how he was brought like an animal in a general class compartment by train from Rajasthan to Thiruvananthapuram in extreme heat. It took four days to reach their destination. Subsequently, they were sent by air to Colombo and then to Male in Maldives. He used to work as a mason in Rajasthan and earned around 10,000 rupees per month. None of these men were unemployed in India or Bangladesh. They came because they were lured for greener pastures. Upon arrival, the Immigration in Male cleared their papers and the agents took away their passports for being kept in safe custody. They were also shocked to find their return tickets cancelled. Not a single inmate in the guest house wanted to stay despite the fact that they would get a placement.

Indian Labour Migrants

A freshly recruited Indian group belonged to the state of Rajasthan. These trapped victims did not have their passports (hence were illegal migrants), did not know the local language nor had anybody to share their concerns with. They were too happy to express their heart out before the researcher during the field visit, as it was for the first time that somebody wanted to know their problems. This lot is not about a particular country or community but crosses all administrative borders and regions across South Asia and beyond, touching upon the vulnerable lot from India, Bangladesh, Sri Lanka, Nepal, Indonesia and others. A common pattern which emerged is that they belong particularly to a vulnerable lot which is in search of livelihood options, that too menial work, even at the cost of foregoing their land and life's savings. It is evident that they were brought here by agents who assured them with false promises, deceit and cheating. Most of them have had to pay an enormous amount of money which they generated either by selling their land or by borrowing from local moneylenders by mortgaging their land.

Many of them especially from India were pure vegetarians and the food offered to them at the guest house was mainly fish and beef. As a result most of them starved. They had no money to eat outside and managed to survive with a small amount of rice and sugar. Two of them got a job assignment to construct bridges in the middle of the sea. Belonging to a desert region of India, one of them had never had an opportunity to see the sea. The sea itself was shocking and the living was even more frightening. He was asked to stay inside a pipe throughout the night and work in the sea immersed in water. They were asked to bathe and even drink the same sea water after filtering it. The very next day, he left and returned back to the guest house. Several of the men were longing to return back to their homes despite the fact that they would have to dish out money from home to pay for their fare, but alas they did not have their passports with them.

At the Indian High Commissioner's office, a letter dated 25th April 2011 was written to the Human Rights' Commission, Maldives, regarding the 1,400 complaints received since 2008. They expressed concern and brought to their notice the inhuman living conditions and other fake work visa permits being issued to the expatriates. The Councillor from the Indian High Commission talked about an agent who was arrested in Tamil Nadu. His name was 'Abrar', who faced imprisonment for barely three months. He had been let free and had started the same business all over again. They feel that instances like this one, let down the morale of the people who put in so much effort and time to nab the culprits. There were people who wanted to help but the end result was always depressing. They are disappointed at the insignificant punishment meted out to a person who plays with the lives of thousands. The Indian High Commission stated that they do not have any records as to how many Indians are working or how many have left. The Detention Centres or the Immigration deals with it. There was no tripartite agreement in place. There were instances where people (around 45) have returned home and some money also has been recovered but there are instances where cases have been lingering on for the last nine years. An example of an Indian man was quoted who was found in an island and working since the last five years. He simply did not have any other option. The Indian High Commission has started some welfare camps in the islands. The Indian professionals working in Maldives as doctors and teachers report back to the High Commission whenever they come across any Indian who is under stressful conditions. They have cases that are reported from Vaghara island resort where men have been forced to work in the middle of the sea under extreme conditions.

According to the Councillor at the Indian High commission, Sri Lanka does not allow any of its people to go out for menial jobs. They have fixed a minimum wage limit of 140 USD per month if anyone wants to work outside. The same unfortunately cannot be applied for India as it is a signatory to the ECNR (Emigration Check Not Required). There was a rush of development activities post-Tsunami such as construction, etc. This was the time when the NGOs also became active. Earlier, Indians came for jobs from the southern part of the country but now it has been observed that people even migrate to the Maldives from the northern part of the country such as Rajasthan, the eastern part such as Kolkata, Azamgarh in UP and so on. There have been instances of violence by young Maldivians towards the Indians. Worse is, that people have now started arriving without any work. The Ministry of Overseas Indian Affairs has undertaken an initiative to study the condition of the Indians abroad. Pictures have been taken to show how they live in Maldives. People just arrive hoping to earn huge amounts of dollars and pay a lot of money to the agents. When they are given a job here, it is not more than 70–80 USD. With their passports taken away, they are like bonded labourers who have been trafficked into servitude. The employers usually get away scot free and the Employment Tribunal and Labour Tribunal are unable to do anything under the law. Out of an estimated 28,000 Indian expatriates in Maldives, only 600 are registered and have a regular work permit.

The only park in Male is usually thronged by the labour migrants, especially on a Friday. This tiny park gets overcrowded and there is hardly any space to sit. The men in the park stated that they felt extremely angry about the way in which they were being treated. Only one of the men was lucky that he had got a job at the right time and placed with a good employer who was with a water-processing plant at the RO Company. However, it was extremely alarming and distressing to see others who were at the park trying to kill their time on a Friday. Even this park has to be vacated after 8 pm and people were thus asked to leave. The police station was located right next to it and the police were prompt to arrive by 8 pm for making the people vacate the park. One of the men stated, "Only if we were allowed to sleep in the park, most of our troubles would be over".

The men complained that although they were promised to be paid in dollars, they were being paid in rufaiya (local currency). Moreover, the bank had a policy that not more than 500 dollars could be exchanged at a time per month and hence if their people back home needed more money for an emergency there was no way of sending the same. Every time they changed their earnings from rufaiya to dollars, they were subjected to the exchange rate and a bank charge thereby making them lose more money. The migrant workers are also prey to the fall in the dollar rate prevailing in the economy. They would now have to pay more for a dollar.

Bangladeshi Labour Migrants

A focussed group discussion with the Bangladeshi trafficked victims was held at the office of the High Commissioner. People were visibly upset and looked traumatised. Some of them were in tears and wanted to return home immediately. Each of them had paid around a sum of 200,000 Bangladeshi taka to the agents. As per the rules of the government of Maldives, a sum of 8000 rufaiya (15 rufaiya = 1 dollar) per head has to be deposited by the employer with the Ministry of Human Resource for security just in case the workers need to be deported back plus their food and living expenses. This sum gets deposited only to be withdrawn when needed. However despite such a system, people are unable to break free. The Immigration Department stated that there were flaws in the names in their passports or other flaws and hence they cannot obtain the money to purchase a return ticket. They thus continued to stay back in Maldives without a proper job, no medical facilities and under inhuman living conditions.

The Bangladeshi High Commissioner was extremely bitter about the state of affairs and simply lashed out at the authorities stating that there is a nexus existing in place. He even stated this seems to be the second highest sector contributing to the GDP after Tourism. He showed all the numerous documents he had collected about the law and other papers and letters that he has written to the authorities to which he has not received a single reply. He threatened to call a press conference and reveal all, in case he did not receive responses to his letters and the three reminders. The 29 men were literally on the roads and helpless. The Immigration and Emigration Department however suggested that they were keen to send such people back and it is not a problem to buy their tickets—passport or no passport. But the Labour Minister of Bangladesh had personally requested the Maldivian government not to deport back the Bangladeshis as it would be a huge problem for Bangladesh to take them back. The Immigration Department stated, "How can we send them when Bangladesh is not willing to take them?" This fact remains to be verified.

Another group of ten Indian men were in a jubilant mood as they had managed to get a return ticket from their homes and had a copy of these in hand. But, they were distraught with anxiety when their agent refused to hand over their passports saying they have to first pay up for their food and living expenses during the past seven days. It was obvious that there was a huge gap between what the law said and what was in practice.

Law Enforcing Machinery

In the areas of creating a legal framework, Immigration has amended the Immigration Act, 2007 to include trafficking as an offence, which was not mentioned earlier in the Immigration Act, 2007, but it is still very important to draft a new legislation on trafficking to combat the issue effectively. One key ingredient missing in the legal area is victim protection and the definition of human trafficking as a criminal act which violates the very core of human rights. The Immigration Department with the assistance of the Department of Immigration and Citizenship of Australia (DIAC) has been working on a draft legislation for human trafficking and human smuggling which would specify human trafficking as a criminal act and would allow severe punishments for offenders. It would also state victim protection and other necessary provisions such as safe houses for victims.

The Law Enforcing Machinery was studied through the Constitution and the laws that prevailed in the country. Unfortunately, there are no laws on human trafficking although there were laws on theft, robbery, rape, etc. These laws do not cater to the problem of human trafficking from a holistic approach. Punishments are light and lenient with hardly any implementation. An analysis of the immigration laws, the labour laws and the social protection measures were studied at length. Information based on interviews with the Prosecutor General and the officers from the Tribunal courts revealed that the existing system of prosecution was controlled by the Attorney-General and his/her office. The punishments implemented with the help of data from the concerned offices, referred basically to Crime against Women and many others from the police records and the Department of Gender. The missing gaps as regards what is lacking and what has been achieved needed to be identified. An Action Plan was in the pipeline or getting drafted probably in collaboration with the international agencies as was being suggested by the Prosecutor General during the interview.

Undoubtedly, there exists a large expatriate community in Maldives. This is vital for the rapid economic growth of the country. However, there are several trafficked victims within the expatriate community who had been promised opportunities for better wages and living. Although the constitution prohibits some forms of exploitation, the government has not developed a law that defines or criminalises the offence of trafficking. There are no established protective homes or shelters for the rehabilitation and reintegration of the trafficked victims. Trafficking has been taking place in Maldives specifically in the exploitation of migrant workers by the employers and sponsors. The Immigration Department is trying hard in taking every additional step necessary to prevent this. Recently, the mandatory security deposits for foreign workers by their sponsors had been raised for the sole purpose to prevent and protect the foreign workers from being trapped as trafficked victims in the Maldives. This would allow the department to ensure a reintegration of the victims with their families which at the moment has been a great challenge because of the financial burden.

Maldives is still a long way off the road. It still lacks the necessary legal tools to define human trafficking as a criminal act and to protect the victims of these criminal acts. They lack the resources like safe houses for the victims. The 2009 Trafficking in Persons Report states that to a lesser extent women from Sri Lanka, Thailand, India, and China get trafficked to Male for commercial sexual exploitation. This implies that trafficking for sexual exploitation is also prevalent in the Maldives. The country lacks even proper and adequate facilities and training for the law enforcement officers who would eventually play a vital role in identifying the victims of these criminal acts at the borders where cross-border trafficking takes place. At present, there are no government facilities or services for the in-care reception of the cross-border trafficked persons pending their repatriation. It is also important to develop human resources at the borders to combat these transnational organised crimes like human trafficking. There is no national policy or bilateral mechanisms for the rescue and repatriation of the cross-border trafficked victims. Nevertheless, the Maldives Immigration with its limited capability and capacity has made some arrangements to prevent, suppress and punish human trafficking.

Recruitment Processes

The system of recruiting the migrant workers in Maldives involves the registered employers/employment agencies, which seek permission from the Labour Department for the number of labourers they need. This is easily sanctioned and the respective agents usually hire such workers through agents and sub-agents from the labour-surplus countries. This lot mostly belongs to the poorest of the poor and is illiterate. Bangladesh and India top the list. When a migrant worker does not get his salary for months together or gets very little salary he often runs away to the islands or simply takes up other jobs such as collecting garbage from homes or does other menial work. The workers usually prefer this kind of work to other insecure jobs. However, this change in the work gets declared as illegal and the previous employer is quick to inform that the employee is missing. The employer can then ask for a fresh lot of workers and so on. The passports of these workers continue to be with the authorities and they are never able to return back home. Many such instances were reported by the Indian High Commission's office in Male.

The Recruitment Process, Gaps and Vulnerability were studied on the basis of interviews with the Immigration Department, Ministry of Human Resources, Ministry of Education and the Employment Agencies. The retaining of passports from the immigrants causing severe hardships to the expatriates was highlighted in the interviews. The prevailing illegal practices by the unregistered employers and rouge agents, both in Maldives and the source countries, were a major challenge for the Immigration Department. There were instances such as the one in which an old Maldivian's name was being used to recruit the migrant workers illegally without his knowledge. The gaps in the Recruitment Process and Areas of Vulnerability such as the lack of Regulation, Coordination and Monitoring under the LRA (Labour Regulation Authority) and the minimal punishment imposed on the defaulters were highlighted by the

Immigration officers. Nevertheless, none of the stakeholders could ascertain if there were any such defaulters till date and whether any prosecution had happened.

International Commitments and Regional Cooperation

The Government of Maldives has complied with a whole set of international commitments such as the ICCPR,[12] ICESCR,[13] ICERD,[14] CEDAW,[15] CAT,[16] CRPD[17] and CRC[18]. It also became a signatory to the Convention for the Protection of All Persons from Enforced Disappearance (CED) in February 2007. In addition, it is a party to the Optional Protocols to the ICCPR, CEDAW and CAT, and to both the Optional Protocols to the CRC. Maldives supported the adoption of the Optional Protocol to the ICESCR by the UN General Assembly in November 2008 and the ratification was being considered in due course along with the Optional Protocol to the CRPD. It would be important to understand the implications of all the conventions.

However, Maldives is yet to be a party to the International Convention on the Rights of Migrant Workers and Members of their Families (ICRMW). It has expressed its reservations under the ICCPR, CEDAW and CRC. However the Government is supposed to actively review these reservations in the light of the changes brought about by the new Constitution. It is understood that the Maldives officially notified the UN on March 26, 2010, of its decision to withdraw its reservation to Article 7a of the CEDAW, following the removal of the constitutional bar that had prevented women from running for presidency.

In May 2009, Maldives become the 183rd member of the International Labour Organisation (ILO) and is currently working with the ILO Secretariat on the implementation of the Framework Proposal covering labour law reform, labour administration and a plan of action to ratify the core conventions. This was confirmed by the Labour Department during the interview with stakeholders. The Maldives was also to become party to the Rome Statute of the International Criminal Court. Under the new Constitution, parliamentary approval must be obtained for international human rights treaties entered into by the Government. The Maldives seemed to have a dualist legal system. Nevertheless, Maldives is a member of the Commonwealth and works closely with its Human Rights Unit to promote human rights in the country. The Maldives is a member of the South Asian Association for Regional Cooperation (SAARC) and has signed a wide range of human rights-related SAARC

Conventions as well. It was to host the 17th SAARC summit from 10–11 November 2011, as was stated on the website[19]. For the first time, SAARC had nominated a woman secretary-general who hailed from the Maldives.

A report on the Maldives in the South Asian Association for Regional Cooperation (SAARC) Review of the Convention on Preventing and Combating Trafficking of Women and Children for Prostitution has highlighted that the Maldives is a destination country for human trafficking, "where the primary form of trafficking is forced labour." The SAARC report, funded by the Asian Development Bank (ADB) and produced by the International Organisation for Migration (IOM), suggested that the country's main offenders were "registered employment agents who fraudulently recruit low-skilled migrant workers and subject them to conditions of forced labour once they are in the country."

The other major offending group was of the "wealthy families who subjected domestic servants to forced labour," the report noted.[20] "A new bill on trafficking in persons was being initiated with support from the Government of Australia, and a shelter for the victims of human trafficking is scheduled to be opened in Malé shortly".[21] This would be a great opportunity for the Maldives in supplementing the United Nations Convention against Transnational Organized Crime (Palermo Protocol). The Palermo Protocol is an international legal instrument that specifically addresses the trafficking in persons from a holistic approach considering prevention, protection and promotion of cooperation.

However, many of the conventions are yet to be ratified by the Maldivian Parliament. Several reservations have also been raised for some of the conventions which are in the process of discussion. The Government of Maldives is jointly embarking upon several projects and is drafting processes with the International Labour Organization (ILO), the Australian government and others.

Conclusion

The study revealed that the working conditions of the trafficked victims were inhuman and appalling. The kinds of jobs undertaken were basically menial and the wages earned were meagre. The shift from the legal to illegal status was swift due to the prevailing compulsions in the system and as a result of salaries not being paid on a regular basis. The living conditions of the trafficked victims (based on interviews and focussed group discussions [FGD] with the victims) highlighted major problems in the food supplied by the guest houses, lack of washing and bathing and the sick being left with no medical support. The interviews with the hospital staff revealed that especially for emergency cases there was nobody who could sign on behalf of the patient, hence the medical care was restricted for the expatriate. Migrants and other locals running guest houses were with no regulation or/and monitoring and such owners of the guest houses seemed to be in league with the agents. Violence was inflicted on the inmates by the owner. The presence of such a large proportion of guest houses in Male and their demand suggested a large proportion of the immigrants' presence in the country. The practices adopted for the dead were even uglier with no government support.

The whole place seemed weird and a sense of insecurity prevailed among the expatriates. The local Maldivians (young ones) have been violent with the migrant workers on many occasions but these instances have been brushed aside by the authorities as non-racial. Stakeholders were reluctant to even acknowledge that trafficking was happening. Even if they did, they felt that it is a headache of the source countries and that they are responsible for rectifying the problem as well. Everyone seemed to blame the other department and shrug their responsibilities. The stakeholders' meetings revealed that they were all in the knowledge of the living conditions of these trafficked victims but did not think much of it. They even stated that many Maldivians also live like that and that this was nothing new.

The secondary sources of information available were far and few. Many of the data needs permission from higher-ups which was an arduous time-consuming task. The Human Rights Commission—an independent organisation—was also cautious and did not openly criticise any system that was not functioning. It even justified the taking away of passports, the living conditions and several actions of the authorities.

Recommendations

- Draft and enact a legislation prohibiting and punishing all forms of trafficking in persons;
- Develop and implement systematic procedures for government officials to identify victims of trafficking among vulnerable groups such as undocumented migrants and women in prostitution;
- Ensure that identified victims of trafficking are provided with the necessary assistance and are not penalised for unlawful acts committed as a direct result of their being trafficked;

- Increase efforts to investigate and prosecute the trafficking offences and convict and sentence the trafficking offenders;
- Raise public awareness of human trafficking through media campaigns;
- Take steps to ensure that employers and labour brokers are not abusing the labour recruitment or sponsorship processes in order to subject the migrant workers to forced labour.
- A network needs to be created among the government-level stakeholders. By utilising resources and obtaining assistance from the Maldives Police Services and the hospital staff, the Immigration authorities will be able to bring all on a common platform.

NOTES AND REFERENCES

1. UNODC (2010): UN.GIFT, https://www.unodc.org/documents/data-and-analysis/tocta/TOCTA_Report_2010_low_res.pdf, Pg 40
2. UNODC (2006): Trafficking in Persons; Global Patterns, Vienna
3. http://en.wikipedia.org/wiki/Geography_of_the_Maldives
4. http://en.wikipedia.org/wiki/Maldives
5. US Department of State, 2010: Trafficking in Persons Report, Tier Placements, http://www.state.gov/g/tip/rls/tiprpt/2010/138377.htm
6. Discussion with the Department of Immigration and Emigration revealed that many of them upon arrival asked, "Is this Malaysia?"(Discussion held on 7th May, 2011, Male)
7. Human Rights Commission of the Maldives, 2009: Rapid Assessment of the Employment Situation in the Maldives. http://www.hrcm.org.mv/Publications/otherreports/TheEmploymentSituationintheMaldivesEng.pdf
8. As stated in the stakeholders' meetings with Employment Agencies, Ministry of Education, Department of Immigration and Emigration dated 4–10 May,2011, Male.
9. Interview held on 6th May 2011, with trafficked victims in the guest house owned by a Bangladeshi national named Jehangir.
10. Information obtained from the Indian High Commission, The Maldives, May 2011.
11. FGD with 21 trafficked victims on 5th May 2011 in the office of the Bangladesh High Commission, The Maldives.
12. International Covenant on Civil and Political Rights
13. International Covenant on Economic, Social and Cultural Rights
14. The International Convention on the Elimination of All Forms of Racial Discrimination
15. Convention on the Elimination of All Forms of Discrimination against Women
16. Convention against Torture

17. Convention on the Rights for Persons with Disabilities
18. Convention on the Rights of the Child
19. http://news.xinhuanet.com/english2010/world/2011-01/02/c_13674011.htm
20. Robinson J. J., (2010): Minivan News, 20 April.
21. United Nations, General Assembly: Report of the Working Group on the Universal Periodic Review, Maldives, 4th January 2011.

PART III

Energy Security

10

Energy Security in South Asia: Issues in Regional Cooperation

B.C. Upreti

ABSTRACT

The energy resources of the world—both fossil and non fossil—are depleting fast due to their extensive uses and ever increasing demands, resulting in a deep energy crisis for the countries whose economies are extensively dependent on the energy resources. Therefore, energy security has become a critical issue all over the world. Some of the fast-growing economies of the developing world like India and China need a huge pool of energy, which is not available to them. The external dependence of energy resources has become a critical issue for most of the countries. The South Asian region is characterised by a lack of vital energy resources, external dependence for energy, uneven distribution of energy resources in the region and a lack of resources and capacity to exploit the available pool of energy resources. It is obvious that the energy security is a critical issue for the countries of the South Asian region. The oil politics and the great game for energy affect the countries which are extensively dependent on the external sources of energy. The future economic growth of the South Asian countries depends on finding alternative sources of energy supplies, utilisation of their available energy resources, finding alternative sources of energy, building a regional energy pool and in learning the efficient uses of energy.

To what extent SAARC can be a viable instrument in dealing with the regional security crisis in South Asia and ensuring the energy security in the region is not a critical, though important, issue. The SAARC has not stood up to its expectations. But whether it is possible to meet the crisis of energy in South Asia through regional efforts and with the SAARC becoming an instrument to that, is a significant and relevant issue.

Keywords: comprehensive security, South Asia, environmental security, energy consumption patterns, energy dependency, regional energy cooperation, SAARC, regional energy grid.

Introduction

The notion of security has undergone a fundamental change in the last few decades due to several reasons ranging from development needs, welfare of the people to the natural hazards of various sorts. The phenomenon of security, in fact, has no more remained confined today to the security of the state and its territory through the conventional approaches of war and defence but the whole concept has undergone a change. The security of human beings has acquired much more importance today in comparison to the traditional notions of security, although, the traditional security paradigms are still relevant in the overall context. Nevertheless, the comprehensive security approach incorporating social security, economic security, political security, environmental security, energy security and the security of the state has become a necessity in the context of democracy, human rights and development.[1]

Energy security has become a highly significant component of the comprehensive security approach in the recent years. The fact is that the modern economies are extremely dependent on the energy resources and it has resulted in a fast depletion of the energy pools in various parts of the world. Therefore, the question of energy security has become a critical issue in the global context.[2]

The emerging economies, particularly in the Asia-Pacific region, have created a strong demand for an adequate and reliable supply of energy, while these countries are facing the challenges of imbalance between energy consumption and energy resource availability.[3] The increasing population resulting in a higher rate of energy consumption, external dependence for energy supplies, price hikes, etc. create problems for a large number of countries—particularly many of the developing countries which are dependent on the external supplies of energy and do not have much paying capacity. It may also be added here that the overgrowing consumption of fossil fuels and its serious implications for the environment has added new dimensions to the energy security challenges, as there is always a need to maintain a balance between energy resource utilisation and environmental protection. The exploitation of energy resources and distribution has become a highly politicised issue and it acquires a significant position in contemporary global politics. The threats of disruptions in energy supplies and the vulnerability of the security of energy infrastructures are other critical issues.

In the Asia-Pacific region, energy security issues have acquired a high significance over the years due to the following reasons:

(i) Increasing demand for energy due to rising economies like China and India.
(ii) Heavy population concentration in the region.
(iii) Increased energy consumption.
(iv) Available sources of energy in abundance in certain sectors but a lack of technology or capital resources to explore it.
(v) Uneven distribution of energy resources.
(vi) Lack of research.
(vii) External interferences for a hold over the energy resources: the great game.
(viii) Challenges of energy independence.

One would also like to add here that the energy map of the world has undergone a change in the post-Cold War phase. The great game is shifting from West Asia to other parts of Asia which are rich in energy resources. The Central Asian and the Caspian regions are becoming the new frontiers of oil politics. The world powers are contesting for their hold over the energy resources of this region and that has made it a hot spot of international politics in the recent decades. But, then there are a sizeable number of countries which are struggling for the energy resources and they are likely to struggle more in the years to come if no alternatives are found.

The countries of the South Asian region are at crossroads in terms of energy security. There is a growing need for energy in almost all the countries of the region and how to ensure sustainable energy security is a big challenge for them. There are countries like India which has a huge demand for energy. But, on the other hand, there are countries like Nepal and Bhutan which have a tremendous potential for generating hydropower but no resources to do so.

What are the challenges and prospects of energy security in South Asia? What role can the larger countries of the region like India and Pakistan play in this regard? Whether SAARC can play an effective role in forging a broad-based regional cooperation for energy security and what are the prospects and challenges of interregional cooperation for the energy security in South Asia are some of the issues that appear interesting in the context of the theme of this paper.

What is Energy Security?

In its simplest form, energy security may be understood as an attempt on the part of the government or a condition to ensure an adequate and reliable supply of energy at reasonable and affordable prices. The emerging economies, lifestyles and needs, welfare states and the impulses of globalisation have made a secure and reliable supply of energy a necessity. If there is any disruption in it, the people and the state become vulnerable. One may state that in today's world the strength and stakes of a state are judged on the basis of its energy pool, its command over the energy resources and its ability to provide energy to the people as the economies of today depend on energy.[4] Energy security thus includes:

- Adequate and stable energy supplies.
- A suitable distribution network of energy.
- State command over energy resources.
- Affordable price structure.

There can be broadly four drivers of energy security:

Economics	Market fundamentals of demand and supply.
Geopolitics	Ways and means of cross-border energy supplies.
Politics	Price structures, etc.
International relations	Regional and international cooperation for energy security.

Energy Resources and Consumption Patterns in South Asia: An Overview

South Asia constitutes one of the most vulnerable regions of the world. There are social divides, underdevelopment, unemployment, poverty, systemic divergences and asymmetries, discontent and distrust between the countries of the region. There has been a persistence of a conflicting situation in most of the countries of the region for one or the other reasons. The two major countries of the region, India and Pakistan, have still not been able to overcome the hangover of the partition, thereby hampering the growth of regional cooperation in South Asia. The other countries of the region also have issues and problems with India primarily due to the Indo-centric nature of the region.[5]

The South Asian region is home to nearly 23.2 per cent of the world's population. It shares 2 per cent of the total land area of the world and accounts for 6 per cent of the world's total primary energy use and 5 per cent of the total world energy production. The increase in the energy uses in South Asia can be understood from the fact that the energy consumption was 51 per cent between 1980–1990, which had increased to 53 per cent between 1990–2007, at an average annual growth rate of 4.1 per cent. The steady economic growth, industrialisation, urbanisation impacts of globalisation, etc. have increased the energy use in South Asia.

With regard to the energy resources there is a mixed situation in South Asia. The region is quite rich in respect to some resources but poor in the case of others. Secondly, these resources are unevenly distributed in the region and there are strong complementarities as well.

The South Asian region is not rich in fossil energy resources, particularly oil and natural gas.[6] The total estimated oil reserves of South Asia are 6.2 billion barrels, which constitute 0.6 per cent of the world reserves. India alone accounts for 5.7 billion barrels out of this pool. It means that the rest of the countries of the region share 0.5 billion barrels of oil. South Asia's natural gas reserves were estimated at 81.3 trillion cubic feet in 2006—almost one per cent of the world's total gas reserves. India, Pakistan and Bangladesh alone share 37.9 trillion cubic feet (icf), 28.1 tcf and 15.3 tcf respectively.

The region accounts for 10–11 per cent of the world's total coal reserves. Most of these reserves are in India and it is one of the major coal producer and consumer countries in the world.

There is a huge untapped hydropower potential in South Asia, particularly in Bhutan and Nepal. Nepal ranks next to Mexico in terms of the estimated hydropower potential, which accounts for 83,000 mw. It provides a vast scope for hydropower energy uses between India and Nepal. The India–Bhutan cooperation for hydropower development has already set an example that hydro-energy can be an asset to economic transformation and prosperity. However, except for the India–Bhutan cooperation for hydropower development, it has not been successful elsewhere. Nepal has not been able to exploit its vast water wealth in collaboration with India. It has not been possible to implement the 1997 Mahakali treaty till date. In fact, between India and Nepal, the whole issue of river waters is highly politicised.[7]

The energy consumption is also uneven in South Asia depending on the demand and resource availability. Commercial sources dominate South

Asia's energy consumption pattern. In 2007, the total energy consumption of South Asia was 584.6 mt which constituted 72 per cent and the remaining 28 per cent included biomass. The dominant energy consumption patterns of the South Asian countries are as follows:

India	: Coal	: 50 per cent
Bangladesh	: Natural gas	: 68 per cent
Afghanistan	: Oil products	
Maldives	: Oil products	
Nepal	: Oil products	
Sri Lanka	: Oil products	
Bhutan	: Hydroelectricity	: 70 per cent
Pakistan	: Natural gas	: 55 per cent

The total installed power-generation capacity of South Asia (2007) was 728 billion kilowatt hours, dominated by India (85%) and followed by Pakistan (12%). The different means of power generation are as follows:

Conventional thermal power plants	: 81 per cent
Hydropower plants	: 16 per cent
Nuclear plants	: 02 per cent
Renewal resource based power plants	: 01 per cent

The priority sources of power generation in different countries are as follows:

Thermal power	: India, Pakistan and Bangladesh
Hydropower	: Nepal, Bhutan and Sri Lanka

It may be emphasised here that renewable energy contributes only 1 per cent to the installed power-generation capacity in South Asia. It may also be added here that nearly 600 million people of the South Asian region still do not have access to electricity. The electricity demand is likely to grow at an annual average of 9 per cent.

Energy Dependency Syndrome

The South Asian countries are heavily dependent on import of oil and petroleum products ranging from 25 per cent for India and other countries to 100 per cent in the case of Maldives. It clearly shows that some countries of the region are very much dependent on the external supplies of oil and gas.

The transport sector in Nepal, Bhutan, and Maldives totally depends upon the import of oil. The regular hikes of oil prices, political dynamics, etc. are serious issues for the countries of the South Asian region. Countries like India, Pakistan and Sri Lanka are trying to make use of hydro and gas resources in order to reduce their import dependency in energy but for others it is a big problem as they do not have the capacity to explore and utilise their energy resources without external collaboration.

Some studies have indicated that energy consumption is likely to increase in South Asia. The World Energy Outlook 2004 estimated that the energy consumption in South Asia is likely to increase from 470 mt in 2002 to 726 mt in 2020 and 880 mt in 2030. The annual average growth rate of total energy consumption is projected to be 2.3 per cent in South Asia for the period till 2020.[8]

The bulk of demand for energy is likely to come from India, Pakistan and Bangladesh. The sectoral growth rate of different energy resources is likely to be:

Coal	: 0.4 per cent
Oil	: 3.5 per cent
Gas	: 4.2 per cent
Electricity	: 4.9 per cent

Issues in Regional Cooperation

The energy demands of the South Asian countries, the available pool of energy resources and the projected energy demands clearly indicate that the countries of the region are facing commonly a formidable energy security crisis. Due to the uneven distribution of energy resources and external dependence on oil energy, countries like Nepal, Maldives and Bhutan face serious challenges, while India, Pakistan and Bangladesh face higher energy security risks because of rising economies and population pressures.

Electricity is an important source of industrialisation in Nepal, Bhutan, etc. However, untapped hydro-resources and management of electricity transportation and distribution are a big challenge. The South Asian countries have been so far totally dependent on West Asia for oil imports. Further, countries like Nepal and Bhutan need huge funds for hydropower generation and also a potential buyer that can be India alone. Similarly, Bangladesh also needs funds for the exploration of its natural gas reserves. In the given situation, regional cooperation through SAARC seems to be the best alternative. It is though a well-known fact that SAARC has been ineffective due to the political tangles among the countries of the region—particularly India and Pakistan.

Nevertheless, there is a rationale for energy cooperation in South Asia. The following aspects are relevant in this regard:

1. Development of regional energy planning.
2. Collaboration for hydropower generation between India–Nepal and India–Bhutan.
3. Developing regional energy trade: Indo-Nepal-Bhutan, Bangladesh and Myanmar, Central Asia, Afghanistan, Pakistan–Iran, Iran–Pakistan, India–Sri Lanka, etc.
4. Collaboration for exploring the energy resources.
5. Cooperation for natural gas supplies through pipelines particularly between India-Pakistan-Afghanistan and further.
6. Collaboration for development of renewable energy potentials. The South Asian countries can take advantage of India's expertise in this field.
7. Collaboration for diversification of sources of external oil imports.
8. Facilitating inter-country energy development opportunities.
9. Cooperation for evolving a common strategy to address the regional energy security issues.

Efforts and Achievements

Some efforts have been made towards regional energy cooperation. However, most of it exists at the bilateral level. Some of the examples of collaboration for energy security are:

1. India–Bhutan cooperation for hydropower production and trade.
2. India–Nepal electricity trade.
3. India–Nepal joint development project in oil and power sectors.
4. India–Sri Lanka collaborations assisted by ONGC, IOC and NTPC.
5. India–Nepal and India–Bhutan cooperation for oil and gas supplies.
6. Bangladeshi imports of diesel from India.

There is further scope for regional cooperation in petroleum products. It may be noted here that India has emerged as a major exporter of petroleum products. India's export of petroleum products increased from 3 million tonnes to 40 million tonnes from 2003 to 2011. India's major exporting countries are UAE, Singapore, etc. Pakistan and Bangladesh import petroleum products from these countries. If these countries expand their trade for these products at the regional level, they will be able to save money. In 2009, Pakistan agreed to lift the ban from importing diesel from India. Pakistan has also agreed to import petroleum products from

India. The South Asian countries can learn from ASEAN, APEC, SADC, EC, etc. in forging a meaningful regional cooperation for energy security; though, there are vast structural asymmetries between South Asia and others.

Bottlenecks

SAARC is far behind in taking up substantive measures for ensuring regional energy security. The slow progress of SAARC has been due to the political hangovers and animosities among its member countries. However, there is a need that has been felt to activate SAARC in this direction. The problem is that SAARC has yet to come up as an active regional organisation in comparison to the other regional organisations. The lack of confidence and cooperation among the member countries has also reflected in the working of SAARC.[9]

In January 2000, energy cooperation was brought under the purview of the SAARC Integrated Programme of Action (SIPA). In 2004, a Technical Committee on Energy Cooperation was constituted. The SAARC Energy Centre has also been established. However, SAARC has yet to prove to be an effective means of regional energy cooperation. There are serious bottlenecks:

1. Geopolitics of the region.
2. Lack of cooperation among member countries, distrust and ill-feelings.
3. Emphasis on bilateral arrangements.
4. Regional asymmetries and unevenness.
5. Outward-looking approach of the countries of the region.
6. Slow progress of SAARC and lack of initiatives.

Looking Beyond the Region

Despite these challenges, it may still be argued that there is vast scope of interregional cooperation for energy security in South Asia. It has already been pointed out that the South Asian countries need to diversify the sources of oil imports and reduce their dependence on West Asia. Central Asia can be not only an alternative source of oil imports but also there is a vast scope for multi-sector energy cooperation with the states of Central Asia. The Central Asian countries are rich in hydrocarbons, oil, gas, hydropower, etc.

Pakistan and Afghanistan are important countries from the point of view of energy sector collaboration and energy trade with Central Asia.

India's disadvantage is that it has lost direct surface links with Central Asia. India is also not a major player in Central Asia. However, India is involved in the energy resources exploration in Kazakhstan, Turkmenistan, Kyrgyzstan and Uzbekistan. There is vast competition among the major powers in Central Asia. India can be a viable alternative in certain respects, provided:

1. Regional cooperation for energy security in South Asia is strengthened, SAARC is activated and the South Asian region attains stability and peace.
2. Stronger India–Pakistan ties get built and a mutual understanding for cross-border energy cooperation attained between these two countries.

The supply of natural gas through pipelines is a significant issue. The Iran-Pakistan-India Gas Pipeline, Central Asia-Afghanistan-Pakistan Gas Pipeline, Myanmar-Nepal-Bangladesh-India Gas Pipeline are important projects, which would again need a closer cooperation between India and Pakistan.

The question of energy security and regional energy cooperation appears to be a high priority of the new government in India under the leadership of PM Modi. In the 18th SAARC Summit held in Kathmandu in November 2014, India accorded top priority to energy along with connectivity and trade. It could not be taken up in the agenda of SAARC as Pakistan did not agree to it. But it clearly reflected in India's approach and concerns to the energy issues.

India is also emphasising on subregional cooperation for energy development and it is also open to multilateral cooperation for hydro-resources development.

Summing Up

On the whole, one may say that energy security is the core of the future economic growth in South Asia. There are serious challenges but there is a vast scope for attaining the goals of energy security through regional and interregional cooperation.

As pointed out earlier, there is an uneven distribution of energy resources in South Asia. Therefore, there is a need to strengthen regional cooperation not only for exploration, research and development planning of the energy sector development but also for regional energy trade. One advantage with the South Asian countries is that there are multiple sources of energy and few of them are quite in abundance. However, there has been a lack of political will among the countries of the region to cooperate with each other. It has not been possible to implement the Mahakali treaty between India and Nepal, concluded as early as 1997. The India–Pakistan discontent and discord has caused a slow progress of SAARC. In fact, the India–Pakistan relations are key to regional peace stability and cooperation.

There is a need to pool up the energy resources of South Asia. Suggestions have been given for the formation of a Regional Electricity Grid and a Regional Gas Grid. The harmonisation of energy policies including pricing are other issues that have been emphasised by a number of scholars. There has to be a regional regulating structure for this purpose. There is no regional framework for the promotion of regional energy trade other than SAARC.

A South Asian Energy Charter Treaty has also been suggested by some. There is a need to tap the renewable energy potential like wind, solar, etc. India has done some progress in this regard. The other countries of the region can learn from India's experiences.

The South Asian countries are extremely poor in energy efficiency projects.[10] a lot of energy goes waste due to lack of awareness and management. It is essential that we learn a lot in the fields of energy efficiency and energy management. Private sector involvement in energy resource development is also an important issue and needs to be encouraged. Some steps have been taken at the bilateral level. But, such measures need to be encouraged at the level of SAARC.

Lastly, at the core of energy security in South Asia is the mutual understanding and cooperation among the constituent countries in a regional and broader perspective.

NOTES AND REFERENCES

1. For theoretical discussions on the comprehensive nature of security see, Abdur Rob Khan (ed.), *Globalization and Non-Traditional Security in South Asia*, RCSS, Colombo, 2011; Rajesh M. Basrur (ed.), *Security in the New Millennium*, India Research Press, New Delhi, 2001; Dipankar Banerji (ed.), *Security Studies in South Asia: Changes and Challenges*, Manohar, New Delhi, 2000; Dev Raj Dahal and Nischal Nath Pandey (eds.), *Comprehensive Security in South Asia*, Manohar, New Delhi, 2006; V.R. Raghavan (ed.), "Comprehensive Security in South Asia: Seminar Proceedings", Delhi Policy Group, New Delhi, January 2001.
2. "South Asia Development and Cooperation Report", RIS, Oxford University Press, New Delhi, 2008: 115-116.
3. For details see, V. Gupta & Chan Suan Kwa (eds.), *Energy Security: Asia-Pacific Perspectives*, Manas, New Delhi, 2010: 10-13.
4. For the changing dynamics of energy as a security aspect and the politics of

energy, see Rashmi Doraiswamy (ed.), *Energy Security, India, Central Asia and the Neighbourhood,* Manak, New Delhi, 2013.

5. For more elaborations see, B.C. Upreti, *Contemporary South Asia,* Kalinga Publications, Delhi, 2004.
6. For details of the energy resource situation in South Asia, see Energy Information Administration, "South Asia Energy Fact Sheet", Department of Energy, United States of America, March, 2007.
7. See, B.C. Upreti, *Politics of Himalayan River Waters,* Nirala, New Delhi, 1994.
8. "Status of Renewable Energy and Energy Efficiency in South Asia", WEC, 2004; referred from South Asia Development and Cooperation Report, no. 1: 120.
9. For a comprehensive overview see, B.C. Upreti (ed.), *SAARC: Dynamics of Regional Cooperation in South Asia,* 2 Vols, Kalinga Publication, Delhi, 2009.
10. For some references in this regard, see "Energy and Security in South Asia: Cooperation or Conflict", the Brookings Institution, Washington DC, November, 2011; http/www.brooking-ed/research/books/2011.

Table 1: Some Basic Data

	India	*Pakistan*	*Bangladesh*	*Nepal*	*Sri Lanka*	*Bhutan*	*Maldives*	*SA Av.*
Population (2009) (mm.)	1198	181	162	29	20	0.7	0.51	15927
Annual Population Growth Rate (%) (2000-09)	1.6	2.2	1.6	2.1	0.8	2.4	1.4	1.6
GDP Growth (%) 2009	9.1	3.6	5.7	4.7	3.5	7.4	-3.0	8.0
HDI 2010	0.519	0.490	0.469	0.428	0.568	-	0.602	0.511
Energy use per capita (kg of oil Equivalent) 2008	545	499	175	340	443	-	-	497
Total Electricity Production (Billion kw 2008)	830.1	91.6	35.0	3.1	9.2	-	-	969.0 T
Electricity Consumption/POP (Kwh)/ capita 2006	480.00	456.0	147.0	69.0	379.0	-	-	-
Total Primary Energy Supply (Mtoe)	537.31	76.33	24.19	9.17	9.37	-.	-	-
Hydropower (MW)	301000	40000	775	42915	2000	50000	-	-
Oil (Mtoe)	740.0	39.0	0.9	0	0	0	-	-
Gas (BCM)	920	795.0	434	0	0	0	-	-
Coal (Mtoe)	91631	3100	724	5	0	0	-	-

Source:"Human Development in South Asia 2010/2011", Oxford University Press, Karachi, 2011; "South Asia Development and Cooperation Report", Oxford University Press, New Delhi, 2008.

Table 2: Energy Consumption Pattern in South Asia (2007)
(Million Tonne Oil Equivalent—mtoe)

	Afghanistan	*Bangladesh*	*Bhutan*	*India*	*Maldives*	*Nepal*	*Pakistan*	*Sri Lanka*	*South Asia*
Commercial fuels	6.91	16.64	0.29	106.00	0.19	7.40	23.36	3.58	164.37
Coal	0	0	0.01	171.00	0	0.17	3.30	0.00	174.48
Oil products	0.21	3.71	0.04	124.00	0.27	0.77	15.21	3.01	147.22
Natural gas	0.11	8.20	0.00	28.00	0	0	27.39	0	63.79
Hydro Electricity	0.03	0.23	0.12	18.00	0	0.14	6.47	0.83	25.82
Nuclear/renewable Electricity	0	0	0	8.50	0	0	0.42	0	8.92
Total primary Electricity	0.03	0.23	0.12	26.50	0	0.14	6.89	0.83	34.74
Total commercial energy	0.35	12.20	0.17	349.50	0.27	1.08	52.79	3.84	420.20
Total energy consumption	7.26	28.80	0.46	455.50	0.46	8.48	76.15	7.42	584.60
Per capita commercial energy consumption	16.00	89.00	243.00	335.00	759.00	44.00	355.00	200.00	302.00

Source: South Asia Cooperation and Development Report, 2008.

Table 3: Energy Demand in South Asia and the Growth Rate Forecast, 2019–20

	Electricity	*(Bkwh)*	*Oil Product*	*(Mtoe)*	*Gas*	*(Mtoe)*	*Coal*	*(Mtoe)*
Afghanistan	3.9	(13.1)	3.5	(19.1)	0.9	(14.5)	0	(0)
Bangladesh	72.8	(8.2)	11.6	(7.3)	44.0	(11.0)	0.9	(3.7)
Bhutan	6.9	(15.0)	0.6	(16.0)	0.0	(0)	0.1	(16.0)
India	1756.0	(7.1)	246.9	(4.8)	101.8	(8.0)	447.6	(6.2)
Maldives	1.6	(5.9)	1.7	(12.0)	0.0	(0)	0.0	(0)
Nepal	8.1	(8.0)	1.6	(4.9)	0.0	(0)	0.8	(10.0)
Pakistan	251.1	(7.5)	30.9	(4.5)	72.8	(6.2)	13.9	(9.4)
Sri Lanka	23.9	(7.2)	7.8	(6.2)	0.0	(0)	7.0	(..)

Source: RCE, 2008.

11

Geopolitics of Energy in India-Kazakhstan Relations

Mukesh Kumar Mishra

ABSTRACT

The geopolitics of energy is returning, once again, to the core of international relations. In this context, energy is an important element in what is described as the "New Great Game" of the twenty-first century. In the present times, energy is universally recognised as one of the most critical inputs for economic growth. Therefore, the energy security is emerging as a vital issue in the era of fast economic growth. Same is the case with Central Asia where energy has become a major factor in the geopolitical game of regional powers. In Central Asia, Kazakhstan occupies a leading position in the energy sector. It has added a new strategic dimension to the geopolitics of the whole region, particularly to that of India and China. This region contains key global hydrocarbon reserves. About 70 per cent of these reserves are found in the western regions of Kazakhstan which has all the potential and opportunities to become a major supplier of big volumes of petrochemicals for the leading economies of the world. India too has sought to improve its access to the Central Asian energy resources, particularly in Kazakhstan, as its demands are growing. The increased price of crude oil has also forced India to search for alternative sustainable resources of raw materials and Kazakhstan is being seen as a reliable source of hydrocarbons. As part of cooperation in the energy sector in 2011, India and Kazakhstan signed a nuclear cooperation agreement during the former Indian Prime Minister Manmohan Singh's visit to Astana. The nuclear agreement came after a 2009 MoU signed during a visit by the Kazakh President Nursultan Nazarbayev to India, which provided for Kazakhstan to supply uranium to India. Therefore, the main aim of this article is to highlight the energy cooperation between India and Kazakhstan in the context of the geopolitics of energy in Central Asia. Because of the fact that the geopolitics of energy in Central Asia has been witnessing a New Great Game involving major the regional and global powers, it is important to deal with the situation that prevails in the energy cooperation between India and Kazakhstan.

Keywords: Geopolitics of energy, New Great Game, energy security, Kazakhstan's Strategy 2050, recoverable uranium.

Today, energy is universally recognised as one of the most critical inputs for economic growth and, therefore, energy security has emerged as a vital issue in the era of fast economic growth. This has essentially led to what is called as the geopolitics of energy which has become the core of international relations in the twenty-first century. Central Asia, too, is a case in point where energy has become a major factor in the geopolitical game of the regional powers. Among the Central Asian countries, Kazakhstan occupies a leading position in the energy sector. It has added a new strategic dimension to the geopolitics of the whole region, particularly to that of India and China. This region contains key global hydrocarbon reserves of which about 70 per cent are found in the western regions of Kazakhstan which has all the potential and opportunities to become a major supplier of big volumes of petrochemicals for the leading economies of the world. India too has sought to improve its access to the Central Asian energy resources, particularly in Kazakhstan, as its demands are growing. The increased price of crude oil has also forced India to search for alternative sustainable resources of raw materials and Kazakhstan is being seen as a reliable source of hydrocarbons. Given the situation, it is pertinent to understand Kazakhstan's growth strategy at first.

Kazakhstan's Growth Strategy

Kazakhstan is the largest economy in Central Asia and the second largest after the Russian Federation among the Commonwealth of Independent States. In the national economic field, Kazakhstan has led the Strategy 2030 and Initiative. This is an ambitious plan to transform Kazakhstan into an Innovation Nation and bring it amongst the 50 most competitive economies of the world by 2015. Strategy 2030 has recently been expanded to Strategy 2050 to take Kazakhstan to new heights of economic growth and prosperity. Kazakhstan's economic initiatives have produced significant results that have helped to spread prosperity among all segments of the population.

In his National Day Address to the Nation on December 16, 2012, President Nazarbayev laid out a strategy for the country, calling for better governance, improvement of welfare and tax systems, support for small- and medium-sized businesses and development of infrastructure. Currently ranked as the 51st most competitive country in the world, Kazakhstan, he said, should work towards and aspire to be ranked among the 30 most advanced nations by 2050.

However, in order to do so, Kazakhstan will need to integrate its economy into the global and regional economic systems by capitalising on its transit potential and on bolstering its information technology capabilities. As an oil-rich country and a reliable international partner, Nazarbayev said that Kazakhstan will lift the existing subsoil-use moratorium in an effort to become "a regional magnet for investment." This would be done in exchange for advanced technologies and creation of new production. Nazarbayev directed the government to lift all licenses and permits not directly affecting safety in the first half of 2013. He also said that it was necessary to redistribute responsibilities so that a second wave of privatisation of the non-strategic enterprises could begin. The goal is to preserve the nation's high rate of economic growth.

Nevertheless, the single most important challenge that confronts Kazakhstan today is the overcoming of its predominant reliance on the natural resources so as to diversify into sectors such as telecommunications, financial services, transport, construction, pharmaceuticals, food processing, etc. With the possibility of development of many key industrial sectors and modernisation in the services sectors, Kazakhstan offers enormous opportunities for trade and investment. The situation is complicated by the fact that Kazakhstan is fortunate to have been endowed with large commercially viable deposits of most minerals. For example, it is the second largest source of uranium, chromium, lead, and zinc reserves and among the top ten sources of coal, manganese, copper, iron and gold reserves. Kazakhstan also has the 11th largest proven reserves of both oil and natural gas. Mining accounts for 61.6 per cent of the industrial output.

With energy prices reaching new heights, the sources of oil and natural gas outside the unstable West Asia are now more important than ever. The Caspian region has the third largest oil and gas deposits in the world after the Persian Gulf and Russia. In contrast to the Gulf region, it shows a relative political stability and a lower level of terrorist threats and religious strife. Kazakhstan is a country of great importance to the West and the region. With estimated oil reserves of 39.8 billion barrels, proven natural gas reserves of 105.9 trillion cubic feet (3 trillion cubic metres)[1] and other natural resources such as uranium, coal and metals, and a fast-growing services sector, Kazakhstan's future looks promising to its people and attractive to foreign investors. However, the great powers and regional actors are playing a "New Great Game"[2] around the Caspian's energy resources. In this new geopolitical reality, the region is drawing an increasing attention from the US, Russia and China as well as Iran, India and other regional players. It is also attracting multibillion-dollar investments and becoming the subject of international intrigues.

Kazakhstan is convinced that its position as an important supplier of oil to the international markets has enabled it to develop an assertive foreign policy. The country is capable of defending and promoting its strategic national interests from the standpoint of a stable and independent regional player. Nazarbayev described Kazakhstan's approach and principles in the hydrocarbon sector in his 2006 statement which is as follows:

> At this time, our country is among world's top-ten countries by recoverable oil reserves. Kazakhstan holds the second largest oil reserves outside OPEC... Apparently, such resources potentially place Kazakhstan among the world oil powers. We must become aware of our new geostrategic role in the global energy market, and develop our energy policy accordingly over the next ten to fifteen years. We find it essential to conduct an optimal, balanced, and transparent foreign policy. In the future, we are going to strengthen the reputation of Kazakhstan as a forward-looking, reliable international partner that contributes to global energy security with due consideration to its national interests.[3]

Such a statement underlines the fact that the Kazakh leadership is striving for consistency and predictability in its geostrategic posture in general and in the oil and gas sector in particular. Since the early 1990s, Kazakhstan has put a great deal of effort into developing an international policy that ensures its national interests and regional security in all four principal directions: North, South, East and West. The foreign policy course followed by the country's leadership has thus far allowed Kazakhstan to develop foreign economic ties and maintain high GDP growth rates despite the unfavourable geopolitical situation in Central Asia and especially in the neighbouring West Asia.

Geopolitics of Energy in Central Asia: The New Great Game

The competition among the global actors in the Caspian and Central Asian regions has prompted many scholars and analysts to compare the situation with the nineteenth century "Great Game" played between the Russian and British empires for influence in Central Asia. In the twenty-first century, however, more players are competing for presence in the region, and so it is now known as the "New Great Game". In order to maintain a balance of external interests, Kazakhstan has chosen a path of transparency concerning the country's foreign policy. Over the years, Nazarbayev, regardless of the geopolitical climate at the time, has undertaken Eurasian integration initiatives as well as consulting with the political leadership in Moscow, Washington and Beijing on all important projects in the oil and gas sector. This multi-vector policy course has thus prevented a single global political player from achieving a complete hegemony over Central Asia. Basically, the four key powers dominating the geopolitical landscape around Kazakhstan's sector of the Caspian Sea are Russia, China, the US and Europe.

Kazakhstan's principal geoeconomic value and role is that of a major oil and gas producing economy. Exports are projected to rise from 1 million barrels/day (mbd) in 2005 to an anticipated 3 mbd in 2015 (from 50 million tonnes/year to 150 million tonnes),[4] putting Kazakhstan in the same category of oil exporters as Kuwait, Iran and Iraq. However, despite its large reserves of coal, uranium, gold and other precious metals, the newly established country faced a deep economic crisis when the Soviet Union collapsed. Though Kazakhstan was a potential global hydrocarbon supplier, with the collapse of the USSR it faced energy shortages and for several years was unable to meet its domestic demands for oil, gas, fuel, electricity and even water. In the late 1990s, oil prices were low, and the benefits of having oil and gas fields for exploitation were limited. With crude prices falling to a minimum ($10/barrel) in the wake of the Asian economic crisis, the landlocked republic's energy industry remained on the edge of self-sufficiency. By 1998, oil production in neighbouring Russia fell to its lowest point at 250–300 million tonnes a year, which at that time was less than 10 per cent of the global production.[5]

It is imperative that Kazakhstan could take the road to full nationalisation of the oil extractive industry, as has been customary in West Asia and in other oil provinces, or it could transfer some energy assets to the private sector, which is what happened in Russia in the 1990s. Both scenarios imply turning Kazakhstan's oil resources into a geopolitical tool. In particular, privatisation involves the identification of potential partners based on the geostrategic balance of the era. At the time, Kazakhstan was in a position to seek partnerships from among the global and regional players, including the American, Russian, European, Chinese, and Middle

Eastern energy companies. However, all scenarios included risks. In his 1997 annual State of the Nation address, Nazarbayev emphasised that the opportunities offered by the Caspian mineral wealth included potential dangers:

> Our natural resources are an enormous wealth. Ironically, world experience shows that many countries with natural resources were not able to dispose of them properly and never came out of poverty. The East Asian countries, poor in natural resources, have demonstrated the most dynamic development. These examples highlight that the people, their will, motivation, persistence and wisdom, primarily determine the development outcome.[6]

Eventually, Kazakhstan opted for a balanced approach, with proper consideration for the interests of all the world powers involved in the region, by opening access to the international oil companies. The Kazakhstani leadership considered this strategy to be consistent with the country's foreign policy priorities, believing that Kazakhstan would be able to maintain partnerships with the key players in the region and utilise oil revenues towards the achievement of sustainable economic development. In deciding in favour of foreign direct investment, according to the *Financial Times*, "Kazakhstan was becoming one of the few oil-rich countries that are open to foreign companies."[7] In a short time, Kazakhstan undertook a series of legislative initiatives and became the most attractive CIS country for foreign investment.[8] Interestingly, the country did not apply the model it was using in opening the energy sector to foreign capital to other sectors of the economy. Thus, protectionism and reliance on internal resources dominated the financial sector, the media and other markets.[9]

The Kazakh government gave preference to internationally recognised companies which were interested in developing long-term projects and ready to take into account the country's domestic interests. They had to emphasise environmental safety programmes, train local staff and exercise corporate social responsibility. Transnational companies, such as ChevronTexaco, ExxonMobil, Agip/Eni, Royal Dutch Shell, British Group, TotalFinaElf, Impex and others emerged as the winners in this race. China's desire to strengthen its role became more obvious in 2005 and 2006, with Russia's presence on the increase and the American influence on the wane. With Chinese and Indian extractive and financial corporations entering the scene, the interests of all major world players were represented in the Caspian region.

The arrival of foreign corporations demanded the construction of a system of export oil and gas pipelines. Kazakhstan had gained independence, but it lacked a sufficient hydrocarbon infrastructure to develop the giant fields and connect them to the international oil markets. This underdevelopment of the petroleum transportation system still limits the exploration and production of the largest Caspian fields. In order to realise the full potential of its oil fields, Kazakhstan had to assure export routes that would guarantee its ability to fill the demand for "black gold", particularly to the West and China. The role of Kazakhstan as a reliable supplier of hydrocarbons to the global market has greatly increased since the beginning of the decade. The attacks of September 11, 2001, growing destabilisation in the Middle East and an increased demand for energy throughout the world, especially in China and India, have all led to an insatiable thirst for oil.

Energy Factor in the India–Kazakhstan Relations

It was the visit of President Nazarbayev as the Chief Guest on India's 60th Republic Day celebrations from 23–26 Jan, 2009, that imparted a significant impulse to the India–Kazakhstan bilateral ties. Discussions were held on providing a big push to the bilateral commercial and economic ties as well as in the area of energy cooperation. A breakthrough was made in bilateral relations when the Agreement between the ONGC Mittal Energy Limited (OMEL) and KMG, the National Oil Company of Kazakhstan, was signed in respect of the offshore Caspian Sea block of Satpayev. A significant achievement of the visit was the signing of an MoU between the National Company KazAtomProm and the Nuclear Power Corporation of India Limited for cooperation between the two sides on the supply of uranium to India.

The much-needed impetus to bilateral relations came in April 2011 when the Indian Prime Minister Manmohan Singh visited Kazakhstan. One of the most significant achievements of Singh's visit was the signing of the agreement for cooperation in peaceful uses of atomic energy. It provided a legal framework for cooperation in fuel supply, nuclear medicine, use of radiation technologies for healthcare including isotopes, reactor safety mechanism, exchange of scientific and research information, exploration and joint mining of uranium and the design, construction and operation of nuclear power plants. The agreement can be viewed in the context of India's growing energy demands. According to India's 12th Five Year Plan, nuclear power will play a major role in meeting the country's energy demand which needs an additional 1,00,000 MW of power during the 12th Plan (2012–17).The much-awaited agreement on energy cooperation was also finalised during that visit. A package of three agreements—participating share assignment agreement, carry agreement and joint operation agreement—on the Satpayev exploration block was signed between ONGC Videsh Ltd. and National Company "Kazmunaigas" (KMG).

India has been trying to gain a foothold in Kazakhstan's hydrocarbon sector since 1995. But it was only in 2009 that the agreement was signed between the OVL and the KMG. This was followed by an Exploration Contract between India's Ministry of Oil and Gas and the KMG in 2010. And in 2011, during Manmohan Singh's visit, definitive agreements were concluded between the ONGC and the KMG. This agreement assigned 25 per cent participating interest in the Satpayev Block to OVL as a strategic foreign partner in the project. Thus, the agreement became the first breakthrough for India in the Central Asian energy sector. Manmohan Singh's visit can be considered a major step forward in India–Kazakhstan relations during which the main thrust was given to cooperation in the field of hydrocarbons and the peaceful use of nuclear energy and in finalising the Joint Action Plan for future cooperation for the period 2011–2014. Prime Minister Singh also acknowledged that "Kazakhstan is a very important and influential player in Central Asia" and that India wants to develop this partnership in diverse fields.

Oil and gas represent the most important areas in which India and Kazakhstan can cooperate to mutual advantage. Currently, India imports 70% of its energy requirements. India's demand for fossil fuels and other forms of energy is expected to keep increasing in view of its rapid economic growth. On the other side, Kazakhstan produces about 80 million tonness per year (1.6 million barrels per day). With the development of the Kashagan oilfield, Kazakhstan's oil production is likely to go up to 150 million tonnes per annum by 2015 making it one of the world's top ten exporters of oil. Kazakhstan can take advantage of the rich and vast experience that India has accumulated in downstream processing and refining of crude oil to manufacture petrochemicals and other related products.

Although OVL was hopeful that it will be able to gain an 8.3% stake in the Kashagan oilfield, this share has been given to the Chinese despite the fact that India had indicated its interest in this project much earlier. This has caused an avoidable disappointment and shock to the section of opinion makers and leaders in India who have been speaking out in favour of stronger strategic and economic links with Kazakhstan. But, then the two sides continue to identify and pursue fresh initiatives and opportunities for strengthening and deepening the bilateral partnership.

Another area which presents attractive prospects for further diversifying the bilateral economic and commercial contacts is civil nuclear energy cooperation. Kazakhstan actively supported India for an unconditional waiver for international commerce in civil nuclear energy in 2009 at the negotiations at the International Atomic Energy Agency (IAEA) and the Nuclear Suppliers Group (NSG). Kazakhstan is the largest producer of uranium ore currently with an annual production of around 20,000 tonnes per annum. It has the capacity to continue to be the largest producer with an annual output of 27,000 tonnes by 2015. India has developed nuclear reactors indigenously. Both countries can collaborate successfully to mutual advantage and benefit in this field. Kazakhstan is also keen to use India's expertise for moving up the value chain in production of nuclear fuel pellets.

Given India's growing demand for energy, it needs to be mentioned here that in the field of civilian nuclear energy, India has been planning to increase its nuclear power capacity from 4.7 GW today to 20 GW by 2020, with the annual nuclear fuel consumption projected to increase tenfold to 8000 tonnes. Though some slowdown in the nuclear industry development appears to be increasingly likely in the wake of Japan's Fukushima disaster, long-term plans appear to be unchanged and India's demand for nuclear fuel in the near to medium-term will still be substantial. Much of this demand will need to be met by growing the uranium imports while India develops its domestic uranium deposits. India's hydrocarbon consumption is also projected to increase at a very rapid pace, with the IAEA estimating the growth of demand from 3 to 3.5 million barrels per day in 2011 to over 5 million per day in 2020.

Kazakhstan can help India address these needs because it is the second largest source of recoverable uranium after Australia with an estimated 15% to 19% of the world's total reserves. Extrapolating from the current trends, the Central Asian nation is poised to emerge as the number one global supplier of uranium in the next five years with a presence across the uranium extraction, enrichment and fuel fabrication markets. Kazakhstan's extractable resources of oil are estimated to be 7.8 billion tonnes, and those of natural gas 100 trillion cubic feet. However, the transport of hydrocarbons from Central Asia to India is problematic given the absence of stable and reliable land routes. In the case of the Satpayev field, for example, this means that the oil will not enter the Indian market directly, but will be sold within the region with compensating oil purchases from India's traditional oil market counterparts.

One should also consider that the Kazakh government has laid out the main strategies for the accelerated development of Kazakhstan's gas industry in the *Development Concept of Kazakhstan's Gas Industry Until 2015.* By the end of 2015, Kazakhstan expects to produce 40 to 50 billion cubic metres (bcm) per year, up from 29 bcm of gas in 2007, and to be the third largest producer in Central Asia after Turkmenistan and Uzbekistan. However, while Turkmenistan, the largest Central Asian producer, exports most of its natural gas, Uzbekistan consumes most of its annual production of 65.3 bcm or sells it to the immediate neighbours. By 2014, Uzbekistan expects to export 16 bcm of gas per year, up from the current 14.5 bcm.[10] Kazakhstan is striving to reach some ambitious natural gas goals. In early 2008, then president of KazMunayGaz, Uzakbay Karabalin, announced plans to increase the national gas output from 29.6 billion cubic metres in 2007 to 114 bcm in 2020, while exportable production should reach 30 bcm in 2020, up from the current 12.9 bcm. Over the same period, the government expects Kazakhstan's domestic consumption to grow by some 5.4 bcm and reach 18.7 bcm per year.[11] Today, Kazakhstan exports most of its gas to Europe through Gazprom's pipeline system. An attractive option would be to connect Kazakhstan's gas system to the Baku–Erzurum gas pipeline, which links to the Turkish gas system and would continue further, via the proposed European Union-sponsored and US-supported Nabucco pipeline project, to Central and Western Europe. All these are matters of concern for India as far as the Kazakhstan–India energy cooperation is concerned.

Conclusion

While competition among the global actors in Central Asia particularly for oil and natural gas has turned the region into a zone of the "New Great Game", one major point of understanding here is that this geopolitics of energy has strengthened Kazakhstan's geoeconomic importance in recent years. But in order to maintain a balance of external interests, Kazakhstan has preferred to follow transparency in its foreign policy. Despite the existing geopolitical climate, Kazakhstan's Eurasian integration initiatives as well as consultations with the American, Chinese, Russian and European leaders on important projects in the oil and gas sector have resulted positively. In this regard, Kazakhstan's multi-vector foreign policy has contributed much to its favour as it prevented a single global political player from achieving a complete hegemony over Central Asia.

As regards the energy factor in relations between India and Kazakhstan, it is an important aspect and energy cooperation between the two countries is developing at a significant pace, though the future holds an even greater promise and potential. It needs to be pointed out here that India's three-year uranium purchase commitment constitutes less than 4% of Kazakhstan's likely uranium production volumes over the same period. Therefore, India's long-term energy security calls for a longer planning horizon and a broader view of the India–Kazakhstan relationship. The current political, strategic and economic scenario, both regionally and internationally, presents an immense potential for India and Kazakhstan to qualitatively and quantitatively enhance their engagement to bring it to a higher level. As far as the geopolitics of energy in Central Asia is concerned, both India and Kazakhstan are factors of peace, stability, growth and development not only in their regions but also in the world. Stronger and deeper relations between these countries may contribute to the increasing prosperity and security for the peoples of the two countries as also for the Central Asian region as a whole. Thus, further talks between India and Kazakhstan must continue to go beyond the immediate energy concerns.

NOTES AND REFERENCES

1. British Petroleum, "BP Statistical Review of World Energy," June 2007, pp. 6, 20, 22 at *www.bp.com/productlanding.do?categoryId=6848&contentId=7033471* (August 20, 2007).
2. "The Great Game" was a term apparently introduced by Arthur Conolly, a British intelligence officer, in the first half of the nineteenth century. It describes the strategic conflict between the British Empire and czarist Russia for control over Central Asia. The classical period lasted from 1813 to 1907. The Great Game renewed after 1917. Peter Hopkirk, *The Great Game: The Struggle for Empire in Central Asia*, Kodansha International, 1992.
3. Nazarbayev, Address at the Ceremonial Meeting dedicated to the 15th Anniversary of Kazakhstan's Independence.
4. Crude oil measurement units conversion: 1 million barrels per day = 49.8 million tonnes per year; 1 metric tonne = 7.33 barrels; 1 barrel = 0.133 metric tonnes. Natural gas measurement units conversion: 1 billion cubic metres (bcm) = 35.3 billion cubic feet (bcf) = 0.9 million tonnes oil equivalent (mtoe); 1 billion cubic feet (bcf) = 0.028 billion cubic metres (bcm). Source: British Petroleum, "Conversion Calculator", at *http://www.bp.com/conversionCalculator.do?&contentId=7033429&categoryId=9017919* (May 25, 2008)
5. Edward L. Morse, James Richard, "The Battle for Energy Dominance", *Foreign Affairs*, March-April 2002, at *http://www.foreignaffairs.org/20020301faessay7969/edward-l-morse-james richard/the-battle-for-energy-dominance.html* (December 20, 2007).
6. Nazarbayev, Annual Address to the People of Kazakhstan, 2008.
7. Gorst, "Kazakh President to Visit UK".
8. Clinton R. Shiells, Presentation "FDI and the Investment Climate in the CIS

Countries", IMF, November 2003, at *http://www.imf.org/external/pubs/ft/pdp/2003/pdp05.pdf* (February 22, 2007).

9. Kazakhstan's law allows foreign investment in any sector of the economy. However, the foreign capital share is limited to 25 per cent in the banking sector and to 20 per cent in the mass media. Source: The Heritage Foundation, "Index of Economic Freedom", at *http://www.heritage.org/research/features/index/country.cfm?id=Kazakhstan* (January 12, 2008).
10. Shamil Baigin, "Uzbekistan to Raise Natural Gas Exports in 2008", *Reuters*, May 13, 2008, at *http://in.reuters.com/article/oilRpt/idINL1351337820080513?sp=true* (May 30, 2008); Energy Information Administration, "Country Analysis Brief: Central Asia", updated February 2008, at *http://www.eia.doe.gov/emeu/cabs/Centasia/Full.html* (May 28, 2008)..
11. "Kazakhstan is Determined to Up Gas Production and Lessen Dependence on Import from Uzbekistan", *Ferghana.ru*, February 28, 2008, at *http://enews.ferghana.ru/news.php?id=122&mode=snews* (March 10, 2008).

12

Nuclear Power Expansion and its Safety and Security Risks in East and South Asia: A Regionally Based Comparison with the European Union

Thomas Jonter

ABSTRACT

The latest global data on the states' ongoing nuclear power reactors under construction and future plans demonstrates that the Fukushima accident has had little, if any, negative effect on the development of the nuclear power globally. Asia was in 2011, and still is today, the main growth area for nuclear expansion. Is the present global nuclear non-proliferation system or the so-called NPT regime consisting of the Treaty on the Non-proliferation of Nuclear Weapons, its appurtenant export control regimes and the IAEA (International Atomic Energy Agency) strong enough to handle the enormous work and responsibility involved in making possible a significant expansion of nuclear power? The purpose of this paper is to analyse the nuclear renaissance in Asia, its potential and security risks, against the backdrop of the experiences gained in the European Union to develop an effective and integrated nuclear non-proliferation and nuclear security system.

Keywords: East and South Asia, European Union, nuclear nonproliferation, nuclear security, regional governance.

Introduction

In 2011, shortly after the Fukushima accident, many international observers believed that nuclear power would not have any future at all. The German government announced a three-month shutdown of seven of its 17 nuclear power plants and commissioned a review of its nuclear strategy. As a result of this review process, the German Bundestag decided to phase out nuclear power by 2022. Many believed that several other states would follow the German example.[1] However, a quick look at the latest global data on the states´ ongoing and future nuclear power plans shows that these predictions were inaccurate. In the year 2015, there were about 437 nuclear power reactors in the world and 60 new ones under construction.[2] In addition, more than 100 new reactors have been planned to be built all over the world and many of these states have little or no experience in the nuclear field.[3]

It seems that the states do not currently see the other viable alternatives to meet the growing demand for energy. The World Nuclear Industry Report, for example, estimates that the global population growth combined with the industrial development will lead to a 45 per cent increase of electricity consumption by 2035.[4] Another reason for the renewed interest and increase in nuclear energy is the acceleration of climate change, which has resulted in the countries trying to reduce dependence on fossil fuels to mitigate the greenhouse gas emissions. Europe and Asia are by no means exceptions to this global trend; quite the opposite. Within the European Union, there are currently 131 reactors in operation in 14 of the 27 EU member states, and several new nuclear power plants are under construction or planned.[5] In Asia today, there are 119 nuclear reactors in operation, 49 under construction, about 100 more planned and proposals for many more have been put forward, according to the World Nuclear Association. In fact, the building of nuclear power reactors is a key energy strategy component for many Asian countries. The largest increase in the nuclear activity is in China, South Korea and India.[6] This makes Asia the most expansive nuclear power region in the world.

One consequence of the expanding nuclear power is a corresponding increase in trade and movement of fissile fuels via land, air and sea, between the states and within national borders. The task of the global non-proliferation system is to control and ensure that nuclear material is not used for nuclear weapons manufacture (the nuclear proliferation dimension). Furthermore, the growing numbers of nuclear energy facilities and the storage of uranium, plutonium and other fissile material across the world require measures to prevent these materials falling into terrorist hands or theft (the nuclear security dimension).[7] The Nuclear Security Summits in Washington, D.C. 2010, in South Korea in 2012 and in The Hague in 2014 have demonstrated that the international community perceives the nuclear terror threat as a growing concern. These summits also recognised that nuclear terrorism could significantly damage the political, security and economic interests of all the countries, regardless of the specific target and location.[8]

Is the present global nuclear non-proliferation system, the so-called NPT regime, consisting of the Treaty on the Non-proliferation of Nuclear Weapons (NPT) and its appurtenant export control regimes and the IAEA, strong enough to handle the enormous work and responsibility involved in ensuring a safe and secure nuclear power development? Today the NPT regime is being questioned by many. Some critics even claim that it has or is in the process of losing its preventive force. They assert that the NPT regime has failed to prevent North Korea from conducting nuclear weapons tests or Iran from pursuing nuclear weapons capability and may lead to a proliferation spiral.[9] The purpose of this paper is to discuss the nuclear renaissance in East and South Asia and its potential safety and the security risks against the backdrop of the experiences and hindsight of the European Union (EU) experience in developing a functioning and effective nuclear non-proliferation and nuclear security system. The central argument in this paper is that in order to allow an expanded role for nuclear power, a new system of global non-proliferation is needed. A central component in such a new system would be a greater role and responsibility for the regional bodies. A division of responsibility between the IAEA and other regional bodies will have to be instituted, since the IAEA cannot handle this task on its own. A new approach is needed, one that is capable of going beyond the complex legal and regulatory arrangements based on international regimes to create a more effective and flexible system. In this proposed flexible system, a reformed NPT regime will form the core. Regional bodies must assume greater responsibility to ensure that effective measures are taken to prevent the spread of nuclear material. The EU with its European Atomic Energy Community (EURATOM) can in many respects serve as a model for how such regionally based systems can be developed and can work effectively. EURATOM has in many respects played an important role as a building block in the European integration process and today a coherent non-proliferation system with common strategies and regulations are binding the member states´ nuclear activities together. It is, of course, not realistic to believe that regional bodies in Asia could play the same role as the EURATOM has done and still does for the economic and political integration in Europe. Asia is a huge continent with different regions with their own geographical and historical traditions making an overarching, single, functioning, regional body controlling the nuclear development and its proliferation and security issues a utopian and naïve goal. However, it is worth mentioning that many small steps have already been taken in some Asian regions to create nuclear energy communities that could be considered as important building blocks in a process to stimulate a broad regionally based cooperation in Asia. In order to move forward, the regionalisation process has to be strengthened. This paper presents a couple of ideas on how this process can be promoted.

The European Union

Currently, almost 30 per cent of the electricity consumed in the EU comes from nuclear power.[10] Eleven EU member states are among the fifteen countries in the world with the highest share of nuclear energy in their total national electricity generation, making the EU the most nuclear power-dependent region in the world. Furthermore, the EU is now planning an energy policy that will determine its strategy until 2050, and according to these plans nuclear power will account for 20 per cent of the electricity production by then. Needless to say, many things can happen that could change the outcome. On the other hand, since the EU has decided to secure energy needs and simultaneously cut down the greenhouse gases, many member states seem to be reconciled to the fact that they have to be dependent on nuclear power for an unforeseeable future.[11]

From a nuclear non-proliferation point of view, the situation in the EU is satisfactory. The EURATOM Treaty has, for example, a supranational power that includes the ownership of nuclear material and the power to carry out sanctions on EU states that violate the safeguard rules and norms. After many years of fruitful collaboration between the EURATOM and the IAEA, the two organisations are carrying out inspections in cooperation with national authorities to avoid duplication of work tasks.[12] In 2003, an overarching common EU non-proliferation strategy was adopted which in many respects has strengthened the structures to prevent the spread of illegal nuclear-related technology within the EU.[13] A nuclear non-proliferation community involving governmental bodies, supranational entities and non-government organisations has emerged over the years, to create an effective system. Regulatory authorities within EU, companies, universities and research institutes collaborate in a number of organisations and networks in the nuclear energy field to solve common problems.

It is, however, important to understand that this nuclear community is a product of 60 years of efforts to integrate Europe against the backdrop of the challenges from the Second World War, the political tensions during the Cold War and the breakdown of the Soviet Union. The Treaties of Rome and the creation of EURATOM in 1957 became two of the key factors in a strategy to integrate Europe and create a common market with one-energy system. The first step in this process of integration was taken in 1952 when the European Coal and Steel Community was founded with the goal to bind the arch-enemies France and Germany together with Belgium, Luxemburg, Netherlands and Italy in a peaceful cooperation that would ensure lasting peace and economic prosperity.[14] EURATOM established the grounds for the development of nuclear power and at the same time guaranteed that a system of surveillance and control of nuclear material and technology would be established. Through a number of vital objectives such as promoting research, establishing uniform safety standards and ensuring regular and equitable supply of nuclear material to all users, EURATOM guaranteed that the nuclear material would not be diverted.

Since the signing of EURATOM Treaty, a road to a well-functioning nuclear community has been paved by overcoming many challenges and obstacles. During the first period, between 1958 and 1968, the main task was to launch the EURATOM Treaty, a work that met severe resistance from the member states. In the period 1969–79, EURATOM supported ambitious programmes to build nuclear reactors, and between 1980 and 1990 much of the work was focused on how to design and develop safer and secure systems following the nuclear accidents at the Three Mile Islands (1979) and Chernobyl (1986). Following the demise of the Soviet Union in 1991, the tasks have in many respects been oriented towards assisting the newly established states in Eastern Europe to develop new nuclear infrastructures and to make the enlargement of EU possible, with the goal to open up an internal market of electricity within the EU and also to tackle the environmental problems due to climate change.[15] As a result, no one today would seriously believe that a nuclear renaissance within the EU would increase the risk of spreading nuclear weapons.

This success story does not mean that there are no problems in the EU in the nuclear area. Europe as a hub of global nuclear commerce would have a great deal to lose from nuclear terrorism directly or indirectly. Indeed, the EU has long recognised this vulnerability, dating back to the Ghent European Council meeting of October 2001 following the terrorist attacks on the United States. In December 2002, the EU adopted the 'Programme to improve cooperation in the European Union for preventing and limiting the consequences of chemical, biological, radiological or nuclear (CBRN) terrorist threats'. Later, EU initiatives have taken the agenda forward, such as the European Commission's 2009 CBRN Action Plan, which focuses on the core competencies of prevention, detection, preparedness and response.[16] Through joint actions by its Council and through contributions from its member states, the EU is one of the main contributors to the IAEA's Nuclear Security Fund (NSF). Established in 2002, the NSF is designed to support the implementation of nuclear security activities to prevent, detect, and respond to nuclear terrorism.[17] The European Commission (EC) and several member states have also made substantial contributions to the nuclear security work in Russia and in other former Soviet Republics through the G8 Global Partnership threat reduction initiative.[18] Preparing recovery strategies in the event of a nuclear terror attack is also a key part of the challenge confronting the policymakers. Central to this task will be determining the extent to which the European infrastructure and society can be made resilient, where resilience is defined as the 'capacity to absorb disturbance and reorganize while undergoing change so as to still retain essentially the same function, structure, identity and feedbacks'.[19]

How to Create a Nuclear Community in East and South Asia

The following figures and data show clearly that nuclear power is considered as an important present and future energy source in the states' energy strategies in East and South Asia.

- Mainland China has 26 reactors in operation, 24 new reactors that are under construction and many more that are planned.[20]
- India has 21 reactors running and six under construction with plans to build 20 to 30 new reactors by 2020 as part of its national energy policy. India is trying to develop the necessary technology to allow the country's abundant thorium reserves to be used in the civilian nuclear power reactors.[21]
- South Korea's 24 reactors produce one third of the state's electricity, and under its strategy to increase the capacity of nuclear power by 59% by 2022, it has plans to construct additional new reactors. Moreover, South Korea plans to be a major exporter of nuclear technology. For example, recently South Korea won a contract to supply the United Arab Emirates with four reactors.[22]
- Taiwan has six reactors in operation. After the Chernobyl accident, the future of nuclear power was questioned in Taiwan as in many

states.[23] Given what happened at Fukushima many voices within the country now demand the abolishment of nuclear power or a review of its future role in Taiwan. On the other hand, Taiwan, as is the case with Japan, does not have alternatives if the goal is to be less dependent on coal, gas and oil.

- Vietnam has signed agreements with Japan and Russia to build nuclear power reactors. If these plans materialise exactly as they exist on paper, Vietnam will have 14 reactors running by 2030.[24]
- The future of nuclear power in Japan is unsure. However, it is difficult to imagine an energy profile without any role for nuclear power, given that the country has few natural resources of its own and imports 84 per cent of its energy.[25] Until recently Japan had ambitious plans to build 15 new rectors to meet its estimated future energy needs and to reduce its dependence on imported energy and to decrease CO_2 emissions. The present Prime Minister, Shinzo Abe, is also pushing hard to restart the dormant nuclear plants and to keep nuclear power as an essential part of the future Japanese energy system. For example, in the country´s new energy plan, nuclear power is described as an important "baseload" electricity source which is to produce electricity at a constant rate at a lower cost than alternatives like solar and wind power.[26]

Since the end of the Cold War, globalisation has generated a larger process of global structural change, one in which regional cooperation and regionalism play a more important role than in the past. In several parts of the world, regional bodies have taken over functions that were the the responsibility of international and national institutions during the Cold War. This transformation process has been the most extensive in the EU area. It is true that Asia is not Europe, and it would be naïve to uncritically replicate an EU model of nuclear community for a number of reasons. First, the actual risks of proliferation of nuclear weapons are much higher in Asia compared with Europe, where this problem hardly exists. The nuclear weapons states of India and Pakistan, which are not parties to the NPT, have been in conflict with each other for many years, and nobody can guarantee that nuclear weapons will not be used in a future war if conflicts between the two governments cannot be settled. When North Korea withdrew from the NPT in 2003 and carried out nuclear weapons tests in 2006, 2009 and 2013, thereby becoming the ninth nuclear weapons state, many international security experts feared a chain-reaction of proliferation among the neighbouring states. Japan and China have their border disputes that, according to some security analysts, might trigger a nuclear weapons programme in Japan. Second, many states in Asia have serious domestic problems with ethnic, political and religious conflicts. For example, Pakistan is considered to be one of the most dangerous places on earth due to the fragile political situation combined with a weak regime that possesses nuclear weapons and is not able to cope with the religious and political problems that the state is facing.[27] Indeed, the tensions are ongoing and the potential conflicts in Asia are manifold.

On the other hand, when Europe started its long march towards an integrated Europe with the goal to develop a common nuclear energy market, the continent had experienced the worst war in history. In fact, major parts of Europe lay in ruins when the first ideas about integrating Europe were being discussed. The Association of Southeast Asian Nations (ASEAN) was founded in 1967 to promote economic and political cooperation, and a comparison with Europe shows that the institutionalism of political cooperation (or regionalism) has been much slower in Asia. The process to promote regional collaboration in Asia did not take off until the late 1990s when China, Japan and South Korea started to organise regular meetings with the goal to stimulate economic collaboration within ASEAN. The end of the Cold War and the new geopolitical situation opened doors for such a regional cooperation. In that respect, one can compare this to the early integration process in Europe, where the driving force for the process came from outside Europe, namely the foreign policy of United States in the immediate post-Second World War period and the Cold War dynamics.[28]

If, however, the causes for a greater role for regionalism are the first and foremost to be found in the changes in the international system after the Cold War, it does not mean that ideas and political actions have no impact whatsoever. The structural and geopolitical preconditions can be viewed as the outer limits for how far cooperation within a region can reach. Björn Hettne and Fredrik Söderbaum distinguish between the de jure forms of cooperation, which are characterised by formal political undertakings, and a de facto regional process, in which the forms are based on informal collaboration without expressed political agendas.[29] The EU cooperation is based on the de jure forms, which means that the decisions made are legally binding, and over the years this collaboration has developed a sense of regional identity, which is not the case in Asia. The EU is a grand demonstration that a regional identity transformation is possible, but it is important to stress that shortly after the Second World War such a development seemed most unlikely. How can East and South

Asia move from the de facto forms of regional cooperation to a situation where more integration of a formal character takes place?

Is it really realistic to expect more of integration in Asia given the troubles and conflicts the huge continent faces? Yes, there are good reasons to believe that now is the time to take a step further, but the areas chosen for potential progress in cooperation are crucial. In Europe, the vision to create a common energy market and use nuclear energy as the vehicle became a starting point for a successful integration process. Given that Asia´s energy demand will increase dramatically in the future, and that response to such a development needs to be coordinated among several states in order to be successful, the energy sector evidently constitutes a potential strategic area of integration.[30]

In fact, some initiatives have already been taken in the different regions of Asia over the last ten years. ASEAN has promoted collaboration, and other organisations and network communities have been created to push for extended nuclear collaboration. Worth mentioning are the Forum for Nuclear Cooperation in Asia (FNCA), Asia Pacific Regional Cooperative Agreement (RCA), Asia Nuclear Safety Network and Asia Pacific Safeguards Networks (APSN). However, positive results have been hampered due to a rather poor interest and short-sightedness by the governments.[31]

Furthermore, the prospects for an extended collaboration among the Asian states have increased after the Fukushima accident, which highlighted the need for stronger international cooperation. The Fukushima safety issue, which occurred in the highly technologically advanced and well-organised Japan, clearly demonstrates that nuclear power development cannot be treated as only a national affair. Nuclear accidents have regional and even international impacts, and states have to cooperate to prevent them from happening or mitigate their effects. How can a successful regional collaboration for safety and security be designed and what is needed to put such a framework in place?

A new regional collaborative framework has to be instituted with the capacity to meet the nuclear non-proliferation and nuclear security challenges that will arise when nuclear power acquires a dominant role in Asia. If we start with the non-proliferation aspect, a new approach has to be introduced to tackle the problem from an angle that facilitates and promotes a greater role for regional cooperation to replace the nation-centred policies.[32] This strategy will need to focus on the individual nations' abilities to develop nuclear non-proliferation structures and subscribe to the international treaties and control regimes. A starting point in this direction is nuclear power development based on cooperation among states to promote *multilateral arrangements* regulating the development and/or ownership of technology and fissile materials. The main idea behind this type of an arrangement is to either set up a globally-controlled common nuclear materials bank, or to promote cooperation among states to prevent any one actor from achieving exclusive control. The concept of a common bank could not be realised during the Cold War because of the absence of the necessary political and historical preconditions.[33] One can ask whether the preconditions are better today. It could be argued that the conditions ought to be more favourable in today's world, when the demand for energy intensifies by the day and states need to be more willing to consider pooling their nuclear sovereignty to ensure a greater control and access to the much needed energy supply. In the event that this idea of creating a common bank cannot be realised, however, there is the somewhat less stringent option of a *multilateral arrangement* where several states sign up to a joint-use arrangement for obtaining nuclear energy from a common nuclear energy system. It may be a question of three or four states jointly owning a reactor and/or an enrichment facility. Since several nations would be cooperating in this way there would be less risk of diversion, because the different parties will monitor each other and have a collective interest in not breaching the NPT regulations. There has been a trend in the recent years for discussions on such arrangements. For example, Poland and the Baltic countries are currently planning a common nuclear energy system. The fact that all four states are members of the European Union would facilitate such a solution, since they would be in a position to receive assistance from EURATOM. This example shows the value of having a network of multilateral institutions with an overlapping membership.

Another way to mitigate the proliferation risks would be obtain nuclear power without owning any nuclear facilities. From a non-proliferation perspective, it is more feasible to have an arrangement where a regional or international organisation assumes the responsibility for nuclear energy production, while a state merely buys the energy. Alternatively, another state under international control and enjoying widespread respect for its non-proliferation commitment might produce and supply the energy. In these two scenarios, the energy importing state, is not a potential nuclear weapons proliferator because it neither owns nuclear facilities nor has the need to possess nuclear materials. In this context, Turkey is an interesting example. Russia is planning to build, own and run a nuclear power plant in Turkey.[34] Turkey has no nuclear infrastructure of its own, and to construct an entire nuclear power system from scratch at the cost of enormous resources in the form of capital and technical development does not make sense. It can be argued that many states do not consider this approach as especially attractive today, given the recent Russian occupation of Crimea and Russia's use of its energy supply as an economic weapon to exert political influence. However, there are other potential states in Asia that can play a similar role as Russia does in Turkey. What if China and South Korea took the same initiative with states in Asia as Russia is doing in relation to Turkey, for example?

A second approach lately discussed by experts consists of investing in new proliferation-resistant nuclear fuel and technologies. The technology that exists today has been developed within the framework of a military paradigm, since nuclear power was originally used for military purposes. It was not until the 1960s that nuclear power came to be used for civilian power production. Nuclear technology is said to be "dual-use"—in other words, equipment, facilities and fissile fuel may be used both for civil and military purposes. Some experts are of the opinion that it might be possible to develop nuclear power systems where each step in the process of nuclear power production would be specifically designed to reduce or eliminate the proliferation risks. However, it is important to stress that even if this new technology was developed on a large scale, and was adopted, it would not suffice to make the nuclear facilities absolutely proliferation-proof.[35]

Besides the proliferation risks, the growing threat of terrorism, theft, and sabotage owing to the expanded role of nuclear power is an issue that has to be taken seriously. When more states opt for new or renewed nuclear power programmes in Asia, one of the main challenges over the coming decade will be to ensure that new nuclear facilities are integrated into the robust plans for nuclear security from inception, and not just safety and safeguards against state-level proliferation. The Asian states, however, are characterised by different security traditions, threat perceptions and views on how to deal with nuclear and other forms of terrorism. This creates a challenge in terms of the prioritisation of threats as well as the strategies for their mitigation. Preparing recovery strategies in the event of a nuclear terror event is also a key part of the challenge confronting policymakers. A first goal would therefore be to determine to what extent the Asian states' infrastructure and societies can be made resilient.[36] To date, resilience in the context of nuclear security is a relatively unexplored field, which the Fukushima accident has demonstrated. The states in East and South Asia have to collaborate to coordinate collective efforts to design a more resilient nuclear security system.

A second goal would be to ensure that all the states comply with international agreements. For example, not all Asian states have implemented the UN Resolution 1540 which is legally binding on all UN members and notes that all member states have to provide "appropriate effective" nuclear security for all nuclear material and related technology, and to "to establish domestic controls to prevent the proliferation of nuclear, chemical and biological weapons. The Resolution also encourages enhanced international cooperation on such efforts, in accord with and promoting universal adherence to existing international non-proliferation treaties."[37] If the words "appropriateeffective" meananything, as Matthew Bunnargues in an article, "they ought to mean that security measures must be put in place that can effectively defeat the threats that terrorists and criminals in that country have shown they can pose."[38] The third goal would be to make sure that the states in East and South Asia meet world standards in the management of nuclear technology even if the international obligations do not require that. The Convention on the Physical Protection of Nuclear Material and Nuclear Facilities and other efforts to strengthen the nuclear security by the IAEA has many weaknesses. For example, the Convention on the Physical Protection of Nuclear Material and Nuclear Facilities is very generally formulated and leaves much room for the states to interpret how the physical protection should be designed, which most likely may result in insufficient systems.[39] A regional collaboration such as the EURATOM system could serve as a model along which such a standardisation system could be designed. Finally, in order to achieve the above-mentioned goals to create an Asian nuclear community, one important and decisive factor has to be added: regional collaboration has to be based on a real decision-making authority that makes the cooperation formally binding. In this context, the nuclear industry in the region has to be more extensively involved in these efforts.[40] The more the collaboration among the Asian companies dealing with nuclear-related production and services that could be stimulated, the greater the possibilities that such a development would lead to more regional interdependence: for example, joint investments in the building of reactors and in the sharing of powergrids, etc. Such a positive development might lead to a situation where the political leaderships in the different Asian states are more or less forced to enter into a cooperation which is formally binding. Only the future, however, can tell whether there is a willingness among the East and South Asian states to move in such a direction.

NOTES AND REFERENCES

1. Caroline Jorant (July 2011), "The Implications of Fukushima: The European Perspective", *Bulletin of the Atomic Scientists* 67 (4); Mycle Schneider (9 September

2011). ""Fukushima Crisis: Can Japan be at the Forefront of an Authentic Paradigm Shift?", *Bulletin of the Atomic Scientists.*

2. http://www.world-nuclear.org/info/current-and-future-generation/plans-for-new-reactors-worldwide/ (updated May 2015).
3. International Status and Prospects for Nuclear Power 2012, 5 August, 2012, IAEA, http://www.iaea.org/About/Policy/GC/GC56/GC56InfDocuments/English/gc56inf-6_en.pdf.
4. http://www.worldnuclearreport.org/Who-we-are.html, 8 June, 2015.
5. World Nuclear Association, October 2014, http://www.world-nuclear.org/info/Country-Profiles/Others/European-Union/, 22 May, 2015.
6. World Nuclear Association, http://www.world-nuclear.org/info/Country-Profiles/Others/Asia-s-Nuclear-Energy-Growth/, October 2013.
7. The related concept of 'nuclear security' encompasses any activity or system that contributes to the protection of nuclear (highly enriched uranium and plutonium) and high hazard radioactive materials and associated expertise from unauthorised access, theft, diversion or sabotage by terrorists or other non-state actors, including inter alia the guarding, physical protection, facility design, personnel vetting, information technology security, technical measures, among other things. It also incorporates any activity or system that can contribute to the detection of preparations for the perpetration of a nuclear terrorist event, and responding to and recovering from the after-effects of such an event if prevention fails.
8. "Nuclear Security Summit: Countering New Global Threats",http://www.america.gov/relations/nonproliferation.html; *Tariq* Rauf, "Looking beyond the 2014 Nuclear Security Summit 2014", SIPRI, March 2014, http://www.sipri.org/media/expert-comments/rauf_mar2014.
9. William Walker, *A Perpetual Menace: Nuclear Weapons and International Order* (Routledge, 2011); Joseph Pilat, "The End of the NPT regime?" http://www.chathamhouse.org/sites/default/files/public/International%20Affairs/2007/83_3469-482.pdf.
10. http://ec.europa.eu/energy/en/topics/nuclear-energy, 8 June, 2015.
11. Ian Anthony, "Exports of Dual-Use Chemicals to Syria: An Sssessment of European Union Export Controls", Non-proliferation Paper No. 35, Jan. 2014, 13 pp. http://www.sipri.org/research/disarmament/eu-consortium/publications/non-proliferation-paper-32.
12. Piotr Szymanski, "The EURATOM Regional Safeguards System", http://www.iaea.org/newscenter/focus/iaeanwfz/euratom211111.pdf
13. "EU Strategy Against Proliferation of Weapons of Mass Destruction", Council of the European Union, Brussels, 10 December 2003, <http://register.consilium.europa.eu/pdf/en/03/st15/st15708.en03.pdf>.
14. Gunnar Skogmar, "The United States and the Nuclear Dimension of European Integration", Basingstoke: Palgrave Macmillan, 2004.
15. *Euratom: 50 Years of Nuclear Energy serving Europe*, European communities, 2007.
16. "Communication from the Commission to the European Parliament and the Council on Strengthening Chemical, Biological, Radiological and Nuclear

Security in the European Union: An EU CBRN Action Plan", Brussels, 25 June 2009, COM(2009) 273 final, <http://ec.europa.eu/home-affairs/summary/docs/com_2009_0273_en.pdf>.

17. "Nuclear Security Fund", International Atomic Energy Agency, <http://www-ns.iaea.org/security/nsf.asp>.
18. Alan J. Heyes and Wyn Q. Bowen, "Silent Partnership: The G8's Nonproliferation Program", *The Bulletin of the Atomic Scientists*, 66/2 (March-April 2010), pp. 17-26; "G8 Global Partnership Against the Spread of Weapons and Materials of Mass Destruction", US Department of State, <http://www.state.gov/t/isn/c12743.htm>.
19. Brian Walker, C. S. Holling, Stephen R. Carpenter and Ann Kinzig, "Resilience, Adaptability and Transformability in Social-Ecological Systems", *Ecology and Society*, 9/2 (2004).
20. http://www.world-nuclear.org/info/current-and-future-generation/plans-for-new-reactors-worldwide/
21. Ibid.
22. "Nuclear Power in South Korea", http://www.world-nuclear.org/info/Country-Profiles/Countries-O-S/South-Korea/ (updated May 2015).
23. http://www.world-nuclear.org/info/Country-Profiles/Others/Nuclear-Power-in-Taiwan/ (Updated May 2015).
24. "Nuclear Power in Vietnam", http://www.world-nuclear.org/info/Country-Profiles/Countries-T-Z/Vietnam/ (updated May 2015).
25. "Nuclear Power in Japan", http://www.world-nuclear.org/infoCountry/-Profiles/Countries-G-N/Japan/ (Updated May 2015).
26. "Reversing Course, Japan Makes Push to Restart Dormant Nuclear Plants", *New York Times*, A6, February 26, 2014.
27. Ramesh Thakur, "The Global Governance Architecture of Nuclear Security", The Stanley Foundation Policy Analysis Brief, March 2013.
28. Mark Breson, "Re-thinking Regionalism: Europe and East Asia in Comparative Historical Perspective", Paper presented at the Oceanic Conference on International Studies, Canberra, July 14-16, 2004.
29. Björn Hettne and Fredrik Söderbaum, "Theorizing the Rise of Regionness" in *New Political Economy*, Vol. 5, No. 3 (December), pp. 457-473.
30. For example, the International Energy Association (IEA) estimates that the electricity demand in the ASEAN region will increase 76% between 2007 and 2030; "Nuclear Renaissance in Asia", http://www.prlog.org/10941323-nuclear-renaissance-in-asia.html.
31. Asia Pacific Leadership Network for Nuclear Non-Proliferation and Disarmament. Discussion Paper: The Concept of an Asian-Pacific Nuclear Energy Community, 18 February 2013, http://a-pln.org/sites/default/files/apln-analysis-docs/APLNEnergyCommunityPaper18ii13.pdf.
32. Vitaly Fedchenko, "Appendix 13C: Multilateral Control of the Nuclear Fuel Cycle" in *SIPRI Yearbook 2006: Armaments, Disarmaments and International Security*, Oxford: Oxford University Press, 2006.
33. However, the 1956 IAEA Statute provides for the creation of an international

nuclear fuel bank that could guarantee the supply of fuel to those states that need it but don't want or are not able to produce the nuclear material themselves. See Fedchenko (2006): 691.

34. http://www.panarmenian.net/eng/world/news/69440/.
35. Fedchenko 2006.
36. Brian Walker, C.S. Holling, Stephen R. Carpenter, and Ann Kinzig, "Resilience, Adaptability and Transformability in Social-Ecological Systems", *Ecology and Society*, 9/2 (2004).
37. 1540 Committee, UN, http://www.un.org/sc/1540/.
38. Bunn, G. (2003), "The Nuclear Non-proliferation Treaty: History and Current Problems" in *Arms Control Today*, December <http://www.armscontrol.org/act/2003_12/Bunn.asp>. Bunn, M. (2005), "Incentives for Nuclear Security", Conference Paper at the Conference on Incentives for Nuclear Security, Belfer Center, Harvard University, 30 August, 2005, ", http://belfercenter.ksg.harvard.edu/files/inmm-incentives2-05.pdf.
39. Ibid.
40. Gretchen Hund and Amy Seward have argued that the industry can be more effective in preventing the spread of nuclear material and technology and can be a strong ingredient in the efforts to enhance the nuclear security aspects of the non-proliferation regime. Gretchen Hund and Amy Seward, "Broadening Industry Governance to include Nonproliferation", *Pacific Northwest Center for Global Security Publication*, 11 November 2008, http://cgs.pnnl.gov/pdfs/IndustryCorporateGovernance-Security_11-12-08Final.pdf.

PART IV

Tourism, Trade and Economic Cooperation

13

Tourism in Kazakhstan: Opportunities and Challenges

Malini Prava Sethi

ABSTRACT

Tourism is one of the largest and dynamically developing sectors of the international economic activities. Its high growth and development rates, large volumes of foreign currency inflows, infrastructure development, innovation of a new management and educational experience actively affect the various sectors of the economy, which positively contributes to the social and economic development of the country as a whole. The potentials of mountain tourism are especially useful where a large-scale basic industrialisation is not possible or where the ecology of the area is fragile. The purpose of the present paper is to study the relationship between tourism and development in Kazakhstan. The contribution of the tourism industry to the GDP in 2013 has been 5.3% in Kazakhstan (WTTC, 2014). Every region in Kazakhstan is a distinguished destination by itself and is unique in attracting tourists for its rich potential in sports and adventure tourism like rafting, trekking, mountaineering, hunting and fishing. Cultural tourism on the Silk Route i.e. travelling to places of pilgrimage and on traditional tourist routes of historical and architectural importance attracts tourists and encourages travellers. Kazakhstan is a land through which passed the famous Silk Route—the "Golden Road". It is one of the developed countries in terms of Attraction, Amenities and Accessibility facilities. Therefore, the development and formation of tourism in Kazakhstan as one of the most important economic and social policies requires the specific regulations of economic relations and measures of State support for the travel industry.

Keywords: Tourism, Kazakhstan, Attraction, Amenities, Accessibility, Silk Route, tourism potentials.

Introduction

Tourism is a significant activity which had existed long before it was actually identified. Evidence of the very early conscious travels has been documented by scholars (Robinson, 1976; Pearce, 1981). The tourism industry like any other industry contributes towards the economic uplift of a region. This industry is encouraged in certain region largely due to the fact that it brings economic prosperity and acts as an accelerator to economic growth and a source of employment generation—direct or indirect.

Kazakhstan lies to the north of the Central Asian Republics and is bounded by Russia in the north, China in the east, Kyrgyzstan and Uzbekistan in the south and the Caspian Sea and part of Turkmenistan in the west. It has almost 1,894 km of coastline on the Caspian Sea. The territory is mostly steppe land with hilly plains and plateaus. A population inflow due to mass deportation from Siberia and other Soviet regions had led to the formation of large labour camps where they were held under captivity. Kazakhstan has the potential for becoming one of central Asia's richest countries because of its huge mineral and oil resources and its liberalised economy, which encourages Western investment. The total population of Kazakhstan was 17,037,508 in 2013 (WDI, 2014).

The political and economic situation after the collapse of the Soviet Union was not stable and this influenced the tourism sector. Tourism became seen as a luxury—a commercial product—and social tourism declined. The tourist councils and bases of accommodation which had functioned during the former Soviet Union were abolished over time. The number of sanatoriums and rest houses dramatically decreased. The majorities of tourist buildings were privatised and changed their profile; others just closed because of a fall in demand. For comparison, only 30% of the tourist accommodations which had been used during the former Soviet Union were still in use in 2000 in the CIS countries. 70% of these required reconstruction, renovation or were destroyed (Voronkova, 2004). Tourism in Kazakhstan after the collapse of the former Soviet Union developed slowly. Before 2000, tourism was mainly outbound and the main tourists were traders. After 2000, the economic situation became more stable and the state started to pay more attention to social welfare issues; Kazakhstan is to be considered as one of the most stable countries with

Map 1: The Silk Road (eighth–fourteenth Centuries)

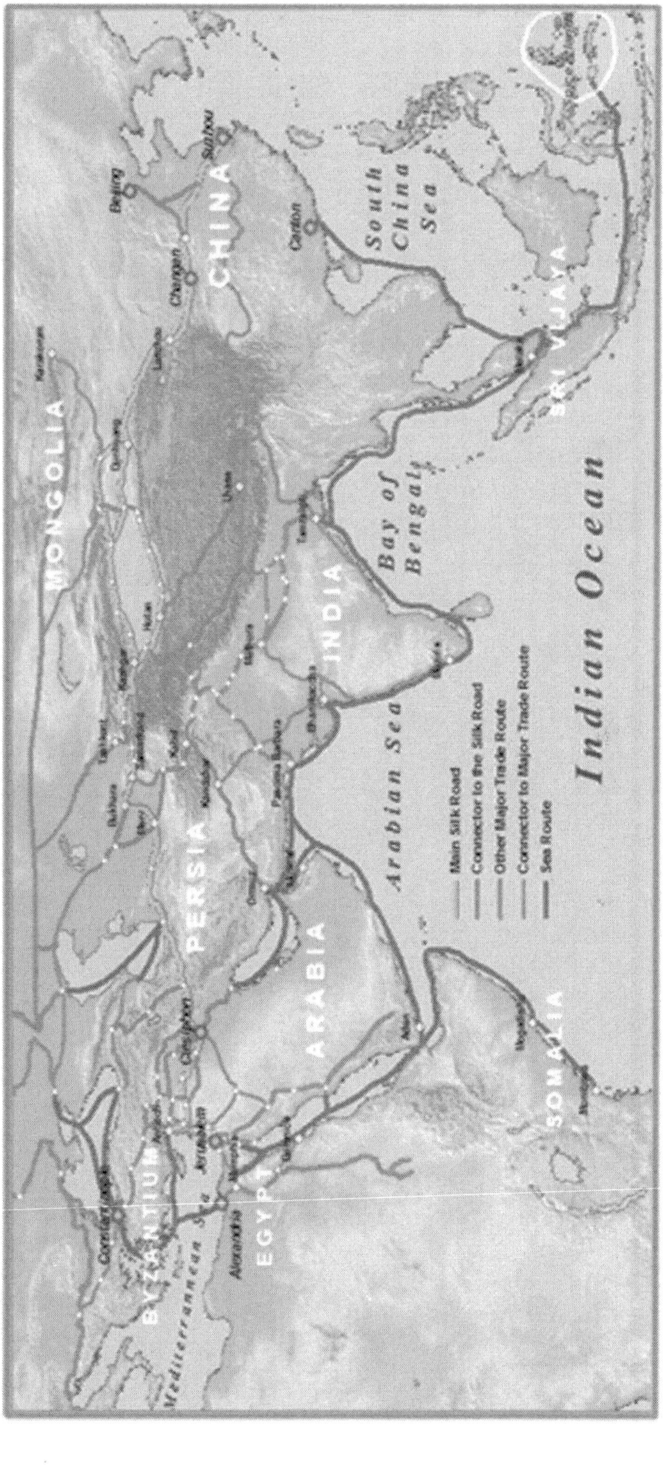

Source: Sethi, M.P. (2011): Unpublished MPhil dissertation entitled, "Impact of Tourism Sector on the Economy of Kazakhstan"

unique tourism opportunities. Besides, the same foreign experts believe that tourism will also be promoted by the characteristics of the republic in terms of the hospitality and goodwill of the Kazakhstani citizens, the natural sights of the country, its history and richness of a cultural and ethnic diversity and also in developing the tourist infrastructure (Birzhakov, 2008).

The Silk Route and Cultural Linkages

The historic Silk Road was the most important land route connecting Europe and Asia. Consisting of many different routes and stretching over a vast geography, the Silk Road was a unique path that not only became a source of prosperity and trade relationships but also promoted an exchange of knowledge and experience as well as cultural interaction among the different communities. Science, arts and literature as well as crafts and technologies were thus shared and spread to the societies along the lengths of these routes, and in this way, languages, religions and cultures developed and influenced each other. The history of these maritime routes can be traced back thousands of years, to links between the Arabian Peninsula, Mesopotamia and the Indus Valley civilisation. Map 1 shows the ancient land routes and maritime routes. The ancient Silk Road emerged as a natural outcome of the large and small-scale market conditions, supply and demand and the needs of people who lived along the Silk Road.

Maritime routes were an important part of the sea links between the East and the West and were used for the trade of spices; they were also known as the Spice Routes. In the middle ages, caravans comprising of horses or camels were the standard means of transporting goods across land along the Silk Roads from Turkey to China; they provided not only a regular opportunity for the merchants to eat well, rest and prepare themselves in safety for their onward journey but also to exchange goods, trade with the local markets and buy local products and to meet the other merchant travellers. In the nineteenth century, new types of travellers ventured onto the Silk Roads who were archaeologists, geographers and explorers looking for adventure. Coming from France, England, Germany, Russia and Japan, these researchers traversed the Taklamakan desert in western China or Xingjian, to explore the ancient sites along the Silk Roads, which led to many archaeological discoveries, numerous academic studies and a renewed interest in the history of these routes (UNSECO, 2012).

At present, for the many countries located on the ancient Silk Road, particularly the landlocked Central Asian countries, the historic Silk Road trade system appears to be the only alternative for their growth and development. Developing industries demand new markets; technological innovations facilitate international cooperation, better transportation and increased trade efficiency and growing energy demands, which require international cooperation. The New Silk Road projects are implemented along the foundation for regional cooperation, for creating political flexibility, improving economic growth, offering trade diversifications, for the mining and energy sectors and for investing in transportation. All of these represent a historically unprecedented chance for the Central Asian republics to become important players in the world economy. The Silk Road had gradually lost its value and importance in the modern period due to developments in maritime transportation and political circumstances in the region.

Tourism Potential

Given the situational conditions, Kazakhstan has made a significant progress in attracting tourists from far and wide and has established itself by a promoting its image as an attractive, tourism-friendly and "dynamic Eurasian destination". Kazakhstan's enormous potential for cultural and nature-based tourism has been accentuated especially due to its geographical attributes, its amazing history and its location on the Silk Road. In 2009, Kazakhstan hosted the 18th United Nation World Tourism Organization (UNWTO) General Assembly that showed an "active involvement and contribution of Kazakhstan to the international tourism community". In Kazakhstan, the forest steppe is quite different from the forest steppe in European Russia. The flora and fauna include 155 species of mammals, 480 species of birds, 150 species of fish and about 250 species of medicinal plants including the very rare Santonica that grows nowhere else but in the south of Kazakhstan. The country has an essential tourist infrastructure and a lot of sights for the progress of active, ecological, historical, cognitive, religious and many other types of tourism. The nodes of tourist interest include those which are important from the historical and pastoral view points and also which depend upon their connectivity and accessibility from the important urban centres. The main tourist inventory may also be cultural, traditional, scenic beauty, entertainment-oriented, etc. The tourism potentials have been studied under three major heads—namely, Attractions, Amenities and Accessibility.

The attractions of tourism are to a very large extent, of the nature of scenic beauty. The attractions of tourism are essentially about people and places (Robinson, 1976). Tourist attractions include site attractions, event attractions like Olympic Games and also religious festivals (Pearce, 1981). Many of the world's most accomplished mountaineers are from Kazakhstan. There are several base camps and expeditions to Khan-Tengri at 6,995 metres—the highest point in Kazakhstan. The following rivers run through Kazakhstan—the Irtysh, the Ural, the Chu and the Syr Darya. The Irtysh River is the longest river in Kazakhstan (1,700 km). It has more than 48,000 lakes—the largest one is the Caspian Sea (374,000 sq km) —the Aral Sea and Lake Balkhash. Today, in Kazakhstan there are 10 national natural reserves, 10 state natural parks, 3 state forest natural reserves, 3 state zoological parks and 5 botanical gardens. The total area of the especially protected territory is more than 22,114.5 thousand hectares which is about 8.1% of all the territory of Kazakhstan.

Most are located in areas with much interest to the tourist, such as sports, cultural, historical and archaeological sites and offer developed excursion facilities. Kazakhstan is a charming and energetic country with lots to offer to the visitors, including the ancient Kazakhstani historical monuments, the renaissance-beauty and fashion metropolis cities. In 2011, there were 515 objects of tourism in the territory of Kazakhstan including hotels (385), camps (7), health centre (36), pension (4), recreational zones (29), rest homes (27), tourist centres (24), sanitary camps (35), mountain skiing lodges (4), guest houses (13), hunting houses (9), youth centres (1), recreational complexes (7), museums (6), mausoleums (2), a state enterprise on tourism (1) and other clubs, craftsmen's cities (5) (Statistical Agency report, 2011).The tourists mainly visit about 8–10 separate good quality tourist destinations. These include the capital Astana, The Aral Sea on the border with Uzbekistan, the Caspian Sea and the Baikonour Cosmodrome. In the north are Aktobe, Kostanai, Pavlodar, Karaganda and Petropavlovsk on the Trans-Siberian railway. In the south are Lake Balkhash, Shymkent, Kyzylorda, Taraz, and the mountains of the Tien-Shan. Also in the south is the biggest tourist attraction of this country, the former capital Almaty, which is a city of more than one million people built within the mountains.

Map 2 shows the concentration of the major tourist attractions and other tourist potentials. A major concentration is found towards the eastern part of Kazakhstan and partly on the western part and the central part mainly amidst the cold desert region. Almaty also has a major tourism potential, a ski resort and the famous Medco ice skating rink located at 1,700 metres above sea level.

Many monuments of different cultures and nationalities and ancient civilisations were built on this land. In the territory of Kazakhstan, there

Map 2: Kazakhstan: Attractions

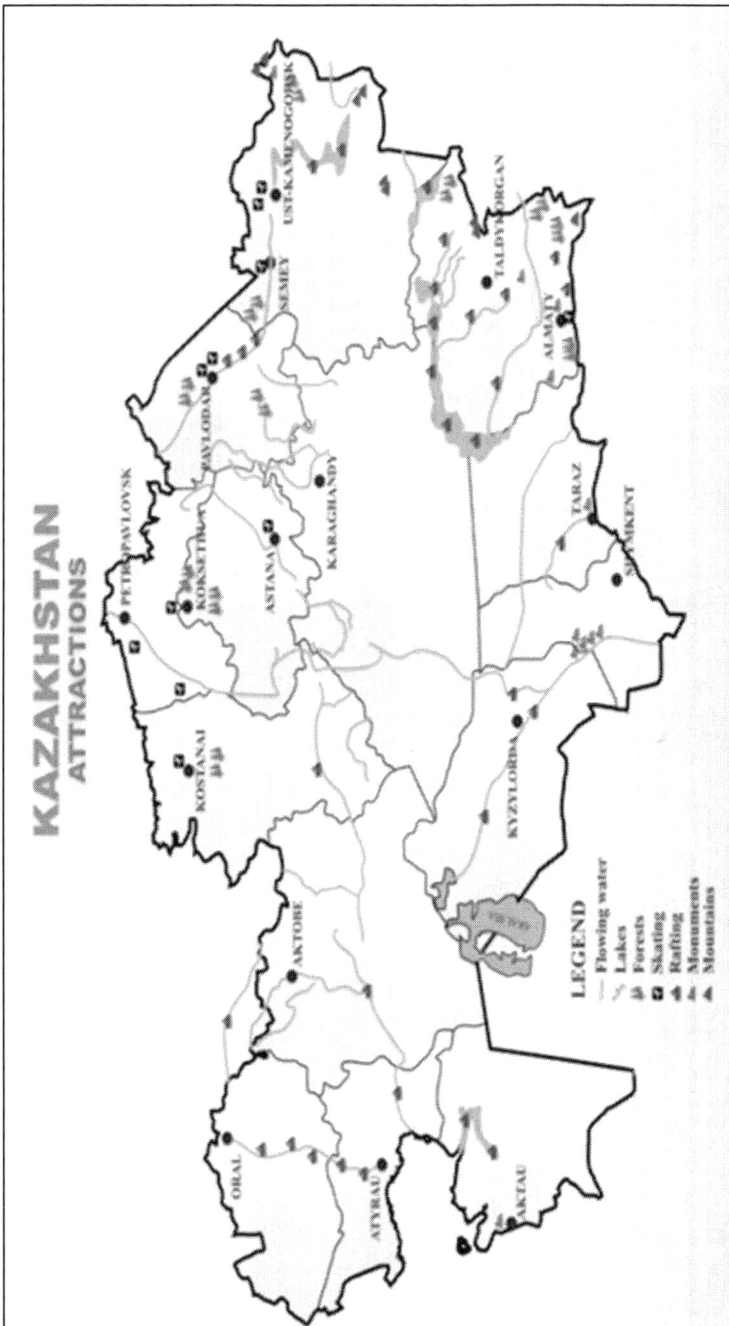

Source: Sethi, M.P. (2011): Unpublished MPhil Dissertation entitled, "Impact of Tourism Sector on the Economy of Kazakhstan".

exist 25,000 registered monuments. Among these archaeological evidences, there are real gems of ancient, medieval and oriental architectural art. Balandy II Mausoleum, fourth–second centuries BC, which is situated in the territory of the Kyzylorda region, is one of the first brick domes in the world. The Aisha Bibi Mausoleum in the Zhambyl region is another unique work of architecture that shows the high level of development of construction technology. The Khodzha Akhmet Yassaui Mausoleum, acknowledged by UNESCO as a monument of universal importance, is an active shrine and attracts a lot of pilgrims. On both sides of the road there are many hills that are the remains of the ancient settlements which were abundant in the Syr-Darya valley. Map 2 shows the major peaks in the south-western part of Kazakhstan. There are several small glaciers on the mountain. Popular climbs in the western Tien Shan include Kyzylbash (4,200 m), Druzhba (4,100 m) and Sairamskii (4,238 m). The forest area in Kazakhstan was 33,034 sq. km in 2011.

Map 2 shows the major forests in the northern border of the eco-region that stretches from the Ural Mountains along the southern end of the West Siberian Plain, and south of Novosibirsk it continues to the foothills of the Altai and Sayan Mountains. The rivers of Kazakhstan have always played an important role in the life and history of Kazakhstan. In fact, almost all main cities were founded on the banks of the major rivers. Nowadays the rivers, especially in the mountains, are attracting tourists for active holidays and recreation. The largest rivers in the country are the Irtysh, Yesil, Tobol, Ural, Syr Darya, Ili and Chu. Map 2 shows the major rivers and lakes in the country. The total length of the rivers is 2,212 km. The majority of the lakes located in the lowlands owe their origin to the erosion–accumulation activity of the rivers in an arid climate. The lowland lakes may be either saline or freshwater. There is a chain of big hollows of salt lakes in Kalibek, Ulkenkaroy, Teke and Seletyteniz in the north-eastern part of the region. In the Almaty region, the largest regional river is the Ili River, which flows almost through the centre of the region, dividing it in two parts, in the middle of which the large artificial Kapshagai reservoir has been built, which is a hydroelectric dam in Almaty.

Any tourist node essentially requires certain amenities and facilities for its successful development for the tourist industry. Kazakhstan is one of the most developed countries in terms of amenities and facilities. The Hotel of Kazakhstan is known as a landmark hotel in Almaty. The economy of Kazakhstan in general and the banking sector in particular, have been closely watched by foreign investors. Three local banks have successfully held IPOs in the London Stock Exchange—the largest by asset value is by the Kazkommerts Bank, the third largest by the Halyk Bank of Kazakhstan and the fourth largest by the Alliance Bank. The system of healthcare in Kazakhstan developed within the Soviet model, which was focused on patient care. Kazakhstan has 913 hospitals and 2752 outpatient circumstances. The state owns 777 public hospitals and 1,825 outpatient organisations (Ainur, Izekenova and Abikulova, 2013). Kazakhstani hospitals currently have a sufficient potential for rendering a range of highly technological services. The demand for accommodation away from one's home is met by a variety of facilities.

Accessibility and Connectivity

Accessibility is a very crucial factor as it is a means by which the tourists can reach the area where attractions are located. Kazakhstan is one of the most developed countries in terms of accessibility facilities. Roads are a key element of the Kazakhstani transport system, playing an important role in providing access to rural areas and in facilitating transit traffic and in-country transport movement. Most of the business in the country takes place in the west, where oil is found, or in the rural areas, where farming is done. The road from Almaty flows through the mountains of eastern Kazakhstan, a rural area which is believed to have a large economic potential with huge oil, gas and mineral reserves. To make it more accessible for business, the Kazakhstani government plans to spend about $19 billion on transport infrastructure in 2014, especially on the links from China to Europe that could help revive towns like Taraz. Map 3 shows the major road connections between the regions. Railway services play a significant role in the transport communication network. They provide up to 70% of cargo and 50% of passenger turnover in the overall transport operations in Kazakhstan. The rail transport is characterised by a high carrying capacity and a relatively low cost. The main rail links which connect Russia and the European countries with the Asia-Pacific, Central Asia and the Middle Eastern region cross Kazakhstan. Map 3 shows the major railway connections between all the regions. The borderline railway network is connected to the networks in Uzbekistan, Kyrgyzstan, Azerbaijan and China.

Kazakhstan can accommodate up to 300,000 tourists per year. There are major hotels in different cities like Almaty, Astana, Karaganda, Aktobe, Kostanai, Ust-Kamengorsk, Pavlodar, etc. There are about 372 hotels of different categories with a capacity of 32,000 rooms. The highest guestroom stock is registered in the Atyrau (50%) and Mangistau (54.1%) regions, while the lowest one is noted in North Kazakhstan (13.5%) and Almaty (13.1%). The Government seeks to transform Kazakhstan into an attractive tourism destination. Business tourism contributes to the development of hotels. The largest number of world-standard accommodation is concentrated in the important tourism centres like the cities of Almaty and Astana. Many of those that visit Kazakhstan are business tourists, especially those who visit the country's largest cities such as Almaty, Astana and Atyrau and Karaganda.

Air transport connects all regions of the country. There is a high demand for using the country's airlines. Kazakhstani air transport corridors are potentially attractive for international air companies operating flights between Europe and South-East Asia, since they help to reduce flight time. There are 22 airports in Kazakhstan for air services including the Astana and Almaty international airports. Map 3 shows the major air connections.

After roads, rails and air, water transportation is the fourth most important element in Kazakhstan's transportation complex, with both state and private companies operating in this field. The Republic of Kazakhstan is one of the countries located around the Caspian Sea. It is located on the Mangyshlak peninsula on the eastern coast of the Caspian Sea. This port is in use throughout the year and is the only seaport of the country built to serve the international transportation of cargo and oil products in the directions of Iran, Baku, Astrakhan, and Europe via the Volga–Don channel and the Dunai system (Catherine, 2015).

Economic Impact

The economic impact of the tourism industry is usually assessed at the macroeconomic level and can be measured in several different ways. The most general measurement focuses on tourism receipts and the contribution of tourism to a country's GDP. The economic indicators of tourist sector show a positive trend in Kazakhstan; there are 1200 small and medium-sized businesses in the tourism sector in Kazakhstan. Each year, between 4 to 5 million inbound tourists visit the country (Tourism in Kazakhstan, 2012). As the tourist industry consists of a heterogeneous group of establishments, many sectors of the economy would be benefited by tourist spending (Archer, 1962). Apart from the benefits from construction, there appear to be few linkages to manufacturing and agriculture or to other sectors of the economy. The economic influence of tourism on the national economy is shown through indicators of the cash flows directed from the country and to the country, which are generated

Map 3: Kazakhstan: Accessibility

Source: Sethi, M.P. (2011): Unpublished MPhil Dissertation entitled, "Impact of Tourism Sector on the Economy of Kazakhstan"

by tourist export and import. The biggest part of the income from the export of tourist services comes from foreign tourists and also from the ticket sale for public travel agencies which serves tourists, 604,699 persons in transport and other services in the country of residence. The tourist import of the country is made by the money spent by the citizens during foreign trips, the payment of transportation costs and other services in the countries of residence and also the payment of dividends to the foreign investors in the tourism industry.

Contribution of Tourism to GDP and Employment

The overall income in the Kazakhstan GDP from the travel industry was KZT 1,748.0 bn in 2013 which was 5.3% of the GDP (WTTC, 2014). The total contribution of Travel & Tourism to employment was 424,000 jobs in 2013, which was 5.0% of the total employment (WTTC, 2014). It included the hotel staff, the employees of travel agencies, transportation companies, restaurants and entertainment companies, i.e. all the employees involved in the direct servicing of tourists. Employment has been an important element in Kazakhstan's development strategy. The Government has also played a direct role in generating employment and in ensuring the minimum qualitative safeguards for the workers. Employment directly in the government expanded with the state assuming the dominant role in providing not only administrative but also social and economic services; "Tourist promotion is the key operation to any regional, state or community development programme". There are many ways to bring money and business into a new given area. These are agricultural activity, industrial activity, transport and communication, accommodation and food service activities which can benefit further from tourism. The interest in the culture of Kazakhstan by foreign tourists has produced a slow but growing revival of handicrafts, with service and handicraft industries for tourism becoming the sources of income for local populations. The needs of the domestic tourist market have become the focus in the development of tourism.

Tourist Flow in Kazakhstan

The demand for world tourism is undergoing considerable quantitative and qualitative changes which are directly influencing the world tourism market. Several economic indicators are used to access the international tourism demand and its effect on the economy such as the number of tourist arrivals at a destination, receipts from foreign tourists, expenditures by tourists travelling abroad and the contribution made by tourism to a region's export earnings. Inbound and outbound tourism have an important impact on a country's financial health. Outbound tourism generates some money in the country of origin. However, outbound tourism takes financial resources out of the home country and gives them to the destination country. The largest volume of incoming tourism, with the prevailing business tourism, is observed in the cities of Astana, Almaty, Atyrau, Aktobe and Karaganda. Outbound tourism is more developed in the cities like Almaty and Karagandaand those in the north-western regions.

Table 1: Number of Foreign Tourists Arrival (Top 10 Countries)

Countries	*2009 (%)*	*2010 (%)*	*2011 (%)*
Russian Federation	14.05	23.07	28.38
France	5.60	6.43	12.78
Germany	14.24	10.88	12.53
China	6.93	13.90	9.12
Italy	6.60	8.00	8.17
India	3.79	6.89	8.06
USA	7.98	8.96	6.92
Great Britain	6.26	7.57	6.89
Turkey	11.48	10.80	5.45
Poland	4.21	3.52	1.67
Total	27,195	26,652	24,700

Data Source: Agency on Statistics of the Republic of Kazakhstan, 2012.

Table 1 shows the percentage of foreign tourist that arrived in Kazakhstan from 2009 to 2011. In 2009, both Germany and Russia were the highest in terms of foreign arrivals while in 2011 Russia and France dominated the scene. The total number of foreign tourist arrivals was accounted as 24,700 in 2011. The total number of tourist inflows to Kazakhstan has continuously been decreasing from 27,195 in 2009 to 24,700 in 2011, indicating a decrease of 2,495 tourists. Russia has always dominated in terms of tourist arrivals due to its past legacy. Germany and France have shown a considerable enhancement in terms of tourist arrivals over the years. Strangely, Turkey has shown a considerable decrease in terms of tourist arrivals in Kazakhstan.

Arrivals of tourists is also because of motivation which can be categorised as price motivation or climate motivation or personal intrest. Price is a major motivating factor in international tourism. Tourism is labour-intensive and salaries make up a large proportion of the product costs. It follows that tourists from the high-wage countries are attracted to the low tourism prices in low-wage countries. Price differential is an important factor in the motivation of the countries' destinations.

Fig. 1: Foreign Tourist Arrivals in Kazakhstan by the Top 6 Countries in 2011

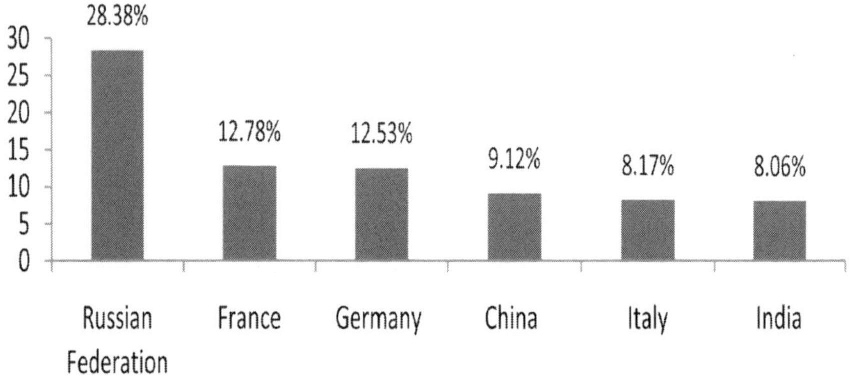

Data Source: Agency on Statistics of the Republic of Kazakhstan, 2012

Table 2: Depature of Domestic Tourists from Kazakhstan

Destinations	*2009 (%)*	*2010 (%)*	*2011 (%)*
Turkey	53.96	55.75	58.98
China	12.67	11.71	15.44
UAE	11.43	12.46	10.09
Thailand	6.35	6.93	5.31
Germany	5.64	3.81	3.20
Russia	4.83	4.69	3.33
France	0.95	0.96	0.67
Bulgaria	1.54	1.55	1.21
Azerbaijan	1.39	0.98	0.45
India	1.15	1.10	1.27
Total	1,66,342	2,17,106	3,45,265

Source: Agency on Statistics of the Republic of Kazakhstan, 2012.

Table 2 shows that the maximum number of domestic tourists from Kazakhstan go to Turkey. In 2011, Turkey registered the highest number of tourists from Kazakhstan (almost 59%); this was followed by China and the UAE. Most of the domestic tourists from Kazakhstan visit the destinations for therapeutic treatments and for visits to thermal resorts. Health trips for medical reasons are made either to receive medical care or for health improvement. Education tourism and the undergoing of training in study centres are also common. Majority of the foreign tourists visit Almaty, Astana, Karaganda, Taraz, Atyrau and Aktau. The objectives of tourists travelling to these regions are mostly for business and professional purposes, leisure, recreation and shopping (Imanbekova,2013)

Fig. 2: "Top Destination Countries from Kazakhstan, 2011"

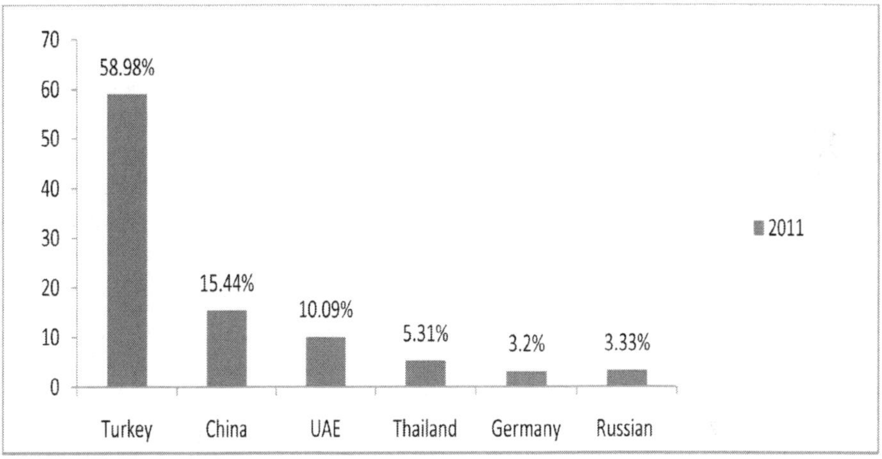

Data Source: Agency on Statistics of the Republic of Kazakhstan, 2012.

Conclusion and Recommendations

The country has a lot of potential attractions in that it has unique natural reserves and more than 9,000 archaeological and historical sites. Strategically, Kazakhstan has a huge potential to link the fast-growing markets of China and East Asia with Russia and Western Europe by road and rail, and through ports on the land-locked Caspian Sea. Kazakhstan is well connected with railways and airways today; there are 7 flights every week between Almaty and New Delhi and several more for the two countries through West Asia and Turkey, etc. The major focus areas in Kazakhstan are Almaty, Astana, Karaganda, Taraz, Atyrau and Aktau. The overall income in the Kazakhstani GDP from the travel industry was KZT 1,748.0 bn in 2013 (5.3%) and the total contribution of Tourism to employment was 424,000 jobs in 2013, which was 5% of total employment. The biggest part of the income from the export of tourist services comes from foreign tourists.

The reason for non-development of the tourist industry is that the states have no personal interest for development. There is no Ministry of Tourism in Kazakhstan; all have region-wise departments of tourism. The problem is that in fact, the places of natural beauty are too much in east Kazakhstan while other places are desert, especially in the central part, which are not very attractive to tourists. On the other hand, mountain tourism and sports tourism is quite developed in this area. Unfortunately, in the areas bordering China, Kyrgyzstan, Uzbekistan and Russia again, there is a strict regime of tourists to enter some places. Here, in Kazakhstan, 2500 thousand tourist spots have been registered as historical and traditional sites but only 200 are to ready to accept tourists. Also, the problem is that in Kazakhstan there is a lack of scientific base and technology to know the scientific development in being first to know how to build and then how to restore. Since 2004, a governmental programme of cultural heritage was started; this programme is intended for the development of students. When the students have finished their course in tourism the government gives training to them to become tourist guides. The foreigners investing in the hydrocarbon industry are not interested in investing in the tourist sector. There are three local NGOs which are involved in some of the tourist activities; they pay the local and rural communities to preserve some sites in the local territory, mostly in the rural areas.

The following recommendations need to be considered in order to strengthen the potential of tourism in Kazakhstan. It draws attention to the northern part of the Silk Road which passes through the southern and western Kazakhstani cities of Turkestan, Sauran and Otyrar that had been the centres of trade, as a new destination for tourists. To create more employment opportunities for the overgrowing unemployed people in the country, there is a need to attract more tourists from abroad and at the same time allow benefits to reach the grassroots. It is important to preserve and enrich the rich cultural heritage of the country, to promote and protect the interests of the people in Kazakhstan by giving various incentives and by encouraging the handicraft sector in the village areas. Social, institutional and medical tourism need to be developed and strengthened so as to improve the tourism access. The number of tourists visiting the western and central regions of Kazakhstan need to be promoted, as their number is much less than those visiting the other regions in Kazakhstan.

NOTES AND REFERENCES

1. Ainur B., Izekenova, A. and Abikulova. A (2013), "Inpatient Care in Kazakhstan: A Comparative Analysis", *Journal of Research in Medical Science*, 18(7); 2013 July.

2. Archer, B. H. (1962), *The Impact of Domestic Tourism*, Bangor: University of Wales Press.
3. Birzhakov, M.B. (2008), *Introduction into Tourism*, 9th Edition, revised and amended, Gerda Publishing House, Saint Petersburg, Russia.
4. Imanbekova, Bagdagul (2013), "Tourism in Kazakhstan: Status, Problems and Prospects", *E-Global*, April, 2013.
5. KITF 2008 Catalogue (2008), Almaty, Kazakhstan
6. Pearce, D.G. (1981), Tourist Development, Longman Inc., New York.
7. Putz Catherine (2015), "Crossroads Asia: Yes, Kazakhstan Has a Navy", *The Diplomat*, http://thediplomat.com/2015/04/yes-kazakhstan-has-a-navy/.
8. Robinson, H. (1976), *A Geography of Tourism*, Harlow, Longman, London.
9. Statistical Yearbook (2009, 2010, 2011, 2012): "Agency on Statistics of the Republic of Kazakhstan".
10. Tourism in Kazakhstan (2011), *National Statistical Data*, Ed. OmarovZh.I., Astana, Kazakhstan.
11. United Nations Educational, Scientific and Cultural Organization (2012): *Silk Road: Dialogue, Diversity and Development*.
12. Voronkova L.P. (2004): "History *of Tourism, National Economy in USSR in 1981*", Moscow Press.
13. World Development Indicators *(WDI)*, September 2014.
14. World Travel &Tourism Council (2014): *"Travel and Tourism Economic impact, Kazakhstan"*, 2014.

14

Trade and Economic Cooperation in South Asia in a Comparative Regional Perspective

Per Hilding

ABSTRACT

The "South Asian Association for Regional Cooperation" (SAARC) was established in 1985. Its basic objectives are to promote the welfare of the people of South Asia by accelerating economic growth and creating mutual trust among its eight member states. Today, 30 years after its inception, it is evident that neither in terms of trade creation nor in lessening the tensions between the members has it reached its objectives. While the European Union generates more than half and the ASEAN a quarter of the total trade in their respective regions, the SAARC generates barely 5 per cent of its total trade. Among the reasons put forward for the failure of intra-regional trade to take off in South Asia are the hostility and suspicion between its members—in particular, India and Pakistan—imbalance of power, tariff and non-tariff barriers, insufficient variation of the commodity composition of trade and the lack of infrastructure and connectivity within the region. By consulting some recent research and statistics, this paper discusses these and other factors that could explain the SAARC's inability to live up to its commitments. In order to put SAARC's performance into perspective, comparisons are made with both the EU and ASEAN and what lessons can possibly be learnt from them. It also deals with China as an extra-regional player, and how its growing presence in the region could be both a threat to the unity of the association and a catalyst of a much deeper integration in the region.

Keywords: Preferential trading, free trade area, regional integration, conflict management, SAARC, ASEAN, EU, China.

Introduction

With multilateral trade negotiations having come to a standstill, as in the Doha round, and with a slowing down of the US and European growth rates in the aftermath of the financial crisis, regional trade agreements as a means to increase trade has received an impetus in many parts of the world. This is the case also in South Asia and the regional organisation "South Asian Association for Regional Cooperation" (SAARC), which inspired by the experience of the EU, has set as one of its long term-goals, the establishment of an economic union.

It was set up in 1985 and consists of eight member states: Bangladesh, Bhutan, India, Maldives, Nepal, Pakistan and Sri Lanka (Afghanistan became a member in 2007). The countries differ widely in terms of land area, GDP and size of population though the living standards and poverty levels are fairly similar.[1] While India occupies 70% of the land area, the remaining seven countries except Afghanistan border only India and not each other. Even though the region is home to a fifths of the world's population indicating a large future market potential, the current low per capita incomes makes the economic size of the region small: 8.4% of the world in terms of the GNI PPP in 2014, and disregarding India, just 1.7%.[2]

SAARC's basic objectives are to promote the welfare of the people of South Asia by accelerating economic growth and creating mutual trust among the member states. Today, 30 years after its inception, it is evident that neither in terms of trade creation nor in lessening the tensions between the member states has it reached its objectives. While the European Union generates more than half and the ASEAN a quarter of the total trade in their respective regions, the SAARC generates barely 5% of its total trade.[3] Among the reasons put forward for the failure of intra-regional trade to take off in South Asia are the hostility and suspicion between its members—in particular India and Pakistan—imbalance of power, tariff and non-tariff barriers, insufficient variation of the commodity composition of trade, and the lack of infrastructure and connectivity within the region.

By consulting some recent research and statistics, this paper will discuss these and other factors that could explain SAARC's inability to live up to its expectations. In order to put SAARC's performance into perspective, comparisons will be made with both the EU and the ASEAN and what lessons could possibly be learnt from them. It also deals with China as an extra-regional player, and how its growing presence in the region could be both a threat to the unity of the association and a catalyst of a much deeper integration in the region.

There is however certain problems and pitfalls with such an approach that needs to be elucidated before we proceed further. One is the view prevalent among the neofunctionalists[4] of the EU as an archetypical model against which integration in other regions could be judged. Another is the divide between old regionalism seen as a planned merger of national economies in the context of a bipolar world and new regionalism as a more open and inclusive process involving both state and non-state actors in a multipolar world.[5] Let us deal with them in turn.

The integrative logic of the neofunctionalist approach is clearly demonstrated by the experience of the EU where the harmonisation of a trade policy led to closer economic integration and by extension also to political integration. The European Union as a political body was the result of decades of economic integration whereas EU's predecessor, the EEC, was principally an economic organisation. The degree of economic integration, according to this approach, ranges from preferential trade arrangements (PTA) to free trade area (FTA), customs union (CU), common market (CM) and economic union (EU). While the EU is well on its way toward becoming an economic union, the ASEAN and SAARC remain free trade areas and even that is an unfulfilled goal as far as the latter organisation is concerned. Among factors seen as conducive to the formation of free trade agreements are the proximity between the countries concerned, a similarity in their GDPs and a large difference in their factor endowments.[6]

It cannot be taken for granted though that the experiences of one region must lead to a better understanding of what is happening or is likely to happen in the other parts of the world. Obstacles which might seem insurmountable on their own can, as pointed out by Shaun Breslin, more easily be overcome when compared with how they have been tackled in the other areas in the past.[7] EEC in the 1950s was a completely different organisation than the EU is today and has had to come to grips with issues of decision-making and conflict management which were not too different from those in South Asia today. This does not mean that solutions must be the same everywhere. ASEAN, for example, dealt with these very issues in its own ASEAN way, which, as we shall see, helped the countries to integrate more closely in spite of the threats to peace and security in the context of the Vietnam War.

In the aftermath of the Asian financial crisis in the late 1990s, East and South-East Asia saw the rise of a plethora of regional organisations, which did not conform to the European pattern described above. Rather, they can be seen as examples of new forms of regionalisms. While the former often had a narrow focus on free trade arrangements and security alliances the latter has been more open, inclusive and influenced by global economic interdependences. A prime example is of course China, whose economy has successively become more closely linked with the wider regional economy through a number of bilateral processes. At the same time, security considerations—both geostrategic and energy related—have become more pronounced in China's foreign policy.[8]

China's involvement in Asian regional organisations such as ASEAN and SAARC demonstrates its increasing interests for regional leadership. Undoubtedly, this approach has had a vital impact on the regionalisation process in South East Asia. In South Asia, China has been much less of a driving force, but, as will be seen in the following account, its potential for regional dominance is growing.[9] While China is developing its multilateral relationships with South Asia through SAARC it is also cooperating bilaterally with its members and is thereby challenging India as the most important trade partner for the SAARC countries.

By adopting a comparative regional approach, this paper seeks to understand SAARC's present dilemma in the light of the achievements of the EU and ASEAN and what new forms of regional cooperation the growing presence of China might call for. The aim is not to provide new factual knowledge on these issues; rather, it is an attempt to make them ineligible by combining some recent research related to the discourse on regional economic cooperation.

Evolution of the SAARC

The idea of a closer cooperation within the South Asian region was proposed by the President of Bangladesh, Ziahur Rahman, in 1980. The countries concerned accepted the proposal, and under the next three years a number of meetings were held with the Foreign Secretaries of the respective countries.

When the Foreign Ministers met for the first time in New Delhi in 1983, a declaration of regional cooperation was signed. Two years later a charter was set up, and an association for regional cooperation in South Asia—SAARC—was formally established.

The aim of the association is to promote economic, social and cultural development of the member states. It is not seen as a formal means of conflict management, but was set up mainly to harmonise the trade policy.

Decisions are taken unanimously and all bilateral and contentious issues are excluded from the negotiations of the SAARC.

The association has had a sluggish start mainly due to the many conflicts in the region, such as the one between India and Pakistan over Kashmir, nuclear rivalry, border disputes, trade and migration issues, etc. among its members.[10]

The SAARC region has a poorly developed communication infrastructure and some countries are rather restrictive in developing regional communication links. Capital markets, banking, IT and aviation are insufficiently integrated in the region. In particular, there are lacking complementarities between India and Pakistan, which hampers integration also among their neighbouring countries.[11]

In 1993, the countries decided to establish the South Asian Preferential Trade Area (SAPTA), which became operative in December 1995. Even though the preferences obtained were very limited, the negotiations between the members kept the dialogue going. The fast spread of trade arrangements around the world in the years that followed stimulated the countries, especially India, to negotiate a preferential agreement also on a bilateral basis, as for example with Sri Lanka, Thailand and Singapore.

This development gave rise to the formation of the South Asian Free Trade Area (SAFTA) in 2006 which aims to transform South Asia into a free trade area. It is an agreement between the SAARC governments to successively bring down their duties with special concessions to the least developed countries among the SAARC. A fairly large number of products, however, are exempted from the scheme and put on a sensitive list. This involves further negotiations between the member countries and has proved to be a very slow process.[12] More recently, in 2012, the SAARC countries entered into an agreement on trade in services (SATIS). It constitutes a promising area for further liberalisation considering the fact that services account for more than half of the region's economy.[13]

What then motivated the member countries to create a free trade area in South Asia? One inducement was probably the general trend towards the proliferation of free trade areas around the world. The political leaders in the region may have sensed that they were being outdistanced by other regions of the world. With the creation of trading blocs such as the EU (Fortress Europe) and NAFTA, incentives were created to form similar blocks in other areas of the world as a defensive or offensive reaction. Undoubtedly, the South Asian countries were also hurt by the trade diversion due to the formation of these and other free trade areas.

Chart 1: Trend in Merchandise Export and Imports Share of SAARC in World Total

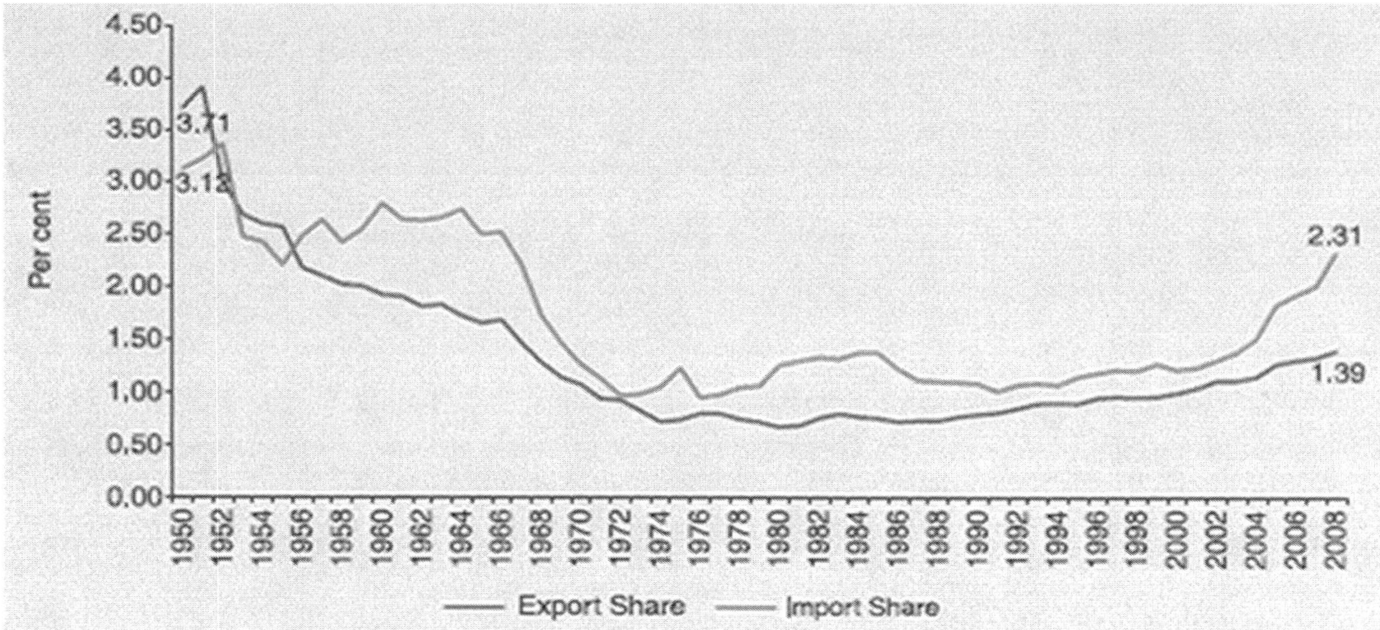

Source: Jain, R. and Singh, J.B, *Trade Patterns in SAARC Countries,* Reserve Bank of India, Vol. 30, No. 3, 2009.

Trade Patterns among the SAARC Countries

In the years following their independence, the intra-regional trade among the countries in South Asia was quite substantial. This was largely a consequence of the protectionist trade regime in the developed countries during the interwar period, but also of the then low barrier to trade in South Asia. When subsequently the developed countries opened up their markets, trade between them and with other countries surged. At the same time the countries in South Asia adopted a more inward looking policy. Import substitutions with heavy investments in the public sector were the main elements of the development strategy that dominated the region henceforth.[14]

This policy, combined with restrictive trade and industrial rules, resulted in a prolonged decline of the intra-regional trade as a share of the world trade. The decline lasted until the mid-1970s and then levelled off. Only in the 1990s did the subregional trade start to increase, but the share was still lower than in the 1950s. See Chart 1 above.

Table 1: Tariff Rate, Applied, Weighted Mean, All Products (%)

Year	*1990*	*1999*	*2005*	*2009*
Bangladesh	(88.4)	18.2	19.8	(13.0)
India	54.0	28.6	13.4	8.2
Nepal	..	13.3	14.3	14.3
Pakistan	..	(39.7)	12.2	9.5
Sri Lanka	27.0	..	7.7	7.6
China	..	14.5	4.8	4.2
Indonesia	13.3	6.1	4.4	3.2
Germany	5.1	3.1	1.8	1.5
USA	4.0	2.0	1.6	1.6

Note: Figures in brackets refer to the tariff rate one year ago.
Source: World Development Indicators 1989–2012, World Bank.

In the wake of a severe balance of payment crisis in 1991, India started to open up its economy with a stronger emphasis on the private sector and a dismantling of tariffs. Other countries in the region followed India's example and began deregulating their economies in the years that followed. The formation of the South Asian Free trade Area (SAFTA) in 2006 gave a further impetus to these changes.

Table 1 demonstrates the substantial lowering of tariff rates that has occurred since 1990, but as can be seen, South Asia is still less open than the other Asian countries such as China and Indonesia—let alone the Western countries.

In spite of the lowering of tariffs, the intra-regional trade has not been boosted. This, according to some scholars, is because non-tariff barriers still loom large in the region. While export subsidies and rules of origin provisions are barriers on the export side, import licensing and minimum import price limits are the measures being used for regulating imports. Finally, there are technical barriers like product standards, quality specifications and regulations to uphold food security and preventing the spread of diseases. Agriculture in particular is being subjected to numerous rules and regulations. These have proved difficult to remove since protecting the vast rural population is a goal of prime political importance in the region.[15]

According to the IMF Trade Restrictiveness Index, which grades tariff-plus-non-tariff barriers on a ten-point scale, Bangladesh and India (7) followed by Pakistan (6) are among the countries with the highest score ahead of China (5), Thailand (5) and Malaysia (4). This is not to say that there may be good environmental, health and other motives for imposing certain barriers on trade. The general impression though is that the region suffers from excessive non-tariff barriers to trade, to which should be added the inadequate transportation infrastructure.[16]

South Asia's exports consist to a large extent of labour-intensive manufactures like textiles and clothing products. The region is also a large exporter of agricultural products. Owing to its rapid industrial development, the region has become a net importer of fuel, machinery and mineral products. The fact that the commodity composition of trade is rather similar in all the countries of the region means that they have to compete with each other in the same industries in the international market. This, according to many observers, also explains why the intra-regional trade lags behind the extra-regional trade.[17]

Table 2: Exports of SAARC Countries to Major Importers (%)

	USA		*EU*		*China*		*ASEAN*		*SAARC*	
	2002	*2012*	*2002*	*2012*	*2002*	*2012*	*2002*	*2012*	*2002*	*2012*
India	21	13	22	17	4	5	5	9	5	4
Pakistan	25	22	27	15	2	8	2	3	2	8
Bangladesh	35	26	50	51	1	2	0	1	2	(2)
Sri Lanka	38	23	30	34	0	1	1	6	5	8

Table 3: Imports of SAARC Countries from Major Exporters (%)

	USA		*EU*		*China*		*ASEAN*		*SAARC*	
	2002	*2012*	*2002*	*2012*	*2002*	*2012*	*2002*	*2012*	*2002*	*2012*
India	7	4	20	11	5	11	5	9	1	1
Pakistan	6	2	17	10	7	15	9	14	2	3
Bangladesh	4	2	11	13	11	16	7	19	20	(16)
Sri Lanka	4	1	15	10	5	14	8	15	15	14

Note: Figures in brackets pertain to India, Pakistan and Sri Lanka only.

Sources: Baysan, T., Panagariya, A. and Pitigala, N., "Preferential Trading in South Asia", World Bank Policy Research, Working Paper, 3183, January 2006, p. 26; WTO, Statistics Database, Trade Profiles: India, Pakistan, Bangladesh, Sri Lanka (March 2014); SAARC Group on Statistics, Trade Database, 2002, 2003, 2012 (http://saarcstat.0rg/2014); ASEAN Merchandise Trade Statistics Database (2014); Bangladesh and China Bilateral Trade Statistics 1997/98–2012/13.

Tables 2 and 3 above show the geographical distribution of exports and imports of the larger SAARC countries. As far as exports are concerned, it can clearly be seen that the countries trade much more with the US and EU than with each other or with China and the ASEAN. The trend, however, indicates a shift from the West to the East with China and the South-East Asian countries gradually becoming more important as trading partners.

When it comes to imports, it is even clearer that Europe's position has been challenged by China and ASEAN while trade among the SAARC countries presents a rather mixed picture. As can be seen, India and Pakistan trade vigorously with the EU, China and ASEAN while taking only a fraction of their imports from the region. For Bangladesh and Sri Lanka, on the other hand, the intra-regional trade equals the trade with the other regions. In view of its much smaller size, the overall picture of the intra-regional trade as a small proportion of SAARC's total trade is not upset. This indicates that the object of transforming the region into a free trade area is still far off.[18]

The trade between the countries is mainly inter- rather than intra-industry trade. The latter is to be found mostly in textile and yarn production. With trade being competitive and similar, the lack of diversification has inhibited the economic integration in the region. Moreover, manufacturing has remained stagnant at around 16–17% of the GDP for several decades and the region has therefore been slow in creating jobs for its surplus rural population. Nor does the booming service sector provide much employment in view of its capital and skill-intensive character. This shall not conceal the fact that the greatest increase in trade has actually happened in the service sector.[19]

In view of its more advanced and diversified economic structure, India has the potential to develop production and distribution networks that could increase trade within the region. At the same time, the imbalance of power and the ongoing conflicts between India and its neighbours make the latter reluctant to cooperate with India since they fear that it will only legitimise India's dominance within SAARC. This, in its turn, jeopardises the effectiveness of the trade agreements and serves as an inducement for the smaller countries to act bilaterally rather than multilaterally, which ultimately threatens the organisational unity.[20]

Lessons from the Experience of the EU

From the very start, an overriding goal of the European Union was to suppress conflicts by promoting economic cooperation. This was the case in particular with the EEC, EU's predecessor, whose approach was to proceed sector by sector to build trust and a spirit of cooperation between the member states—in particular the former enemies, France and Germany. As is the case in South Asia today, Europe in the aftermath of WW II faced a political problem that urgently needed a solution.

Another similarity is the neofunctionalist ideas which inspired the founders of the EU to cooperate within certain narrowly defined areas, such as communications or coal and steel. It is mirrored today by SAARC's ambition of finding fruitful areas for cooperation like agriculture, transport and telecommunications. Climate change and natural disasters are other prioritised areas in view of the vulnerable ecosystems in the region.[21]

It is probably more appropriate to compare the integration process in South Asia today with that of the EEC in the 1950s and 60s than with the EU after Maastricht when the institutions and decision-making power were transferred from the national to the supranational level as a response to the formation of the inner market. This is far from the situation in South Asia today where sovereignty, political independence and non-interventions in the internal affairs of the member states must be respected. Moreover, all decisions have to be taken through unanimity while controversial and bilateral issues are to be avoided.[22]

In the EU, on the other hand, there is a general view that adherence to unanimity would result in stalemate. In certain institutions, a qualified majority is needed. By addressing both the majority of the member countries and the majority of the population, the very fact that the countries are equal before the law but different in size is taken into consideration. Likewise, the principle of subsidiarity is supposed to guarantee that as many decisions as possible shall be taken on a national, regional or local level rather than by the EU institutions themselves.

Within the EU there is a continuing discussion of the roles and functions of the principle institutions: the Parliament, the Council of Ministers, the Commission and the Court. The Commission maintains that the European Union should facilitate cooperation between those members wishing to progress faster and those who take a more cautious stance.

Within the SAARC there is no such discussion. There is a Standing Committee of the Foreign Secretaries, a Technical Committee, a Committee on Economic Cooperation and a Council of Ministers. There is almost no will to change or adjust the organisation that was once set up, or its institutions. The principle of subsidiarity which is fundamental for the decision-making process in the EU has no equivalent within the SAARC.[23]

The EU member states are committed to a Common Security and Defense Policy, whose aim is to strengthen the EU for mobilising its civilian and military capabilities in conflict prevention and crisis management. On a number of key issues, the member countries of the SAARC have radically different foreign and security policies. Two of the SAARC members, India and Pakistan, are nuclear powers and regard one another as unreliable and as a threat to the stability in the region.

The European Union attempts to be in the forefront as a defender of democratic principles and human rights. A frequent argument among the citizens, however, is that they have lost influence as decision-making powers have increasingly been transferred from the local to the supranational level. Human rights issues have not been given much space in the deliberations of the SAARC. There is, however, a SAARC Regional Convention on Suppression of Terrorism, and some countries have established Human Rights Commissions.[24]

The Common Agricultural Policy (CAP) is an integral part of the European integration project. Its basic tenet is to give Europe food security and to ensure stable food supplies at reasonable prices. Its critics maintain, however, that by ignoring the rules of supply and demand, the CAP is excessively wasteful and generates a surplus produce which is threatening the livelihood of farmers in the developing countries.[25]

Although there is no common agricultural policy among the SAARC countries, an Agricultural Vision for 2020 has recently been formulated. It addresses the major challenges for regional agriculture, which is to increase and sustain agricultural growth, reduce disparities between agricultural and non-agricultural sectors, reduce poverty, hunger and undernutrition, stop natural resource degradation and increase bio-safety and bio-security.[26]

The economic troubles faced by the EU in the later years coincide with a shift of the world's total wealth towards Asia. Since 1990, the EU's share of the global GDP has declined from 24% to 21%. The relatively slow growth rate in comparison with the emerging markets has weakened its competitive power. Europe is also handicapped by its aging population and rather immobile labour compared to the cheaper and more flexible labour markets of the emerging economies.[27]

In the wake of the present global economic crisis, the EU faces a number of challenges, which according to Fraser Cameron, pose a serious threat to the whole economic project. The first challenge is the delicate task of upholding fiscal stringency in a situation where a number of the EU's member states are economically weakened. In many cases, their situation is only made worse by their adoption of a single currency. They have thus parted with the key policy tool (the exchange rate) that would have allowed them to adjust to external or domestic shocks.

The second challenge is the EU's identity crisis and persistent inability to decide whether the best way forward is through "widening or deepening". On the one hand, the EU has developed from a customs union to a common market and a Eurozone, which today comprises 19 of the EU's 28 member states. At the same time, the EU's political institutions have not developed at a pace which is consistent with the needs of integration and the heterogeneous character of its members.[28]

Considering the many difficulties faced by the EU in later years, one may legitimately ask what the lasting lessons of the European integration model might be. One area where the EU has been successful is in the field of political cooperation and diplomacy. After almost half a century since its formation, the EU has not only minimised the threat of another European war, but moved slowly and surely towards a deeper and closer economic and financial integration between its member states.

It is interesting to note that from the very start, both the EEC, EUs predecessor, and SAARC adopted a cautious gradualist approach to create trust and a spirit of cooperation. But while the EU went ahead and created the inner market, the SAARC has not been able to accomplish anything that goes beyond a piecemeal approach.

Moreover, there is a striking difference of how the decision-making process is viewed by the two organisations. While the SAARC insists on consensus, the EU members have other means of coming to a decision. By adhering to the principles of proportionality and subsidiarity they try to find new areas of cooperation and for avoiding a stalemate.[29]

Within the EU, there is a willingness to discuss the roles and functions of its principle institutions and by so doing facilitating new forms of cooperation and improving the integration of new and old members, or between those who want to progress faster and those who are more conservative. SAARC, on the other hand, has shown little inclination to change or adjust the organisation that was once set up, or its institutions.

Comparing the SAARC and ASEAN

The European model for regional integration, shaped by the continent's history, may not be easily transferable to other regions including South Asia. One example of successful regionalism closer at hand is that of ASEAN, the Association of Southeast Asian Nations. Maybe, its relative success could give some clues as to why it has been able to manage conflicts and integration better than the SAARC. In spite of the many territorial problems and differences of opinion, the member countries have managed to maintain peace and stability in the region. The reasons for these achievements have been discussed by many scholars. Here a few of them will be briefly reviewed.

When ASEAN was being formed in 1967 much of South-East Asia was in a state of turmoil. Indonesia had been at war with Malaysia and Singapore, while the latter two had gone through a difficult separation. A number of countries had border or other territorial conflicts with each other as the Vietnam War was unfolding. In that situation, the leaders of Indonesia, Malaysia, the Philippines, Singapore and Thailand decided to reconcile their differences. For them, it was imperative to find diplomatic and other solutions to their bilateral conflicts and to keep the region of South-East Asia away from superpower conflicts.[30]

Their main concern was thus not so much with trade as with the threats against peace and security in the region. Liberalisation of trade was implemented very cautiously and gained momentum only after the Asian crisis in 1997–98 when the tariffs and other barriers to trade began to be dismantled. Up till then, the states had played a very active role in deciding what sectors and lines of production should be promoted. However, even after the adoption of a more open market-oriented policy the public and private sectors continued to cooperate closely in order to maintain the region's international competitiveness.[31]

The ASEAN member states adhere to the principle of non-intervention in domestic affairs and try to solve all intra-regional disputes by peaceful means. They have adopted an informal mechanism known as the "ASEAN way" to settle disputes. It is based on silent diplomacy where disputes are temporarily pushed aside in order not to threaten the attempts to attain consensus at a later stage. One important principle is "consensus minus x", which does not presuppose unanimity but only that a member abstain from participation in the deliberations without preventing the others from doing so.

That principle was brought to good use in the negotiations that led up to the ASEAN free trade area (AFTA) where the more important economies Indonesia, Malaysia and Singapore went ahead while the less important economies Cambodia, Laos and Vietnam were given more time to implement the reforms that their participation demanded.

One reason that could explain the ASEAN's ability to reconcile inner tensions and external threats is its multilateralism. By associating itself with APEC and becoming a counterweight to EU and NAFTA during the Uruguay Round, incentives were created for the US and Japan to strengthen their ties with ASEAN. In that way, the organisation has posited itself as part of a larger regional project.[32]

Syeda S. Rahman, Research Associate at the Institute of South Asian Studies at the University of Singapore, mentions four factors determining the effectiveness of conflict management in the ASEAN and SAARC:

The first factor is the perception of a common external threat which has welded the core Asian members: Indonesia, the Philippines, Malaysia, Singapore and Thailand. They all saw the advancement of communism in Vietnam and Kampuchea as a threat to their market's liberal growth model. That made them set aside their bilateral antagonism and create a stable environment conducive to export-led growth.

SAARC, on the other hand, has not been forced to deal with external threats, except possibly from China. The threat perceptions which have been depicted have been internal, i.e. caused by the conflicts between the members of the association. India in particular has been regarded with great suspicion by its neighbours.

The second factor is the role of a key state. Within ASEAN, Indonesia under Suharto took over the role as a benign regional leader. Conferring that role on Indonesia was regarded as a concession by the smaller countries which were anxious to harness Indonesia's alleged hostile ambitions towards them.

Although India occupies a similar position within the SAARC, it has not embraced the regional aspirations with the same enthusiasm. When the association was formed it was seen by the Indian leadership as a forum where the lesser states might 'gang up' against it.

The third factor is the role of extra-regional players, which in the case of ASEAN, was originally performed by the US, but with the formation of ASEAN+3 also by China and Japan. As far as SAARC is concerned, some of the countries, notably Pakistan and Bangladesh, have turned to external parties, such as China and the US, to elicit help against India.

The fourth factor is the creation of common norms which can work as mechanisms for conflict resolution. ASEAN decided to adopt an informal, non-legalist approach to manage conflicts between the member countries, including a method for temporarily removing contentious issues from the negotiations. SAARC has not showed the same inventiveness in finding mechanisms for conflict settlement.[33]

The ASEAN has also developed financial and economic contacts with cooperating partners outside its region and has recently signed free trade agreements with both China and India.

A very important step to form new coalitions in South-East Asia was taken in 1997–98 when the Asian economic crisis had escalated from a currency crisis to a financial crisis and then to a severe economic and social crisis. Also, the governments in East Asia felt the repercussions of the crisis although they were not as badly hit as their South-East Asian neighbours. There was a consensus among most Asian governments by that time that the IMF in conjunction with the US government had misdiagnosed the problems and had imposed solutions that had only aggravated the problems.

Chart 2: Intra-Regional Trade within SAARC, ASEAN and ASEAN+3

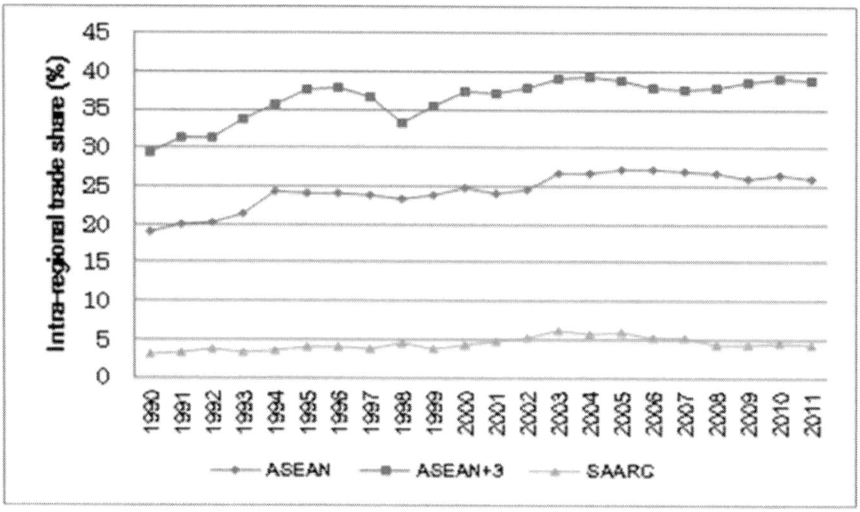

Source: Asia Regional Integration Center (ARIC) Integration Indicators Database (2012)

When neither APEC nor ASEAN were able to assist the affected countries, the idea of forming a wider cooperation between ASEAN and the East Asian countries—China, Japan and South Korea—was raised. They all had a growing trade with and investments in South-East Asia. ASEAN on its part, saw the advantages of developing closer relations with the more developed countries ofJapan and South Korea and to gain a foothold in China's dynamic market. Thus ASEAN PLUS THREE was formed.[34]

Today, the intra-regional trade including the trade with China constitutes close to 40% of the total trade of ASEAN. At the same time, ASEAN's trade with the US has fallen from 20% in 2000 to 10% in 2011, and the trade with EU from 15% to 11% during the same period. On the other hand, SAARC's intra-regional trade has developed slowly. It still represents only 5% of the total trade in the region compared to ASEAN's 25% and EU's 55% in their respective regions. See Chart 2 above.

China as an Extra-Regional Player

The Chinese foreign policy is based on the notion of "China as one of the poles in a multipolar world order" where it holds an increasingly important position. The relationship between China and ASEAN has had a vital impact on the regionalisation process in South-East Asia. It is also cited as an example of how China has managed to obtain a leadership role by getting the other countries to accept a growing Chinese dominance. This is said to have much to do with "Beijing's decision to work within ASEAN-led processes" in order to increase China's role in East and South-East Asia.[35]

In South Asia, China has been much less of a driving force. This is no doubt a consequence of the many conflicts and the suspicions that the members hold against each other, but also because of the region's strategic position alongside two of China's problem areas—Xinjiang and Tibet. There are many signs, however, that China is beginning to see SAARC as a catalyst for its economic and strategic interests in the region.[36]

In 2005, China was accorded an observer status in the organisation. This is a position it shares with the US, Japan and the EU amongst others. While India is reluctant to grant China full membership, other members—in particular, Bangladesh, Pakistan and Nepal—want China to join in order to counter India's dominance within SAARC.[37]

Chart 3: SAARC's and India's trade with China, 2001-2012
billion US dollars, current prices

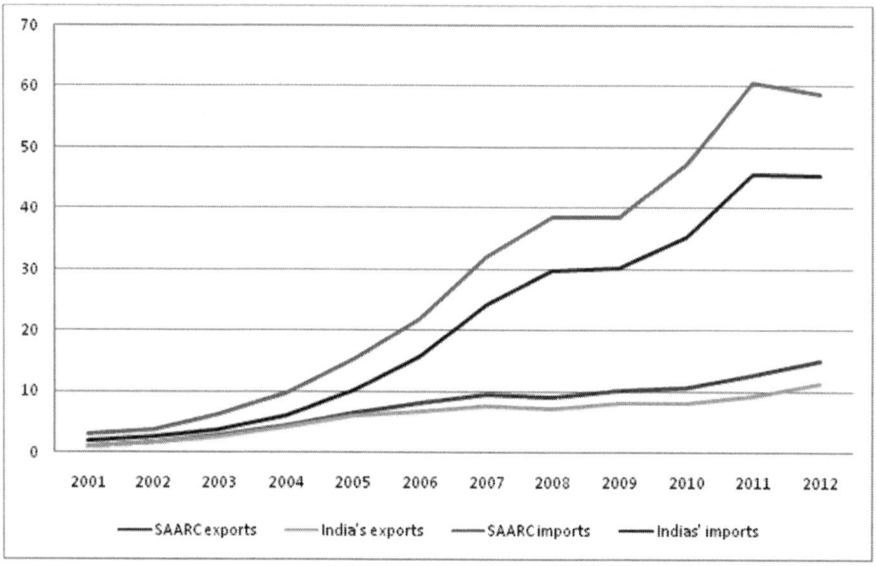

Note: For some years, trade data is not available from Afghanistan, Bangladesh, Bhutan, Maldives and Nepal. Except Bangladesh, their trade with China is of no great significance. When the SAARC data is not available, the Bangladesh and China Bilateral Trade Statistics have been substituted for them.

Sources: Inter-SAARC Imports from Partner Countries 2001-2012; Inter-SAARC Exports to Partner Countries 2001-2012; SAARC Group on Statistics (http://saarcstat.Org/2014); Bangladesh and China Bilateral Trade Statistics 1997/98 -2012/13; Export Promotion Bureau and Bangladesh Bank.

While China is developing its multilateral relationships with South Asia through SAARC it is also cooperating bilaterally with its members. China's old friendship with Pakistan recently resulted in a free trade agreement as well as an investment deal in nuclear energy. China is presently the largest investor in Afghanistan where it has a large stake in copper mining. China has also started to relocate parts of its textile industry to the low-wage country of Bangladesh. In return, China has been given the right to explore the latter country's reserves of coal, oil and natural gas. China's trade with Sri Lanka has doubled in just a few years and is now the fourth largest source of direct investments in power, ports and communications.[38]

India, on the other hand, is accused by its neighbours of being overly protectionist and thus delaying the integration process in the region. Sri Lanka wants an easier access to the Indian market, which it claims is prevented by the caps on imports and rules of origin while Bangladesh accuses India of imposing non-tariff barriers to trade and anti-dumping measures against its exports. At the same time, trade between India and Pakistan is minimal and often routed through Singapore or Dubai rather than directly between the countries.[39]

China's growing economic commitment is therefore welcomed by India's neighbours, which see it as a means to loosen the earlier blockages and to increase trade and investments in the region. This cannot, however, conceal the fact that India by virtue of its size, a rapidly growing middle class and a diversified export structure is the one country that is best equipped to match, and also to gain from China's increased involvement in the region.

Trade between the two countries has grown exponentially during the last decade and constitutes more than 75% of the SAARC's exports to as well as imports from China. See Chart 3 above. As can be seen, imports have grown much faster than exports throughout the decade. Since 2007, India has increased its imports at an of average 13% and exports by 9% per year, which is roughly the same as for the whole of SAARC. This has led to a rapidly growing trade deficit with China for the countries in the region. In India, where the deficit has hovered around 35 billion US dollars during the last three years, it is a hotly debated topic. It has been up for discussion many times when the leaders of the two countries have met as was the case when China's Foreign Affairs Minister visited New Delhi in June 2014.[40]

While India exports mainly iron ore and other commodities, it imports mostly the manufactured goods. Even though both countries now benefit from exploiting their comparative advantages, there may be larger future gains to be obtained from a closer cooperation between them. While China has distinguished itself as a centre for manufacturing industry and construction, India has developed into a centre for knowledge-intensive services such as pharmaceuticals, IT and engineering. Such a focus on the dynamic future sectors could also spillover to the other countries in the region.[41]

ASEAN after the Asia crisis managed to counter the declining demand from traditional export markets such as the US and EU by changing the composition of demand from exports to domestic consumption. It was also able to strengthen the intra-regional trade by actively picking companies that could integrate themselves into the production and distribution networks.[42] Today, China with its large unexploited domestic market faces a similar dilemma. Perhaps the recent deal between the SAARC states and

China's Sichuan province with its modern high-tech industrial base and evolving IT sector could be a step in such a direction.[43]

It must be emphasised though that China has so far gained preciously little from its economic cooperation with South Asia. SAARC, in fact, accounted for no more than 2.7% of China's total trade in 2010, which indicates that China's interest in the region may be driven by more than economic reasons. Of a large strategic interest is China's desire to maintain energy security in the Indian Ocean and to protect the pipelines connecting it with the oilfields in Central Asia.[44]

China is also responsible for building the Gwadar Port in Pakistan. Located at the Arabian Sea coast, it will considerably shorten the distance to the Persian Gulf where China gets 60% of its oil. Access to freshwater is another contentious issue manifested through China's building of dams in the Tibetan Plateau. These are seen as a potential threat to the populations living downstream in both Bangladesh and India.[45]

China's multilateralism involves both economic motives and security considerations, and South Asia is undeniably an area of great geopolitical concern for China. On the other hand, the countries in the region are interested in furthering their relationships with China mainly for economic reasons. For them it is a question not only of trade but also of investments, technology transfers and infrastructure development.

Today, China is challenging India's position as the most important trade partner for the SAARC countries. According to Saman Kelegama, Executive Director of the Institute of Policy Studies in Colombo, Sri Lanka, this development risks alienating India from SAARC rather than strengthening its ties with it. If that happens, SAARC's future development may be endangered and China may not be willing to support SAARC if it can reach its goals by developing its bilateral ties with the countries in the region. On the other hand, if SAARC manages to strengthen its cooperation with China without sacrificing its overall aims, China's participation could be the catalyst of a much deeper integration in the region.[46]

Concluding Discussion

South Asia is a region with enormous human and natural resources. It is home to a fifth of the world's population indicating a large future market potential. Yet, the current low per capita incomes make the economic size of the region small both in terms of the economic size (GDP) and the share in world trade.

Among the economic determinants seen as conducive for the formation of free trade agreements, as mentioned in the introduction, there are proximity between members, a similarity in their GDPs and a large difference in their factor endowments.[47] To what extent do the SAARC countries meet these criteria?

Geographically, the region covers the whole of the South Asian subcontinent thus constituting a continuous land area. On closer inspection, it is clear that India occupies most of that area and that the other countries except Afghanistan border only India and not each other. Besides, communication links between the countries are poorly developed which inhibits the process of regional integration. India's alleged hegemonic ambitions are thus accentuated by its geographical position and is a source of unrest among its neighbours.

The countries differ widely in terms of GDP although their commodity composition of trade is fairly similar indicating a similarity also in their factor endowments. They have thus been forced to compete with each other in the same industries in the international market. This also explains why the intra-regional trade lags behind the extra-regional trade. In spite of a substantial lowering of tariffs, trade has not been boosted, which can partly be attributed to the plethora of non-tariff barriers in the region.

The characteristics of the countries in the region thus seem to be largely at odds with the above criteria, which of course is no more than a pointer. What then do the comparisons with the EU and ASEAN tell us about SAARC's prospects and limitations as a regional organisation? Let us recapitulate our findings and draw some conclusions.

The EU undoubtedly has the best record in terms of *regional integration*. The completion of the single market, the free movement of people and capital across borders and the assignment of the European Commission to negotiate issues of trade on behalf of its members, all testify to this. While the EU is well on its way towards becoming an economic union, the ASEAN and SAARC remain free trade areas, and even that is a distant goal as far as the latter organisation is concerned. They both remain strictly inter-governmental bodies and have shown no interest in sovereignty sharing. The EU's accomplishments do not mean, however, that economic and political integration is free of risks. SAARC and other regions should be well advised to avoid the EU's mistake of rushing prematurely into financial and monetary cooperation, and rather move forward and consolidate step by step as illustrated by the recent financial turmoil in Greece.[48]

Regarding *decision-making*, the SAARC adheres to the view that non-interventions in the internal affairs of the member states must be respected. All decisions have therefore to be taken through unanimity while controversial and bilateral issues are to be avoided. The ASEAN, on its part, has developed an informal dispute prevention mechanism known as the ASEAN way. It is based on silent diplomacy where disputes are temporarily pushed aside in order not to threaten attempts to attain consensus at a later stage. In the EU, on the other hand, there is a general view that adherence to unanimity would result in stalemate. In certain institutions, a qualified majority is needed. Likewise, the principle of subsidiarity is supposed to guarantee that as many decisions as possible shall be taken on a national, regional or local level rather than by the EU institutions themselves.

One problem that has haunted SAARC throughout its existence is the hostility and suspicion between its members, in particular India and Pakistan, who have a long and conflict-prone history. This has jeopardised the creation and effectiveness of regional trade agreements and threatened the organisational unity. The hope that trade could be a means to improve the political relationship between the member countries has so far proved elusive.

The often cited example of *successful reconciliation* is how the creation of the EEC tempered the antagonism between France and Germany in the aftermath of WW II. Europe by that time faced a similar problem as South Asia today, it is argued, and thus presents an example worth following. Some critics, however, see this as a totally false parallel. The European case involved a victorious power, a defeated one and the military presence of an outside superpower. It was thus an altogether different situation than the one facing India and Pakistan today.[49]

What have been the roles of *extra-regional players?* In the case of ASEAN, the US originally performed such a role, and with the formation of ASEAN+3, China and Japan are doing the same. As far as the SAARC is concerned, Pakistan and Bangladesh have turned to external parties, such as China and USA, to elicit help against India. Recently, however, China has increased its presence in South Asia and is beginning to see SAARC as a catalyst for its economic and strategic interests in the region.

While China is developing its multilateral relationships with South Asia through SAARC it is also cooperating bilaterally with its members. Today, China is challenging India as the most important trade partner for the SAARC countries. Whether this development will alienate India from SAARC or be the catalyst of a deeper integration in the region depends on the ability of SAARC to live up to its challenges while maintaining the confidence of its members. If that is not happening, new regional constellations, presently under consideration in Asia, could simply sidestep SAARC or incorporate parts of it.

Already an extension of the ASEAN is contemplated, which in addition to its original members would involve China, India, Japan, South Korea, Australia and New Zealand, with the aim of establishing the world's largest free trade area. Negotiations are planned to be completed by the end of 2015.[50]

Arvind Panagariya, Professor in Economics at the Columbia University, is of the opinion that a South Asian Free Trade Area could only be justified as part of a much broader strategy involving both China and the member countries of ASEAN. The fact that both the EU and NAFTA discriminate against exports from Asia has had a negative impact in terms of trade. A response to this development could be for Asia to move to a block of its own.

The best starting point for an Asian trade block, he argues, would be a free trade agreement between China and India. Both countries already have such deals with the ASEAN, and a working Asian block would not be possible without the participation of both these countries. It would also induce other countries in the region to enter into agreements with them, and bring the US and the EU to the negotiating table.[51]

A word of caution may, however, be appropriate at this juncture. Allowing the Chinese producers an easier access to the Indian market and cheaper imports is not generally welcomed by the local producers, who are already facing stiff competition from China. Such apprehensions were very much in the air when the free trade agreement between China and ASEAN was on the agenda some years back. The fact that the ASEAN leaders were still anxious to sign the agreement depended, according to some viewers, on their conviction that it lay in their countries' long-term interest to join the regional engine of growth. With the present slowing down of China's growth rate, that argument may not convince the Indian business interests as easily.

NOTES AND REFERENCES

1. According to the World Bank Development Indicators, Afghanistan, Bangladesh and Nepal are classified as low income countries; Bhutan, India, Pakistan and Sri Lanka as lower middle and the Maldives as an upper middle income country. Poverty ratio varies from 35.8% in Afghanistan to 6.7% in Sri Lanka, and life expectancy from 61 years in Afghanistan to 78 years in the Maldives, according to the same statistics.
2. "World Development Indicators: Size of the Economy", World Bank, *2015*.
3. The share of intra-regional trade as a proportion of the member countries' total trade as an indicator of the success of a particular regional integration project has been criticised for overestimating the share of intra-regional trade in relatively

large regions as compared to the smaller economic regions: "The reason for this is that the indicator is correlated with the size of the region. Large regions logically trade more within their region and less with the rest of the world". It is thus not surprising that the SAARC shows a low and the EU a high value for this indicator (De Lombaerde et al, "The Problem of Comparison in Comparative Regionalism", *Review of International Studies*, Vol.36, July 2010, pp. 749-750.

4. Neofunctionalism is a theory of regional integration, the purpose of which is to use the European experience of integration to generate hypotheses for testing in other contexts. Jean Monet's approach to European integration, which aimed at integrating the individual sectors in the hope of achieving spill-over effects to further the process of integration, is said to have been based on the neofunctionalist approach.
5. We adhere to Joseph Nye's definitions for region and regionalism in the present paper. According to him, a region can be described "as a limited number of states linked by a geographical relationship and by a degree of mutual interdependence" and regionalism as "the formation of interstate associations or groupings on the basis of regions." Nye, Joseph (ed.), *Inter Regionalism: Readings*, Boston: Little Brown, 1969.
6. Baier, Scott & Bergstrand, Jeffrey, "Economic Determinants of Free Trade Agreements", *Journal of International Economics*, No. 64, 2004, pp. 41-49.
7. Breslin, Shaun, "Comparative Theory, China, and the Future of East Asian Regionalism(s)", *Review of International Studies*, Vol. 36, July 2010, p. 711.
8. Ibid, pp. 717-729.
9. Papatheologou, Vasiliki, Naseer, Rizwan and Amin, Musarat, "China's Engagement with Regionalization in South and Souteast Asia: A Comparative Perspective", *South Asian Studies*, Vol. 29. No. 1, 2014, pp. 282-286.
10. "South Asian Association for Regional Cooperation (SAARC)", *Department of South Asian, Middle East, African Affairs*, December 2013, pp. 1-2. See also: Iqbal, Muhammad, J., "SAARC: Origin, Growth, Potential and Achievements", *Pakistan Journal of History & Culture*, Vol. XXVII/2, 2006, pp. 131-133.
11. Zaman, Arif and Thota, Satish, "Regional Trade in South Asia: Towards Stronger Linkages and Growth", *21st European Conference on Modern South Asian Studies*, 2010, pp. 192-193.
12. Baysan, Tercan, Panagariya, Arvind and Pitigala, Nithal, "Preferential Trading in South Asia", *World Bank Policy Research*, Working Paper, 3813, January 2006, pp. 7-9.
13. Moinuddin, Mustafa, "Economic Integration and Trade Liberalization in South Asia", *Asia Pathways*, August 27, 2013, p.1-2.
14. Baysan, Tercan, Panagariya, Arvind and Pitigala, Nithal, "Preferential Trading in South Asia", *World Bank Policy Research*, Working Paper, 3813, January 2006, p. 2.
15. Bhunia, Abhrib and Nataraj, Geethanjali, "Break Down the Barriers to Trade in South Asia", *East Asia Forum*, 13th March, 2014, pp. 1-2.
16. Kee, Nikita and Olarreaga, "Estimating Trade Restrictiveness Indices, 2009" in Khan, Usman, "Pakistan: South Asia Trade & Non-Tariff Barriers", *DPRC Working Paper*, August 2010, pp. 18-19.

17. Jain, Rajeev and Singh, J. B., "Trade Pattern in SAARC Countries: Emerging Trends and Issues", *Reserve Bank of India, Occasional Papers*, Vol. 30, No. 3, 2009, pp. 7-8.
18. The above tables are an update and elaboration of two tables appearing in Baysan, T., Panagariya, A., Pitigala, N., "Preferential Trading in South Asia", 2006, p. 26. By combining them we can trace the direction of imports and exports of SAARC from 1990–2012. It appears that South Asia's exports to the US and EU peaked in 2002 and then declined while imports from both the regions have declined steadily since 1990. On the other hand, the importance of ASEAN as a trading partner has increased, especially since 2002, while China's rise has been even faster and in 2012 equalled that of ASEAN.
19. Khan, Usman, "Pakistan: South Asia Trade & Non-Tariff Barriers", *DPRC Working Paper*, August 2010, pp. 1-2.
20. Thapar, Raghav, "SAARC: Ineffective in Promoting Economic Cooperation in South Asia", *Stanford Journal of International Relations*, Vol. 7, Issue 1, 2006.
21. McCormic, John, *Understanding the European Union*, Palgrave Macmillan, 2005, pp. 13-23.
22. Iqbal, Muhammad, J., "SAARC: Origin, Growth, Potential and Achievements", *Pakistan Journal of History & Culture*, Vol. XXVII/2, 2006, p. 134.
23. Bhargava, Kant K., "EU–SAARC: Comparisons and Prospects of Cooperation", *Zentrum für Europäische Integrationsforschung*, Discussion Paper, C 15, 1998, pp. 8-9.
24. Ibid, pp. 11-13.
25. McCormic, John, *Understanding the European Union*, Palgrave Macmillan, 2005, pp. 187-193.
26. Chand, Ramesh, "SAARC Agricultural Vision2020" *Agricultural Economics Research Review*, Vol. 23, July-December 2010, pp. 197-208.
27. Cameron, Fraser, "The European Union as a Model for Regional Integration", *Council on Foreign Relations, International Institutions and Global Governance Program*, Working Paper, September 2010, p. 3.
28. Ibid, pp. 4-5.
29. "The principle of subsidiarity determines the level of intervention that is most relevant in the areas of competences shared between the EU and the member states. This may concern action at European, national or local levels. EU may only intervene if it is able to act more effectively than the member states". Similarly, "The principle of proportionality regulates the exercise of power by the European Union. Under this rule the involvement of the institutions must be limited to what is necessary to achieve the objectives of the Treatise" (*The Lisbon Treaty: A Comprehensive Guide*).
30. Siddiqa, Aysha, "An Overview of SAARC and ASEAN", *IOSR Journal of Humanities and Social Sciences*, Vol. 14, Issue 5, Sept.-Oct. 2013, p. 72.
31. Foxley, Alejandro, *Regional Trade Blocs: The Way to the Future?* Carnegie Endowment for International Peace 2010, pp. 24-25.
32. Rahman, Syeda S., "Same but Different: Comparing the ASEAN and SAARC Frameworks", *ISAS Working Paper*, No. 123, 7 March 2011, pp. 5-7.

33. Ibid, pp. 14-18.
34. Stubbs, Richard, "ASEAN PLUS THREE, Emerging East Asian Regionalism?" *Asian Survey*, Vol. XLII, No. 3 May/June 2002.
35. Papatheologou, Vasiliki, Naseer, Rizwan and Amin, Musarat, "China's Engagement with Regionalization in South and Souteast Asia: A Comparative Perspective", *South Asian Studies*, Vol. 29. No. 1, 2014, p. 282.
36. Ibid, p. 287.
37. Chen, Xianming, "China and South Asia: Contention and Cooperation between Giant Neighbors", *European Financial Review*, April/May 2014.
38. Kelegama, Saman, "Economic Cooperation, the Emerging Scenario", *Policy Perspectives*, Vol. 9 Issue 1, June 2012, pp. 107-108. See also Sahoo, Pravakar and Taneja, Nisha, "China's Growing Presence in India's Neighborhood", *East Asia Forum*, 5th February 2010, pp. 1-2.
39. Sahoo, Pravakar and Taneja, Nisha, "China's Growing Presence in India's Neighborhood", *East Asia Forum*, 5th February 2010, p. 2.
40. *Times of India*, 8 June 2014.
41. Kelegama, Saman, "Economic Cooperation, the Emerging Scenario", *Policy Perspectives*, Vol. 9. Issue 1, June 2012, p. 102.
42. Foxley, Alejandro, *Regional Trade Blocs: The Way to the Future?* .Carnegie Endowment for International Peace 2010, p. 36.
43. In 2011, SAARC adopted a nine-point plan for cooperation between its members and China's Sichuan province with the aim of reducing trade barriers and stimulating investments in infrastructure and industrial development. Kelegama, Saman, "Economic Cooperation, the Emerging Scenario", *Policy Perspectives*, Vol. 9, Issue 1, June 2012, p. 98.
44. Kelegama, Saman, "Economic Cooperation, the Emerging Scenario", *Policy Perspectives*, Vol. 9, Issue 1, June 2012, p. 101.
45. Sahoo, Pravakar and Taneja, Nisha, "China's Growing Presence in India's Neighborhood", *East Asia Forum*, 5th February 2010, pp. 6-8.
46. Kelegama, Saman, "Economic Cooperation, the Emerging Scenario", *Policy Perspectives*, Vol. 9, Issue 1, June 2012, p. 105.
47. Baier, Scott and Bergstrand, Jeffrey, "Economic Determinants of Free Trade Agreements", *Journal of International Economics*, No. 64, 2004, pp. 41-49.
48. Monoo, Kamal, "SAARC and EU: Some Comparisons", *The Nation*, January 26, 2011.
49. Baysan, Tercan, Panagariya, Arvind and Pitigala, Nithal, "Preferential Trading in South Asia", *World Bank Policy Research*, Working Paper, 3813, January 2006, p. 12.
50. "Official meeting with the ASEAN+6 Members is Imminent", *Asia Consultants, Strategic Alliance Network*, 20/2 2013.
51. Panagariya, Arvind, "India and China, Trade and Foreign Investment" in Hope, Nicholas, et al (eds.), *Economic Reform in India, Challenges, Prospects and Lessons*, Cambridge University Press, 2013, pp. 135-37.

15

Development of Trade and Economic Relations between India and Central Asia: Traditional and Non-Traditional Barriers

Umarov Khojamahmad

ABSTRACT

Different methodological approaches to the development of trade with neighbouring and far-off countries have led to the fact that practically all over the world because of its higher competitiveness, Chinese goods have become very successful in displacing the Indian goods. It has happened in the Central Asian consumer goods market as well. It is unlikely that in the next 20 years, the Indian goods would be able to restore their image and preferential dominance in the aforementioned regional market unless a proper design and implementation of the strategy of import substitution is introduced along with the tools for protecting the domestic market and the domestic producers besides providing ways to deal with the barriers that create hurdles in the process.

Keywords: Barriers in trade relations, India–Central Asia economic relations, import substitution strategy, China–Central Asia trade, traditional and non-traditional barriers.

Introduction

Following the collapse of the USSR, formation of independent states in the former Soviet Union abolished the state monopoly on foreign economic relations. The non-state sector gave full rights to trade and to the economic cooperation with foreign economic entities. The same right was received by the state-owned enterprises as well. Elimination of the state monopoly on foreign trade was an inevitable consequence of the elimination of the planned regulation of the economy, replacing it with a system of market regulation. These processes have occurred very quickly, because except for Uzbekistan and Turkmenistan, all other post-Soviet countries resounded with the method of "shock therapy" in carrying out economic reforms. The post-Soviet countries, except for Russia, had no experience in creating international economic relations. Each country had its own set up regarding the establishment of international economic relations (Rudneva, 2013). The Central Asian countries with the signing of agreements on the establishment of diplomatic ties proceeded to the signing of agreements on trade and economic cooperation, free trade and the avoidance of double taxation with others, including the neighbouring countries.

During 1991–1992, all the former republics of Central Asia established trade relations with India. The official documents signed by the top leaders of India and some countries of Central Asia contained the idea of providing the most favourable conditions to each other for the establishment of trade and economic cooperation. This allowed for a relatively short historical period of time to develop the trade relations in and for expanding industrial cooperation and other forms of economic links. During the period 1993–2011, the Central Asian trade with India increased 29 times. For comparison, we note that for the same period of time the volume of trade between the Central Asian countries increased 7.4 times. However, there are figures showing multiple and more sustainable development of trade and economic relations with the region's other countries. So, for the above-mentioned period, the volume of trade between the Central Asian countries and China increased by 2370.4 times. Currently, in the Central Asian consumer markets, more than 70% of the commodities are produced by China (except in the case of Uzbekistan). Over the past five years, trade and economic cooperation between the countries of Central Asia and India has been limping. In the Central Asian markets, goods from China, Russia, Turkey and Iran prevail. In terms of turnover, even Afghanistan is ahead of India. During the last few years, rarely has there been any meeting between the representatives of the countries of Central Asia and India on trade and economic cooperation. Conferences, seminars, exhibitions, etc. devoted exclusively towards trade and economic relations are even less likely to have taken place.

However, trade with China was signed only for intergovernmental documents. They were specifically dedicated to the creation of a favourable condition for the development of trade. These included issues of the procedures for obtaining visas for traders, creating favourable conditions for wholesalers, transportation and customs inspection of goods, etc. In a relatively short period of time, China and the countries of Central Asia built relations according to modern European standards and established regular air services—the flights to Urumqi are at present functioning in the world's largest terminals for catering to wholesale consumer goods; specialised hotels for receiving trade tourists from neighbouring countries and having the necessary infrastructure for their full recreation, etc. It may be noted that the physical infrastructure created in China to promote trade and economic relations with the countries of Central Asia was financed from the state budget of the PRC. Currently, this infrastructure works flawlessly and provides a very high level of economic and trade relations between both the sides. There exists a first-hand accurate document stating the regulation of trade and economic relations between the neighbouring countries.

Unfortunately, India does not show a similar example in the regulation of trade and economic relations with other countries. The reason lies in the different conceptual approaches that are being used by the governments of China and India in their economic policies. There is no doubt that in this case the Chinese government adheres to the position of state regulation, and the government of India to a position of market regulation. In India, the government has not adopted any measures to achieve the high rates of trade and economic cooperation with the countries of Central Asia. Over the last 20 years, one has been used to the principle of the "invisible hand" of the market, although it has had an enormous historical experience as well as the tragic experience of the invasion of external market forces on the economy.

Different methodological approaches to the development of trade with the neighboring and far-off countries have led to the fact that practically all over the world because of its higher competitiveness, Chinese goods have become very successful in displacing the Indian goods. It has happened in the Central Asian consumer goods market as well. It is unlikely that in the next 20 years, the Indian goods would be able to restore there image and preferential dominance in the aforementioned regional market.

Let us try to visualise the solution of a problem between some of the Central Asian republics and India. In the latter case, the geopolitical interests of the State need to be kept in mind. The Central Asian countries' main interest has been in achieving a balanced state interest among the geopolitical forces in the region. This eventually would allow them to overcome the economic and political dependence of the region and its individual components from external forces. It is extremely important to keep in mind that countries such as Tajikistan and its regions are already in a dependency mode from China. This itself becomes dangerous in nature, threatening the territorial integrity of the country. Such dependency can take forms which can be dangerous for the interests of India. For example, the possible appearance of military bases of the PRC in the territories of the Central Asian countries can serve as a threatening factor on how to implement the strategic interests of the Indian state.

In this regard, a search for a niche is inevitable by the Indian players that can provide the much wanted geopolitical balance in the Central Asian region. Capturing the consumer market in the region by the Chinese players has been long term and sustained. In terms of effectiveness of the implementation of the approaches it can bring an equilibrium in the markets of the leading geopolitical forces by increasing the participation of India in the import substitution strategies among the different Central Asian countries. Only this alone can bring in sustenance for the Indian goods.

An export orientation strategy, under different names by the providing country offices by the WB, ADB, EBRD, IDB, etc. were compiled and launched for implementation that suffered a complete fiasco. This is evidenced by the fact that in all the countries of the region, from year to year, an increase in the imbalance between exports and imports take place. Preventive attempts that have been made to overcome this dangerous dynamics have been of no avail. While these international and regional financial and economic organisations were kept in complete silence on the noted fiasco, there were voices everywhere regarding the possible ways of wriggling out from this situation, by development and consistent implementation of the import substitution strategy across the region.

Currently, the main directions of the economic ties between India and the Central Asian countries are: trade, investment, external debt, economic assistance, technical and scientific cooperation in the form of transfer of technology, knowledge and experience. In all these areas of cooperation with Central Asia, India differs with a considerable lag in comparison to China. India may have advantages over China in the Central Asian region, in two of its major directions, i.e., about investment and scientific and technical cooperation. This does not mean that the Indian investors are set to outnumber China. The most important is the participation of the

Indian companies in the structural transformation of the economies of Central Asia. Indian firms in contrast to Chinese companies are designed to focus not on the development of physical infrastructure, but on the recovery of the real sector of the economy which was destroyed by the massive influx of the cheap Chinese goods.

Now thousands of enterprises in the manufacturing sector of Central Asia are either completely suspended because the goods they produced were uncompetitive compared with the imported Chinese goods or work at a low level of utilisation of their production capacities. Such enterprises are characterised by a very high level of depreciation of the fixed assets, reaching up to 70–90%. In addition, such enterprises are faced with degradation of human capital, because for many years, the industrial personnel have not been used properly.

The Chinese companies have no desire to restore such companies and to provide them with the latest equipment, to take steps to prepare highly modern industrial personnel and to improve the management among them. Such work could be done by the Indian firms. Refurbishment work in the manufacturing sector in the region could be combined with the creation of a network of new small and medium enterprises for the processing of local raw materials. In this respect, India has favourable economic, scientific and technical capabilities. The latter are more adapted to the climatic and human conditions and development of the manufacturing sector in Central Asia. Restoration and creation of new businesses based on local raw materials should be combined with simultaneous measures of a protectionist nature, i.e. implementation of measures to protect the domestic producers from foreign competition.

Consistent implementation of such measures by the Indian partners in general is useful for sharpening the rates of the Central Asian countries' economy. It will reduce the political and economic dependency of the region on China. This clearly results in a positive assessment, since it leads to a substantial strengthening of the economic and national security of the region. Active participation in the implementation of the import substitution strategy in the Central Asian countries leads to an increase in the international prestige of India as such participation is associated with a decrease in the destructiveness with trade and economic relations among the regions (Umarov et al, 2015).

However, as mentioned earlier, it does not mean that the problem of increasing the trade between India and the Central Asian region should be seen as the last option. Such a cooperation is intended first to create markets in the region and to promote a real competition with the Chinese goods by transferring the competitive field for quality, useful features of the product and low prices. Although, as was stated, a large-scale cross-sectional range of Indian goods can compete with the Chinese goods in the markets of the region. Second, the expansion of the volume of trade between India and the Central Asian countries will have a positive impact on the public opinion. Because, the people will feel the value of the cheaper goods being produced in countries other than China positively. Finally, there would be the strengthening of the assured belief that the production of such goods in the region seems quite real.

However, in terms of the ways for a substantial increase in trade and in other kinds of economic cooperation between India and Central Asia, there are many barriers that need decisive eradication. There are socio-economic and historical barriers and are divided into two large groups: the traditional and the non-traditional. The difference is mainly in the degree of the complexity of their elimination. This study will further show how the traditional barriers historically require a long time to be overcome. In relation to their task, relevant public and private institutions must engage in trying to reduce their impact forces.

Traditional Barriers of Trade

The traditional barriers of trade and economic relations between Central Asia and India may be summarised as below:

(a) *Different levels of market psychology among the people of Central Asia and India*: The people of the Central Asian countries either completely lack a market psychology or a development strategy. This specificity is not only the result of a long-term domination by the planned economy in the region, inherent in the relevant psychology, but also due to the geographical features of the macro-region under consideration. The fact is that a significant portion of the population lives in the mountains, the desert or semi-desert areas. The population living in the vast desert areas or in the deep mountains still remains primarily patriarchal in thinking, which excludes their involvement in market and monetary relations. Although the years of Soviet power and the nomadic lifestyle have been weakened significantly, but due to the inertia, nomadic psychology and behaviour patterns are still being felt. One of the reasons for the failure of the development of micro and small businesses in Central Asia is the inertia of the nomadic psychology. In India, the vast majority of the people living in the peninsula (except forest communities) have developed the market psychology. In this case, the latter is sustainable, because for many millennia this psychology had been strengthened to support the authorities.

(b) *Planned type of organisation of life in Central Asia and India*: A specified widespread type of life in Central Asia relies particularly on its feeling of the state support. The nomadic psychology in India supported by the caste system of social development has played a role. The impact of a clan-type life is expressed in the general orientation of the people in the state as the main source of supply of material and spiritual wealth. Therefore unlike China, people in India and Central Asia in the organisation of trade and establishment of other forms of economic cooperation, expect the blessing of the state, with the perception of human psychology being constantly maintained. Such an attitude towards the organisation of external economic relations acts as an inhibiting factor.

(c) *Traditionally low prices of Chinese products compared to the Indian domestic markets of these countries*: The average salaries of the Chinese workers are higher as compared to the Indian workers. However, transaction costs are much lower in China than in India and this acts as a factor of the higher competitiveness of the Chinese goods in other countries. With regard to the Central Asian market, this factor is enhanced by the fact that due to the smaller community boundaries and medium-sized cargo transportation, transport costs are much less than the corresponding costs of the Indian goods (Umarov et al, 2015).

(d) *Rapid adaptation of the Chinese to the structural needs of the foreign markets*: The Indians have felt such a dynamism to a much lesser extent. The lifestyle of the Indians and the numerous features of their lifestyles act as a barrier to market orientation. The main part of Indian life points to the direct or indirect participation in political activities. The Indian model of democracy is through elections at various levels of state power. Such elections are based on the universal and active participation of the citizens in the discussion of election programmes and individual candidates for the various levels of legislature in India.

According to the impression of the foreign observers during the election campaigns, the people were giving attention largely to the discussions with political opponents, rather than on the specific production problems. During the election campaigns, 50% to 70% of the pages of the national and local media were dedicated to the elections. Forty-six per cent of the voters would support the candidates originating from their clans, while the figure in six states in India ranges from 50% to 60% (*Sunday Times*,

2014). Election festivity serves as the main factor distracting the Indians from issues such as product quality, product compliance with international standards and current market requirements, its competitiveness, the aesthetic perception of customers, etc.

(e) *Among the Indians, a long habit of thinking before making a decision about establishing business abroad*: The Chinese in this regard seem to be more bold and fast. While the Indians take a few months pondering the possibility of a decision, the Chinese not only seize the initiative, but also lay their hands on the corresponding segment of the foreign market. Our observations show that the Indians in decision-making are more sluggish in comparison not only with the Chinese, but also in comparison with the Turks, Czechs, Malaysians, Thais and some other nations.

(f) *Development of a corrupt consciousness*: Here and there, the universally widespread view was that without a bribe it is not possible to solve any serious problem. In Central Asia and in India, there are constant verbal wars against corruption; political opponents accuse those who are in power of corrupt activities in connection with the corrupt and criminal circles. These battles are especially played during the election campaign, but after the elections all such impressions become calm which implies a reconciliation with corruption and economic crimes. According to the latest surveys, 48% of voters in India vote for candidates involved in criminal activities (*Sunday Times*, 2014). The same occurs in the Central Asian countries.

(g) *Absence of favorable routes for the development of trade and economic relations between India and Central Asia*: Geographically, the two sides are close to each other. However, in-between Pakistan and Afghanistan are located, through which, for political reasons, it is not possible to have a regular organisation of commerce. At present, the freight transportation between India and the countries of Central Asia is going through the Iranian port of Bandar Abbas. Transportation of goods via the territory of Iran, Afghanistan and Turkmenistan has met with numerous bureaucratic obstacles, many of which are explained in the terms of corruption. The position may change slightly for the better after the full commissioning of the Iranian port of Chabahar, which is being built with financial and technical assistance from India. However, even after its enactment, the transport freight costs will still remain significant between India and the Central Asian countries. The situation may change dramatically only after the opening of the so-called Pakistan corridor, including distance from the checkpoint of Attari on the India–Pakistan border to the Pakistani city of

Peshawar, located near the Pak–Afghan border. Currently, there is information about the possibility of a solution to this issue, which may have an "explosive" effect on the development of economic cooperation between the countries of Central Asia and India.

(h) *Lack of sufficient knowledge of the Indian business*: There is insufficient knowledge about the economy, geography, ethnic origin, structure and level of consumption of food and non-food products, the development of the social sphere, the image and standards of living of the population of the Central Asian republics. India has not published the illustrated newspapers and magazines in English and Hindi, dedicated to the economy and social life of these republics. The main part of the business community in Central Asia is much more aware of the African countries, New Zealand, South Africa, Canada, etc. compared to the immediate neighbourhood. This is partly because of the authoritarian rule in all the Central Asian countries and also because of the closed eco-systemic nature of some of these republics, particularly Turkmenistan and Uzbekistan.

Overcoming the Barriers of Trade

However, trade and economic relations between India and the Central Asian countries suffer from barriers, which by nature are not traditional. Overcoming them is less resource-intensive than the traditional ones (Chouhan et al, 2013). They can be overcome by improving the institutions involved in them. Such barriers include:

(a) *Capturing the consumer markets of Central Asia by China*: Naturally, such a "seizure" has occurred solely through the market methods. In the mid-1990s, favourable conditions for a mass influx of non-Chinese origin goods had developed which led to those goods flooding the markets of the Central Asian region. Products from other countries were not sufficiently competitive, especially on the prices offered. It is necessary to emphasise that the Chinese side at that time had resorted to dumping actions. At the same time, the World Bank and the International Monetary Fund "taught" the transition countries how to actively use free trade and overcome their protectionist past. The outcome of such an approach is now known to all.

(b) *An active promotion of trade and economic relations with the Chinese government*: Over the past few years, an active use of the above-mentioned financial economic organisations surfaced and the free trade policies were implemented in their foreign expansionist strategy. At the same time, a policy was based on the principle of state regulation of the economy. In this regard, India, exercising broad neo-liberal reforms, both domestically and in foreign economic relations, implemented a policy of market regulation of the economy. There is no doubt that the different rates of economic growth in China and India can be explained through different approaches based on a combined domestic and foreign economic policy. In practice, except for Uzbekistan and Turkmenistan, the Central Asian countries proceeded with their foreign and domestic policies based on the neoliberal recipes of WB, IMF, WTO and regional financial economic organisations.

(c) It is believed that India feels that the existing foreign markets are quite sufficient for a further expansion of foreign trade and maintains its high growth while the emerging markets are risky and unpredictable. Among the countries that are supposed to be dependable include the European and North American markets, markets of the Arabian Peninsula, South-East Asia, Australia, China and Japan. The risky ones include the markets of the post-Soviet countries. This position is incorrect. The US and the European countries' policy over the past 20 years shows that despite the enormous purchasing power in these countries, their leaders have been very selective in their approach. Tools of punishment are there for the changing political relations, based on the inappropriate principles of economic globalisation. As is known, the authors of these principles are the US government and the IFEO which financially depends on the United States entirely.

(d) The war in Afghanistan and the long-term tense political situation in Pakistan, also act as a retarding factor for the rapid development of trade and economic cooperation between Central Asia and India. The southern provinces of Afghanistan are now under the effective control of the Taliban, which prevents the use of the international transport corridors to interdict these provinces with the Central Asian markets. Besides Pakistan, because of poor political relations with Afghanistan and in regard to the unresolved Kashmir issue, also shows no interest in optimising the opening of the Pakistan corridor. It is possible that with the beginning of the transition into the new trade regime between the two countries, the issue of the opening of the corridor will be called in to acquire the features of reality (Muratolieva, 2014).

(e) There is a great influence of criminal structures on the market trade in the Central Asian countries. This factor actually discourages Indian entrepreneurs. In this regard, they have real information that forces them to work anywhere in New Zealand or Canada, but not in the neighborhood of the dangerous countries. By the way, this factor has a negative impact on the investment environment, which has been assessed as not favourable. The situation is aggravated by the fact that commercial disputes are always resolved in favour of the criminal structures, as completely corrupted public officials can bribe any recent court and resolve the dispute in their favour.

(f) The tax laws of the countries of the region also do not encourage the rapid development of trade and economic relations between India and the countries of Central Asia. In all Central Asian countries, the tax burden remains high as compared to those with which India is engaged in developing an intensive trade and industrial cooperation. On national levels, India's private sector compares the tax burden with the other countries and is apprehensive regarding the unreliability factor of a broad development of economic relations with the Central Asian countries. Besides, the development of trade and other forms of economic cooperation with the CA countries also needs to overcome difficulties, and at a high level of risk.

(g) All the Central Asian countries have a high interest rate by banks, which is dangerous for the long-term presence of foreign players in this market. On the contrary, the real interest rates in the region should be low, since there exists an inverse relationship between the level of interest rates and economic growth in all the steps of the hierarchical levels of the economy. In some Central Asian countries, the interest rate is usurious. Interest in such a role cannot act as an engine of development for productive forces. Such high rates are made possible by full-scale market-based regulatory actions in these countries.

The real existence of these barriers does not mean that it is a hopeless situation. There are opportunities to gradually overcome the above-mentioned barriers. Some of them require a long period of time, while others can be overcome in a relatively shorter period. However, a political will and a strong focus on the rapid development of economic and trade relations with India, keeping in mind that the potential for economic cooperation with the Central Asian countries is enormous, is required for the elimination of these barriers (Chouhan et al, 2011).

Conclusion

Enabling factors in this regard relate to a positive attitude among the different population and community groups in Central Asia for India and for the Indian people. Such a positive image of India among the Central Asian population can inspire a leadership of the countries in Central Asia that creates a whole range of positive conditions for the development of trade and economic relations with India. Indian entrepreneurs working in the Central Asian countries can keep good relations with the local people, without fearing for terrorist activities, drug mafia and religious fundamentalism, as in other countries.

However the most important thing is that by facilitating the implementation of the import substitution strategy, India can promote an economic security of the Central Asian states, reducing their dependence on China and other contemporary geopolitical forces. By promoting the rapid development of the manufacturing sector, increasing the degree of protection of the domestic producers from foreign aggressive competitors and a rapid increase in jobs in the industries and other industrial sectors, India can certainly accelerate the dynamics of the socio-economic development and increase the mutual understanding between the society and the state. Simultaneously, the design and implementation of the strategy of import substitution needs to be introduced along with tools for protecting the domestic market and the domestic producers as well as the ways to deal with the barriers that create hurdles in the process.

NOTES AND REFERENCES

Chouhan A.P.S. & Pathania Jyoti M. (2011), *Non-Traditional Security: A Conceptual Analysis in Traditional and Non-Traditional Threats to Central Asian Security*, Knowledge World, New Delhi.

Muratalieva Zamira (2014), "Regional Security of Central Asia: Problems and Prospects" in *Enhancing India-Central Asia Engagement, Prospects and Issues*, Nirmala Joshi (ed.), Vij Books India Pvt. Ltd., New Delhi.

Statistical Yearbook of the Republic of Tajikistan, Dushanbe, 2013.

Sunday Times (2014), "Dance of Democracy", 23 March.

Tajikistan and CIS Countries, Dushanbe, 2012.

Umarov Kh. and K. Warikoo (2015), "Development of Trade and Economic Relations between India and Tajikistan" in *Tajikistan in the 21st Century: Society, Politics and Economy*, Pentagon Press, New Delhi.

Index